CONCEPTUAL ECONOMICS

The Liaising
Role in Politics
and Social
Sciences

CONCEPTUAL ECONOMICS

The Liaising Role in Politics and Social Sciences

Kui-Wai Li

The Kui-Wai consultancy for Economic Development, Canada

 **World Scientific**

NEW JERSEY · LONDON · SINGAPORE · BEIJING · SHANGHAI · HONG KONG · TAIPEI · CHENNAI · TOKYO

Published by

World Scientific Publishing Co. Pte. Ltd.

5 Toh Tuck Link, Singapore 596224

USA office: 27 Warren Street, Suite 401-402, Hackensack, NJ 07601

UK office: 57 Shelton Street, Covent Garden, London WC2H 9HE

Library of Congress Cataloging-in-Publication Data
Names: Li, Kui Wai, author.
Title: Conceptual economics : the liaising role in politics and social
    sciences / Kui-Wai Li, The Kui-Wai consultancy for Economic Development, Canada.
Description: New Jersey : World Scientific, [2020] | Includes
    bibliographical references and index.
Identifiers: LCCN 2020041549 (print) | LCCN 2020041550 (ebook) | ISBN
    9789811222184 (hardcover) | ISBN 9789811222191 (ebook) | ISBN
    9789811222207 (ebook other)
Subjects: LCSH: Economics. | Economics--Political aspects. | Economics--Sociological aspects.
Classification: LCC HB71 .L5482 2020 (print) | LCC HB71 (ebook) | DDC 330--dc23
LC record available at https://lccn.loc.gov/2020041549
LC ebook record available at https://lccn.loc.gov/2020041550

British Library Cataloguing-in-Publication Data
A catalogue record for this book is available from the British Library.

For any available supplementary material, please visit
https://www.worldscientific.com/worldscibooks/10.1142/11881#t=suppl

Desk Editors: George Vasu/Sylvia Koh

Typeset by Stallion Press
Email: enquiries@stallionpress.com

Printed in Singapore

Thoughts for the Day

Ask Not Which Ideology is Suitable, Ask Which Ideology Can Empower People.

Variations in Economic Outcomes are the Differences, Not Inequalities.

Do Not Be a Slave to Your Own Skin.

Preface

The new decade of 2020 experienced the health hazard of corona virus that started in Wuhan in the People's Republic of China in late 2019 but spread through international travels to various parts of the world soon, causing severe health hazard and economic hardship to numerous households and businesses. Subsequently, most governments in corona virus-affected countries massively increased their urgent spending with the aim to contain, control and eradicate the spread of the virus. Such an increase in fiscal spending can be justified in view of the sudden emergence of the health hazard. However, there is a distinction between the need to rescue from a health hazard and the exploitation of the health hazard event by politicians in enlarging the size and power of the government as this would impose a huge burden on the country's fiscal policy. For example, should a government reduce its tax rates to allow households and businesses some breathing space in a time of economic hardship or introduce new spending to rescue not only from the need arising from the health hazard but also the entire economy? The political orientation of the policy choice could be dressed up as a health need.

This book is a timely publication in that it may not involve the medical aspect of the corona virus, but it does highlight the need to focus on the role and size of the government and the government's economic policy given its political content and orientation. Indeed, this book aims to provide an intuitive discussion on the liaising role of economics in political and social activities, thereby giving an intellectual analysis on how economics is related to other social science disciplines. Such an analysis could suggest the possibility of extending and expanding the frontier of economics analysis to a new height and a new dimension and that a new intellectual division in economics science can be created, thereby encouraging other scholars, intellectuals, analysts and professionals to engage and indulge in exploring new research in Conceptual Economics.

The theme of Conceptual Economics falls within the sphere of "political economy of capitalism". Indeed, this book adds to the sequence of books under such a theme. In addition to other refereed journal papers I have published on economic development and political economy, the sequence of single-authored books began with my 2002 publication *Capitalist Development and Economism in East Asia: The Rise of Hong Kong, Singapore, Taiwan and South Korea,* which documented the economic success of the four East Asian economies based on the capitalist mode of production. This was followed by the two books on the Hong Kong economy published in 2002, titled *The Hong Kong Economy: Recovery and Restructuring,* followed by the 2012 publication, *Economic Freedom: Lessons of Hong Kong.* Here, the economy of Hong Kong had been studied extensively as a case of economic freedom under capitalism. The theme is then extended to my next book published in 2017, titled *Redefining Capitalism in Global Economic Development.* By using large amount of global economic data, this book proposed that although capitalism has sailed through various challenges in the last few decades, it has been transformed into its contemporary version, and that capitalism is still the best functional mode of economic production globally.

This book, *Conceptual Economics: The Liaising Role in Politics and Social Sciences,* presents the next intellectual block in the theme of "political economy of capitalism". By employing intuitive and conceptual tools, the analysis in this book widens the discussion to explore the role of economics in politics and other social science disciplines, and highlight the fact that economic activities could be executed for non-economic reasons, and would yield economic outcomes, either favorably or unintentionally. The various dimensions of discussions in Conceptual Economics at best supplement the *status quo* of economic studies and point out the possible inadequacies in economic science. It would be encouraging if the discussion on Conceptual Economics will subsequently lead to new research and intellectual studies on how economics could function in different social science disciplines. As such, to have a university course on Conceptual Economics as an extension of political economy should not be regarded as a remote possibility.

A summary of the key arguments and the chapter layouts are provided here. Although economics is regarded as a "new" discipline in social science studies, it has accumulated decades of analyses through the discovery of various economic theories and empirical studies. Yet, economic problems are emerging periodically and regularly. Indeed, solutions to contemporary economic problems may need to incorporate the wisdom from other social science disciplines in order to come up with a comprehensive and functional solution. Conceptual Economics boldly uses an intuitive approach to examine several aspects in economics and its relationship with other social science disciplines. Believing that economic outcomes are always different from one another, Conceptual Economics argues that analyses should focus more on the *ex-ante* or input end, instead of purely looking at the *ex-post* or output end, of the economic equation. Conceptual Economics examines the *ex-ante* issues by arguing that differences in *ex-ante* factors through the discussion on endowment and opportunity obviously would lead to differences in *ex-post* economic outcomes.

Conceptual Economics thus builds on economic theories and extends analysis to incorporate other aspects, either relating one economic aspect to another or relating the economic discipline to another discipline. One can argue that while theories occupy the surface of the analytical space, concepts are the more fundamental elements that go deeper than the surface in economic theory. One can broadly elaborate the two arms of conceptual economic analysis. The "extensive" arm relates one economic issue with another issue, while the "intensive" arm takes a "vertical" approach to deal with one economic problem in-depth. The "intensive and deep" versus the "extensive and wide" features in Conceptual Economics would provide a powerful framework upon which human problems can be studied through the economic sphere intensively into the deeper root of the problem, as well as extensively by widely incorporating other social spheres in coming up with a lasting solution.

In the division between microeconomic and macroeconomics, the "intra-disciplinary" discussion attempts to merge and integrate the two academic branches of studies because microeconomics can have its implication on macroeconomics and *vice versa*. The simple supply and demand analysis in microeconomics, for example, can be interpreted into "supply-side" and "demand-side" studies in macroeconomics. Secondly, the "inter-disciplinary" discussion relates the economic discipline to other social science disciplines, typically politics, religion, social welfare, psychology, human geography, science and technology and other humanities. It is argued that economics is the commonality among other social science disciplines in that economic instruments have often been deployed in the realization and materialization of social or political activities. Economic resources are "passive" as they can be mobilized only by decision makers. As other social disciplines often do not have their physical form, economics has become the vehicle through which activities in other social science disciplines can be conducted.

Having established the intellectual relationship within the economics discipline and between economics and other social science disciplines, the next level of conceptual discussion adopts a vertical, in-depth approach to examine the nature of "difference" in economics. Economic outcomes are always different from one another. There are several related arguments. Firstly, it is argued that a "value scale" can be established and applied to examine the concept of human value, which would then lead to differences in economic performances. Secondly, the distinction between an *ex-ante* situation and an *ex-post* situation can explain why economic outcomes are different. Analysts often examined the different *ex-post* economic results, such as Gross Domestic Product (GDP), foreign investment and trade, but did not try to understand that different economic outcomes are often due to the differences at the *ex-ante* or the input end of the economic relationship.

The conceptual discussion on *ex-ante* differences relates to the idea of economic endowment, which can differ among individuals, firms, institutions, governments and nations. In addition, while endowment shows the attributes attained or acquired, economic opportunity shows how far endowments can be deployed through market forces. And even with the presence of equal opportunity, differences in economic endowments (*ex-ante*) shall produce different economic results (*ex-post*). The elaboration on endowment and opportunity can explain why economic outcomes are different from each other.

The nine chapters in this book elaborate on the various dimensions in Conceptual Economics, and each chapter carries clear objectives and intentions. The nine chapters are grouped into three sections. The two chapters in Section I begin by examining the difference between economic theories and concepts and discuss the various special features in economics, especially the close connection among economic activities, as one activity shall be related to and have an impact on another, thereby generating waves of economic activities and cycles. As different economic activities have different impacts, it could be true that some economic activities may contradict each other. The arguments in Chapter One are further consolidated into the discussion in Chapter Two, which examines the "liaison role" of economics among different social science disciplines. It is argued that economics is a "vehicle" that permits the realization and materialization of activities in other social science disciplines. The chapter concludes by arguing that analysts should "think outside the box" as conventional economic theories and numerous empirical studies still cannot provide answers to emerging problems. The answer may rest with Conceptual Economics as it shall pioneer an innovative way of analyzing economic and social problems.

Section II elaborates on the "extensity dimension" in Conceptual Economics, in that it relates the two arms of economics in a comprehensive body of analysis. This is shown in Chapter Two which extends the conceptual discussion in the "intra-disciplinary" relationship between microeconomics and macroeconomics and how activity in one will connect to the other. Aspects in microeconomics can have a wider impact on macroeconomics. Similarly, policy decisions on macroeconomics will impact different aspects in microeconomics. Though academically the two areas are distinct from each other, analytically it is impossible to isolate the effect of one without looking at the other.

Among all social science disciplines, the study of political economy integrates economics with politics. Chapter Four argues that economics has been the vehicle to other social science disciplines, and that economic instruments have been used to materialize other social ends. This chapter begins the discussion on the "inter-disciplinary" relationship by examining first the relationship between economics and politics. In dissecting political economy, this chapter clarifies some of the misunderstanding by arguing that the "passive" nature of economics has been exploited by the "active" nature of politics. Politics has no form on its own but needs a vehicle or intermediary through which it can be realized and materialized. Economic instruments have extensively been deployed in political decisions. Indeed, while economic outcomes are different from one another, politics mistakenly dichotomizes the different economic outcomes as "inequalities". The chapter argues that economic differences cannot be solved by political decisions and concludes that while "economic differences" can be improved over time, "political inequality" would be more deadly as it could be permanent. Furthermore, while politicians are elected on an *ex-ante* basis, their performance would only be known on an *ex-post* basis after they have taken up the office, and they are not financially responsible for the economic mess they create through their ineffective or spending policies.

The relationship between economics and politics is further elaborated in Chapter Five through the discussion on the activities and policy decisions by the government. The chapter raises some of the conceptual features in government policies and examines the role of taxation as a political instrument in government's fiscal policy. It is argued that a politicized fiscal policy is unwise because using economic instruments to serve political ends could result in economic distortions and unwanted outcomes. The chapter concludes by proposing a sound fiscal model to promote and enhance economic sustainability and capability, rather than cumulating economic burden for the future generation. The difference between "demand-side" and "supply-side" policies are discussed in depth so that policy makers shall see the consequences of the different adopted policies.

Chapter Six extends the discussion on the "inter-disciplinary" relationship to other social science disciplines. The discussion concentrates on how economics has been the vehicle for cultural, psychological and religious activities, in that these social activities can only be realized and materialized using economics instruments. Like politics, the expression of many social relationships does not have a physical form, and social expressions can only be conducted through the use and deployment of economic resources. This chapter basically highlights some of the "inter-disciplinary" relationships by using examples, but the concept can be extended to incorporate and include other branches of social sciences, humanities and science and engineering disciplines.

Section III goes beyond the superficial or horizontal analyses on the intra-disciplinary and inter-disciplinary relationships.

Chapter Seven elaborates the concept of "value" by incorporating both measurable and non-measurable values and argues that since there are different dimensions in values, they could be judged differently. A "value scale" is used to integrate the various forms of human values. This is an important aspect in understanding Conceptual Economics as it forms the basis of differences and diversities in humanity sciences. With the "value scale", it would be perfect if human activities progress along the scale and can achieve higher human values as civilization takes its path. However, there are imperfections in human activities, and the pace of progress along the scale may be constrained, with progress along the value scale differing among individuals and economies.

Chapter Eight attempts to explain why differences in economic outcomes are inevitable, because it would be correct to examine the "input" end of economic and social relationships. The discussion on the *ex-ante* issues is related to the analyses on endowment and opportunity. Individuals and entities differ from one another because they have different endowments. Typically, the formal education system enriches individuals' endowments through academic qualifications, but the result of an educational system is that individuals have acquired different knowledge, thereby providing them with different marketable endowments, and such differences in endowments should generate different outcomes. Consequently, different academic qualifications are rewarded differently due to market forces, and earnings among individuals are different. Equally, given the same academic qualification acquired by individuals, their employment opportunities would differ, as some would get a higher paid job than others. The difference reflects the availability of economic opportunity, which ultimately arises from the act of investment that mobilized economic resources. These differences simply show the market reaction and so long as all individuals are faced with equal opportunity, such differences are not the same as inequality.

Economic differences have mistakenly been misinterpreted as "income inequality" in political ideologies. Chapter Nine examines the fundamental difference between the two ideologies of capitalism and socialism/communism but elaborates on the more realistic ideology of "civic capitalism" in most democratic nations. The "civic" aspect relates to the presence of numerous apolitical institutions that provide layers of protection and security to the general public, and politics becomes one of the civic channels through which individuals can freely express their opinion and achieve their security. However, politics and governments are the essential components in modern institutions, but politicization of non-political activities should best be avoided because it would be impossible to distinguish between the result from pure economic exercises or those that are the outcomes of policies on other non-economic issues. The chapter concludes that economics should be given a chance to perform, suggesting that it should be left alone so that the economy can take its own undistorted course. Interference from politics should be minimized.

Conceptual Economics is a challenging heading that aims to bring creative, new and intuitive ideas to various existing theories and analyses, providing a deeper and comprehensive approach to looking at contemporary economic issues. There is indeed the need to have new thinking to understand such issues as inequality, politicization, competitiveness and the global economy. Conceptual Economics is therefore a new attempt to ally different areas of analyses to form a new approach to examine contemporary issues. The intuition in Conceptual Economics includes the needed clarity between *ex-ante* and *ex-post* situations, between economic difference and inequality, between endowment and opportunity, and between economic acts and political goals.

In the process of writing this book, I tried to minimize the use of references, citing only the essential ones. This is because much of the discussion in the book shows a considerable amount of creative thinking. It is true that some arguments though dressed differently in different context are being discussed in more than one occasion in the book. The idea is to examine the same point from different perspectives, thereby giving a comprehensive coverage of the topics.

While I wrote this book very much entirely on my own, without assistance, I am thankful to Sylvia Koh, the Acquisition Editor, World Scientific Publishing, for her assistance and guidance, as well as the anonymous reviewers who had supported the publication of this book. Indeed, I am delighted to have my second book published by the World Scientific Publisher. I would like to take this opportunity to show my appreciation and gratitude to all my former research assistants, teaching assistants, research associates and other helpers who had diligently provided help to my research studies, while in reality, they effectively served as the invisible forces that pushed me to think hard and think "outside the box" for new intellectual thoughts, including some ideas presented in this book. The support from my family goes beyond what words could describe.

Both readers and critics are welcome to contact me should a mutual interest arise in discussing Conceptual Economics. While Conceptual Economics can be a newly established course in the economics discipline, especially in the course on Political Economy, there is much room to improve the content of discussion and coverage. Ultimately, it is hoped that Conceptual Economics can become a useful and effective branch of economics that serves the world and promotes humanity in achieving a higher stage of civilization.

About the Author

Dr. Kui-Wai Li obtained his academic qualification in economics from various universities, including the London School of Economics in the UK, and Harvard University in the USA. Dr. Li has taught in several countries, including Canada, Hong Kong, Switzerland, Nigeria, and Lithuania, and has served as a visitor to numerous universities, such as University of Tokyo, University of Toronto, and Yale University. Over the years, he has written numerous academic papers in such macroeconomics topics as political economy, growth and development, monetary economics and financial crises, industries and productivity analysis, globalization, and area studies. Within the theme of "political economy in capitalism", Dr. Li has published several single-authored books on Asian economic development, economic freedom, capitalism, and the world economy. Dr. Li has also worked as an economic consultant to international organizations, business corporations, and professional and government institutions. He was the Director of the Hong Kong APEC Study Center for years and has been interviewed, often live, widely by local and foreign media on different economic issues. He can be reached by email at: *economicfreedomkwli@gmail.com*.

Contents

List of Figures and Tables

Figures

Tables

Section I

The Making of Conceptual Economics

Although the discipline of economics is regarded as "young" when compared to other social sciences and humanities disciplines, there have been numerous developments in the study of economics. Typically, the two divisions of microeconomics and macroeconomics have led to newer forms and branches in the study of economics. There is indeed no shortage of economic theories and models, but equally there is no shortage of economic problems. One would have thought that all kinds of economic problems could be resolved by one economic theory or another. Yet the coexistence of economic theories and economic problems suggests that there could still be a lack of economic theories in solving economic problems, or the solution to economic problems go beyond the wisdom of any economic theory.

Economic development in individual economies worldwide differs considerably. The "resource curse" theory argues, for example, some economies are endowed with rich resources but little economic advancement, while resource-lacking economies such as Japan have experienced technological advancement through productivity, competition and effective management (see, for example, Odagiri, 1994; Ross, 1999;

1

Robinson *et al.*, 2006; Frankel, 2010). As crisis looms, economic growth and performances usually appear in waves and cycles. Economic decisions are made by individuals, enterprises, institutions and the government, and as each economic decision maker reacts differently to the existing economic information, it would be impossible to identify which favorable or unintended consequence in economic performance was the result of which decision. Each economic decision maker would have a different intention in mind. An individual may decide to have a better post-retirement life. A business enterprise may decide to have a larger market share. An institution may decide to promote a certain social cause, while the government may make economic decisions based on political grounds.

This effectively suggests that economic performances and outcomes would be a mixture of all these decisions. Similarly, economic problems could merely reflect the concerns of different economic decision makers. Such a line of thinking goes beyond the application of any single economic theory in solving problems. Indeed, many economic problems are not new, have persisted for a long time, or have re-emerged repeatedly in different forms and styles. Typically, the issue of inequality and poverty has appeared in economic literature for decades, and yet despite the wisdom of scholars, scientists, government officials and international economic agents, the same problem still exists. Similarly, despite the various rescue efforts, economic crises have kept re-emerging through different forms. From the oil crisis and trade protectionism of the 1970s to the financial crisis in 2008, economic turbulences have re-emerged due to cumulated economic decisions by investors and institutions. Indeed, economic instruments have been deployed to fulfill ideological and political ends and the resulting conflicts appeared through economic performances.

References to recent studies and arguments would show the complexities in dealing with contemporary economic problems. For example, "Freakonomics" suggests that economic thinking has been applied to numerous decisions and there is increasingly a lack of clarity in decisions between economics and social sciences. While some scholars extended the political argument of economics into imperialism, others were critical about the argument and suggested that decision and analysis would have to be considered on a case-by-case basis (see, for example, Levitt and Dubner, 2005; Fine and Milonakis, 2009; Gelman and Fung, 2012).

Economics as a "dismal science" (see, for example, Levy, 2002) has been another argument on the growing complexity in economics as it has been substituted by refined areas of studies, such as environment economics and financial economics, which examine issues on specific economic areas. However, the debate on "dismal science" has been challenged intellectually. Coyle (2007), for example, argued that modern day economics is more "soulful" than "dismal" because of its practical and applied nature in human science, and that the improved use of data, technology and computer together with insights from other social disciplines have enriched the analytical capacity in the economics discipline. Relating economics analysis to such social sciences as psychology allowed, for example, Akerlof and Shiller (2009) to put forward a Keynesian belief and argument on transforming economics and restoring prosperity through an active government role in policy-making in order to manage the "animal spirits" in economic decisions.

The complexities in modern day economic analysis have also been captured by Chang (2015) who revealed a range of economic theories, their strengths and weaknesses, and discussed the difficulty in explaining economic behavior in an increasingly global and interconnected world. The reaction to "dismal science" has also been referred in Rodrik (2018) who in response to the 2008 financial crisis argued that economics can still be a powerful tool in global development, but that decision makers have to "focus on getting the context right", and reiterated that the application of suitable economic models is what makes economics a science. Instead of regarding economic analysis as "dismal", Wheelan (2019) acknowledged the complex nature in economic analysis as economic agents do not always behave predictably and it is not possible to conduct laboratory experiments in economic studies.

There is one commonality in these literatures, that economic analyses may have to go beyond the application of any single economic theory, and that due to the multifaceted nature of economic issues and problems, it would be proper to relate economics to neighboring social science disciplines. One can start with an interesting thought as described in "Freakonomics" that economic thinking has been applied to numerous decisions. On the contrary, one can use a reverse argument that other social decisions have used economics as their instrument in deriving their intended goals. One must understand the "passive" nature of economic resources, which can be deployed only by human decisions for different purposes. The use of economic resources may not be for economic purposes, but these decisions would have economic consequences.

Like the more recent developments in economic analysis, Environment Economics concerns resource sustainability in the global environment. Energy Economics studies the effect and sustainability of the deployment of different energy usages. Conceptual Economics is the application of concepts to understand economic behavior, activities and outcomes. Conceptual Economics emphasizes on the intuitive and analytical reasoning in economic activities. Beginning from the fact that economic resources can only be deployed, depleted and renewed by human decisions, one must bear in mind that social decisions can be materialized using economic resources. Hence, someone's birthday party cannot be materialized without sacrificing some economic resources. In order to show some political results, policies adopted by political parties would refer to various economic means for political ends. As such, economic decisions are not meant entirely for economic purposes, but economic resources are used to serve both economic and non-economic goals.

Conceptual Economics comprises a host of concepts and intellectual intuitions that would enrich the understanding of contemporary economic behavior, activities and outcomes. One can begin by arguing that all economic activities are connected like a globe, with one activity impacting another, creating a chain of related activities. To put such a "globe-like" relationship into an intellectual context and perspective, Conceptual Economics focuses on two relationships. The study on the "intra-disciplinary" relationships within economics provides a conceptual discussion between microeconomics and macroeconomics, as one activity in microeconomics is related to another activity in macroeconomics and *vice versa*. There are conceptual linkages between the two branches of economic studies. For example, while there is supply and demand analysis in microeconomics, macroeconomic policies can produce either "demand-side" or "supply-side" effects.

The study on the "inter-disciplinary" relationship between economics and other social science disciplines can be an effective tool in understanding, and therefore solving, complex economic problems. In politics, such economic variables as tax, subsidy, interest rate and export and import have been used as instruments to fulfill political ends. Similarly, economics enters the decision-making process in numerous social activities. The production of cultural artifacts, clothing and related consumer goods use economic resources. The psychology of many individual decisions would be expressed through economic activities. Indeed, one can argue that social and human activities can only be materialized using economic resources. Economics is seen as the vehicle used in fulfilling all other social and human decisions. The point is that economic resources can be deployed for non-economic purposes, and yet we all examine these decisions through economic performances.

The study of these two relationships can give rise to numerous concepts in understanding economic activities. One concept is the term endowment, which can be regarded as a marketable resource held by individuals, businesses, institutions, governments and economies. As people differ from one another, it effectively means that individuals hold different endowments, some perform better than others in academics, while others are enterprising and establish successful businesses. The difference in individual endowments means that economic outcomes are always different, as the more successful and enterprising individuals would acquire a more marketable endowment, leading to a higher return than others. It is the difference in endowments that generates differences in economic outcomes. Hence, when politicians lament about "inequalities" as individuals receive different earnings and rewards, firms make different profits and economies achieve different national incomes, the truth is that the difference lies in the endowments held by individuals, firms and economies. It is the difference in inputs that leads to differences in output in the form of incomes and earnings, profits and national incomes.

The discussion of "*ex-ante*" and "*ex-post*" situations are important in Conceptual Economics. Take education as an example. The education process is meant to promote the academic endowments of individuals so that they can become more marketable. However, the education process itself screens out the academically able students who are supposed to take up professional jobs that are rewarded differently. The *ex-ante* difference in the students' ability generates *ex-post* differences in their career paths. This is effectively the job of an education system, which if politicized could be considered as an engine that produces "inequality". The fact is that *ex-post* differences are the result of *ex-ante* differences. It would then be more appropriate to improve and narrow the *ex-ante* differences, rather than politicizing the outcome differences.

In addition to the "intra-disciplinary" and "inter-disciplinary" relationships, Conceptual Economics applies both "intensive" and "extensive" approaches to analyze economics, with the former aimed at an in-depth search of the problem while the latter is aimed at examining all other aspects related to the problem. Each of the two approaches would lead to several conceptual discussions between competition and competitiveness, and between nominal economy and real economy.

By using intellectual intuition, Conceptual Economics shall add to the debate on the role and position of economics in social sciences. Instead of lamenting how weak economics is in dealing with social problems, Conceptual Economics shows the innate strength of economics in dealing with social problems by widening its analytical scope to incorporate other aspects within the discipline of economics itself as well as venturing into related social disciplines. Conceptual Economics points out that there is no one-to-one relationship in economic activities, rather economic activities represent different aspects of economic trends. In economics, one cause could lead to several consequences, and one consequence could come from different causes.

This section contains two chapters which conceptualize the discussion on the nature of economics as a discipline and how it is related to other social science disciplines. There are specific features one can conceptually find in the economics discipline, and there are also the relationships between economics and other social disciplines. The "intra-disciplinary" relationships deal with the compatibility between the two branches of microeconomics and macroeconomics, while the "inter-disciplinary" relationships concentrate on how economics appears in other social science disciplines, such as politics, social welfare, culture, religion and human geography.

Chapter One deals with some key conceptual features and elaborates on the various possible "connectedness" among the components within the economics discipline itself. In a "pure and simple" form, economics can operate within its own territory, and economic results are generated entirely based on economic performances. However, economics practically operates within the scope of other social science disciplines for their own goals. Chapter Two raises some of the "inter-disciplinary" arguments that will be elaborated in the following chapters. One of the concepts in economics is that economics resources or the factors of productions are "passive" and cannot function without some decisions made on their deployment. The key message in Chapter Two is to argue that economics is a vehicle through which activities in other social disciplines can be realized or materialized.

These two fundamental chapters shall lay the foundation for the conceptual analyses in Sections II and III. Both the "intra-disciplinary" and "inter-disciplinary" relationships are fully discussed in the four chapters in Section II, and the discussion has been focused more in the area of political economy where economics is closely intermingled with politics.

It is argued that politics, so as other social disciplines, does not have a physical form, but in order for its goals to be realized, economic instruments are deployed to show results. As such, many economic activities are in fact meant for non-economic goals. Another concept in economics is that economic outcomes are *ex-post*, economic differences must be explained on the "*ex-ante*" basis. The three chapters in Section III take the *ex-ante* approach to examine why economic outcomes are different.

Chapter One

The Ingredients in Economics

I Introduction

People often look at the discipline of economics differently, with some holding quite extreme views. Some people think that economics is an easy subject as they come in contact with economics on a daily basis: withdraw cash from the bank and use credit cards, shopping in malls and supermarkets, compare prices and look for items which are on sale, acquire property and pay mortgages, earn a monthly wage and build up a credit history, while manufacturers make production decisions and deliver goods to shops. Others think that economics is very remote and can never understand how the economy comes to what it is. Why is there inflation, how come the government can dictate the interest rate, why property prices escalate and oil prices remain so high? There can indeed be endless number of whys in all modern economies. At the global level, one can observe that the world economy can still be divided or fragmented between extremely advanced countries and extremely underdeveloped countries, between fast progressive countries and slow stagnant countries, and between ethically strong free countries allowing diversities and creativity versus countries whose power is concentrated in the hands of the religious state and ideological elites. Indeed, while there are still natural disasters that can cause destruction to human lives, many human problems are indeed manmade, institution-oriented or are controlled by a certain sphere of authority.

The more fundamental concern is given that there are so many economic scholars, so many economic theories, so many branches in the discipline itself, so many years of accumulated economic studies and so many published economic articles, why are there still so many economic problems, many of which are not new, and a lack in the understanding of how an economy functions, and why some economies are even experiencing decline and collapse, while other economies are frozen and have not been able to make progress? In countries with a heavy national debt, such as Greece in 2015, one would have concerns about their economic survivability and sustainability, especially on the younger generation as they would have to suffer for the debt payment accumulated by previous generations. On the contrary, fast-emerging countries such as China are faced with the question of social equity, and openness has been a concern as economic and political powers are unevenly distributed, favoring a minority of governing elites.

Is the discipline of economics itself a problem, or are economic problems ultimately manmade, or is there a need for more theories, or are inappropriate economic policies chosen, are economic practitioners interpreting economics wrongly, or have economics tools been abused for other purposes? Again, there could be many possible explanations, linkages, causations and connections. For example, by referring to the lack of growth in underdeveloped countries, studies on "resource curse" argued that the availability of resources could be a problem when resources were not utilized productively (Ross, 1999; Frankel, 2010; Haber and Menaldo, 2011; John, 2011). Indeed, one can generally observe globally that countries with abundance of natural resources tend to be weaker economically, while countries lacking natural resources tend to be stronger economically, especially with the advancement of science and technology. The economic explanation is that when compared to natural resources, technology advancement tends to achieve a higher "value-added" content, and a higher price subsequently. Typically, agricultural products and most raw materials would carry a much lower price than high-technology products.

The first economic lesson is that economics is a science but unlike physical sciences such as biology and chemistry, economic experiments cannot be conducted in a laboratory. For example, one cannot ask the government to make a certain economic decision to see if the outcome would be desirable. One cannot double the wage of every worker and see if the outcome would be acceptable. Yet, today there is a branch of economics known as Experimental Economics, where sampling studies are conducted to examine certain predictable economic behaviors and outcomes. In economic theory, the presence of an economic equilibrium would provide a certain optimal state, but when do we know there is an equilibrium, where would equilibrium occur, how long would the equilibrium last and how can we maintain the equilibrium? In a market economy, there are possible choices that consumers, decision makers and producers can make. But, how do we assure that the smart or right choices are made for the benefit of all, or what if the choices are "right" for some but not for others?

There is an opportunity cost in all economic decisions and an optimal decision should lead to the minimization of opportunity cost. True, but do decision makers care or know about the opportunity cost, or whom it would affect? "Supply creates its own demand" is the first classical economic concept one learns. It assumes economic freedom of individuals in a market economy, but the ideology of socialism and communism preaches collectivization and the concentration of power in the hands of the state and political elites, while individuals' economic freedom is removed and controlled, if not annihilated. Hence, business-minded leaders would prefer to improve the business environment so that individuals can conduct their own economic affairs. Socialist-oriented political opportunists, on the other hand, would prefer to acquire and accumulate power to exercise control so that they can execute their own political agenda.

Hence, is the economic discipline the cause or the consequence of all this mess? Should we complain about the lack of ability in economies to deal with problems, or should we be sympathetic because economic instruments have been misused and abused for different non-economic purposes? Fortunately, or unfortunately, we cannot do without economics, and a better understanding of economics is preferable than to discard, lament or belittle the discipline, including a freer provision of economic knowledge so that economic complexities could better be understood. In other words, there is a need for the discipline of economics to make progress, but given the state of the art, where shall one start to examine the economics discipline and bring it to a higher stage of understanding, intuition or inject innovative ideas and analyses to existing knowledge?

II Features of Economics as a Discipline

Economics is the study of resource allocation and utilization. It usually begins with the understanding of the three or four broad classifications of resources. Firstly, natural resources are composed of land, minerals, ocean and marine materials. Human resources include all human individuals, especially those at the working age, while human capital shows the quality of the human resources. Capital and financial resources are the monetary and financial instruments and assets used to facilitate the functioning of other economic resources. In market economies, some have argued that entrepreneurship is the fourth group of resources as entrepreneurs pioneer businesses, create employment and investment opportunities and energize the economy. Others argued that entrepreneurs can be incorporated into human resources. There can be more contemporary classifications. Knowledge and advancement in science and technology could be another form of resource, though ultimately it depends on the creativity and innovative ability of intellectuals and scientists, who are included under human resources.

The three ultimate types of resources, natural, human and capital, are referred to as the "factors of production". There are various debatable concerns and features. Firstly, inequality in the three factors of production is obvious among nations. And as such, outcomes in the use and applications of production factors are different and unequal among nations. Countries which have abundance in one production factor may be limited in another. Countries with an abundance of land may face limitation in human capital resources, while countries with a large population may face limitation in capital resources. Furthermore, the pace of development and advancement in each production factor differs within any single economy and across economies. In natural resources, for example, oil exploration enriches the oil-abundant countries, but the science and technology of oil exploration come from other countries. Yet, oil-deficit countries have to suffer due to higher oil prices and economic development would then be restricted.

In other words, if nations possess production factors differently *ex-ante*, economic inequalities are bound to appear among nations *ex-post*. However, such differences should pose no arguments if every nation adopts an "absolute approach" and concentrates in developing and enriching its own production factors, either through domestic improvement or through external connections with trade and inward investments.

Unfortunately, instead of working on improving the country's *ex-ante* situations, the unequal *ex-post* outcomes have often been considered when the "relative approach" is adopted and comparisons are made across nations. Such comparisons are exploited for different ends, often political.

Another feature among the three types of production factors is their different degrees of mobility across nations and geographical regions. Natural resources are the least mobile, as land typically cannot be shifted from one region to another. However, other natural resources can be extracted for economic purposes. Oil, iron ore, diamonds and all kinds of natural resources have been explored to benefit human needs. Human resources are more mobile than natural resources, as individuals are able to move within the country's boundary for employment purposes, or to switch between jobs or learn a different skill. Educational diversity caters to and gears the younger population for different kinds of skills and knowledge. However, cross-country mobility of human resources depends on immigration laws and different professional requirements. Capital and financial resources are the most mobile, especially if the country's currency can be accepted across boundaries. Even in countries with restrictions on capital movements, financial resources can be moved across countries in a matter of hours. Furthermore, capital and financial resources are the most mobile resources because other activities cannot be made functional without financial resources in the first instance. To turn land into a productive resource, financial capital would be needed in construction. To enable productivity in human resources, investments in education and training are needed. Massive financial capital is needed in the building of infrastructures. Thus, financial resources are not only most mobile but are also needed in mobilizing other resources.

The mobility of resources leads to the third feature that economics is a passive discipline in that economic resources and economic variables cannot be activated by themselves without decisions being made by humans. Natural resources can neither move by themselves nor make themselves productive without investment decisions made by businesses. Policies that enhance the quality of human resources also depend on the availability, exercise and execution of financial resource. While the financial resource is the most powerful among the three production factors, economic variables and factors of production typically would be redundant if there were no active human decisions made on their usage. In other words, factors of production can only be made useful and productive through economic policy decisions conducted by individuals, business leaders, government officials and politicians.

While the study of economics tends to focus on how production factors can be used to enhance human's welfare, one must understand that there is no perfection in economic outcomes. In fact, decision makers who work on economic variables might have different intentions and vested interests. Consumers would like to pay a lower price, producers would like to minimize the production cost, while officials and leaders would prefer to expand and extend their own political agenda. Classical economics talks about the usefulness of markets, which provide signals and indications on the direction of the market. The political ideology of the leaders, however, exercises different deployment of production factors. But due to the need to satisfy their ideological goals, production factors could be used sub-optimally. Typically, leaders in the capitalist countries tend to favor the effective use of production factors to enhance people's welfare. On the contrary, leaders in the socialist or communist countries tend to deploy production factors to ensure the continuation of their political authority. A market-oriented political leader would advocate for a lower tax to empower and promote businesses. Socialist politicians would legislate higher tax to have a stronger control on businesses and earnings of individuals. There are mixed cases where left-wing political leaders were elected in the capitalist countries, resulting in the swing of economic policies between regimes. In poor countries where there are abundance of resources, the lack of political stability or an effective development agenda would result in a low utilization of production factors.

What is missing in the "resource curse" argument is exactly the fact that resources cannot be made productive and would remain passive if no effective policy decisions are conducted. And policy decisions have to be made by humans, who have different orientations and interests, depending on their role as to whether they are enterprising individuals, corporates or political leaders; the institutional setting as to whether the production factors are protected by the law and property right; the physical environment as to whether the production factors are remote or close to developed markets and the state of technology as to whether the production factors could have a high value-added content. While the market still presents an "invisible hand" in allocating the use of production factors, many production factors are used for non-economic ends.

Such a passive feature in the use of economic resources could pose problems. Typically, differences in results can be generated. The use of the same production factor would generate different results in time and space. The use of the same production factor in different policies would generate different outcomes. The same production factor used for business purposes versus for political or non-economic purposes would produce differences in outcomes. Even though economic theory makes the difference between "positive" and "normative" economic statements and talks about the "income multiplier", there would indeed be a lack of standard measures in the use of economic resources. Economic maximization based on the theory of lowest opportunity or marginal cost simply means that economic resources should be applied in areas where returns are highest. Therefore, one should not take a simplistic argument because differences in economic outcomes could necessarily imply uneven outcomes or inequalities. The differences could reflect more on the nature of the production factors.

Secondly, decisions in the use of production factors are often made by non-economists, and the purpose of these decisions may not be intended to achieve economic outcomes. Economic resources are used as instruments to enhance and fulfill other social and political intentions and interests. This perhaps is the "weakest link" in the discipline of economics, as economics does not function on its own but needs to be utilized and deployed, or is abused, by decision makers. It would be worse when mistakes result in unintended or distorted outcomes. And instead of admitting to a wrong decision, decision makers put the blame on the economic aspect of the outcome. A policy that provides large or excessive welfare usually ends up with rising national debts and fiscal deficits. But instead of revising down the level of government expenditure, welfare-oriented political leaders would impose a higher tax that generates further economic disincentive on the able individuals and businesses. In the end, one inappropriate policy that produces economic drawbacks would lead to another inappropriate or erroneous economic policy decision. Hence, one layer of economic distortion leads to another layer, thereby choking the proper path for the economy to grow and expand for the benefit of all. Yet instead of admitting the erroneous policies, the poor economic performance would be made the scapegoat. The economy would have to wait for a more economic-minded political leader to rewind the policy, but the economic damage done could take years or even decades to revive before the economy could return to a functional and effective path. In short, the poor or weak economic outcomes could be more due to the incorrect policies than the actual functioning of the economic variables, bearing in mind that weak economic performance will not correct itself without changes or revisions in economic decisions.

Another feature in economics is a lack of a measurable or quantifiable alternative. For example, it is well known that the economy's aggregate measure of Gross Domestic Product (GDP) is not a perfect measurement, because it fails to consider many non-quantifiable or undesirable activities, such as household work, illegal activities and corruption, related cultural specialties, nor does it reflect the different stages of economic development. Additional indicators have been identified, such as the standard of living index, economic freedom index, happiness index and so on, but many of these still rely on the economy's GDP as the ultimate measurement. There is no close substitute to GDP as a comprehensive measurement or indicator of economic activities. Hence, despite its inadequacies, GDP is still reported globally to reflect the economic differences and performances across countries. Conceptually, an economy's GDP reflects an *ex-post* situation, but the differences in GDP across countries is affected by *ex-ante* factors. Hence, while analysts, commentators, critics and leftists lament on the *ex-post* economic outcome shown by the differences in GDP, they should also investigate into the *ex-ante* factors, such as the suitability of economic environment and extent of competitiveness, level of technological advancement and availability of human capital, degree of economic freedom and openness, and willingness of leaders in promoting the capability of the economy or simply aim at amassing and lengthening the leaders' political power and control.

Indeed, economic performances shown in statistics are *ex-post* situations. A country's trade statistics that shows either a trade surplus or deficit is *ex-post* because it gives the "end result" of the trading process, while the *ex-ante* situation should reflect the country's ability to export. The traditional "input–output" analyses in economics concern mainly the inputs used in the production process and the amount of outputs generated for the market, few analyses touch on *ex-ante* studies. In job creation, for example, the statistics often produces the unemployment rate, which is *ex-post*. However, Li (2014) studied the availability of "economic opportunity" as an *ex-ante* condition to growth and development. While numerous studies concentrated on income inequality, Li (2014) argued that equality in economic opportunity should be the more fundamental *ex-ante* issue, which has often been ignored or overlooked. Economic studies focused mostly on *ex-post* analyses, while it should be the differences in *ex-ante* conditions that count.

In addition, another economic feature is the different time lags involved in economic decisions and activities. There are few instances where instant economic results can be seen. Investment activities take time to materialize, productions require time to process, firms take time to grow, government policies take time to see results and so on. Economic decisions conducted today would produce results at a much later time, which could be weeks, months or years. Economics primarily is a long-term activity, and that time is needed for results to materialize, and due to uncertainty and constant changes in the dynamic world, the materialized results might not be the outcome expected or predicted. There can be several problems in such a feature. In the government or political circles, the incumbent decision maker, such as an elected political leader, may not be there to reap the material results of an economic policy decision. As such, the initial incumbent decision maker (for example, the elected political leader for a specified term period) may not consider the outcome too carefully because the decision maker would not be there to make judgments on the results of the policy so decided. Furthermore, estimating future gains of an economic activity has always been difficult, uncertain and risky. Infrastructure construction, for example, has always been costly and the estimated gains would always be debatable. Typically, the estimated future gains of an underground railway, for example, would be compounded back to current gains, but who would know the gains when new urban development along the underground railway would be made in terms of housing settlement, deployment of land around the stations, growth in population and businesses, resulting in exponential rise in the number of passengers, which could lead to the faster recovery in the cost of the construction? In some ways, the gain from key infrastructure projects could be immense and may not be accurately measured because the infrastructure construction could last for decades and centuries and could even lead to new development in related activities.

However, the time lag in the materialization of economic results could be problematic if the initial economic decision was politically oriented, while the economic distortion or negative outcome would be responsible and absorbed by the future generation. One typical example is the accumulation of national debt in some nations with heavy welfare provisions. The overspending in this generation through heavy welfare provision and government deficits would result in the rise in national debt that would become an economic burden for the future generations, thereby weakening the competitiveness of the future economy.

To conclude, the passive nature of economics exposes itself in several problems or inadequacies. When economic variables and production factors are utilized and deployed according to economic predictions, a larger "economic pie" would normally be achieved for all to share. Economic outcomes should be apolitical, but due to differences in *ex-ante* factors, there will always be *ex-post* differences in outcomes. However, the explanations and interpretations of economic outcomes can be different depending on when and how the outcomes are analyzed, received and interpreted. Even among experts within the economics arena, explanations and interpretations on economic outcomes can be diverse, controversial and polarizing. It could even be possible that the economic outcomes are explained and interpreted to suit certain persons, scenarios or ends. As such, when the task of explaining and interpreting economic outcomes falls into unprofessional or biased hands, economic outcomes are often used as scapegoats, as targets or instruments for other purposes. In other words, the problem may not rest within the economics discipline itself, but the user of the discipline in furthering other intentions and interests.

III Comparing Theories and Concepts

The discipline of economics is considered as a young discipline in academic circles. It was the development of the classical economics that has provided the contemporary foundation of the discipline. Early economic theorists concentrated mostly on the political economy. At the beginning of the 20th century, the development of the neo-classical school formalized the study of economics into two main branches, namely microeconomics that dealt with the economic analyses of individual persons, individual firms, individual industries and individual markets, and macroeconomics that examined the development of the entire economy, its growth trend, policy adoption and overall competitiveness, and its global performance and relationships. While microeconomic achievement affects one single individual or entity in the economy, macroeconomic performance affects multiple number of individuals and entities.

Secondly, due to the differences in economic outcomes, economics has been incorporated into social studies and political analyses. The study of social class, for example, uses *ex-post* economic outcomes in the form of income differences as the criteria in a class-society, which is aligned with the two polarized political ideologies of communism and capitalism. The economic criterion in communism is that resources and production factors, including labor and human factors, come under the control of the state, and decisions are made by the party leaders and government officials. Under communism, the party state plays the leading role in conducting and controlling economic affairs. On the contrary, the economic criterion in capitalism is that resources are dispersed, and individuals are free to conduct their own business and economic activities, which are bounded impartially by laws and property rights, regulations, rules, standards and civic ethics. Under capitalism, economic activities are conducted through the market using the "price mechanism" as the available information, protected by numerous well-established civic institutions, while political parties comprise just another form of civic institution. Because political ideologies can only be seen or made explicit through economic activities and performances, economics has become intertwined with other forms of humanities and social sciences. Nonetheless, debates in political ideologies have spilled over to economic performances.

Within the discipline itself, the study of economics has expanded and branched out into various specialized areas. In addition to the traditional areas of economic thoughts and economic history, the use of mathematics and statistical tools has extensively been applied to economic studies. While many believe that mathematical economics shall help to quantify the study, others argue that economic intuition could have been lost in the excessive application of mathematics. Equally, there are new developments in both microeconomics and macroeconomics. Studies on labor economics, environmental economics, real-estate economics, welfare economics, urban economics, managerial economics, game theory, sport economics, industrial economics as well as experimental economics and behavioral economics are the recent developments in microeconomic studies. Studies on growth and development, international trade, international finance, political economy, monetary theories and fiscal policies, globalization and financial crises, country risk analysis and area studies, and open economy macroeconomics are the more popular areas of academic developments in macroeconomics. In addition, cross-disciplinary economic studies exist in such areas as economic geography and law and economics. Furthermore, the principles of economics have been regarded as a core study in business studies, typically in marketing, accounting and management, and increasingly in the science and technology disciplines.

A major feature in the construction of economic models is the use of assumptions. For example, economic models have assumed a closed economy without external trade, a private economy without the government, a constant or a varying return to scale in production, a proxy given to such unquantifiable variables as technology, a residual used in econometric estimations to indicate all possible unknown influences, a certain mathematical value assigned to a variable in order to produce the expected outcome, use of linear or non-linear relationships, use of a short-run or long-run time span, variables selected for inclusion in equations and variations in the number of equations used in constructing a model and so on. Each of these assumptions could be used to analyze certain specific economic aspects.

There are broadly two schools of thought in the construction of economic models. The structuralist school would argue that economic models would be built to incorporate several variables, influences and impacts. Multiple equations and variables would be incorporated into the structural model to explain and predict economic outcomes. As such, structural models have been related popularly to economic planning, especially in the developing countries (see, for example, Taylor, 1979, 1983, 1985; Kendrick and Taylor, 1970; Chenery, 1975; Botta, 2009). On the contrary, the marginalist school considered mainly the incremental impact of an economic variable and would isolate the impact one economic variable has on another economic variable. This might have considerably narrowed down the analysis and examined the performance to one single economic variable. The marginalist school argues that the movement of one economic variable would provide predictions on another economic variable. The presence of a market economy was usually assumed in the marginal school of analyses as price movements in a market economy provided economic directions (see, for example, Streissler, 1972, 1988; Cohen, 2005; Mosca, 2005).

There are several common features in the outcomes of model constructions. One is the feature of "generalization" as economic models tend to produce some discussions which are generally applicable to situations given the assumptions employed. The advantage of such a generalization is that it is static or "time-impartial" and can be applied to any market economy. Secondly, economic models tend to produce predictions that focus on one specific area. Such a "mono-prediction" feature would serve the purpose of concentrating the analysis in one specific economic area, but that may or may not be in alignment with the overall picture. Although the predictions are scientific, their applicability would depend on practicability and reality. Nonetheless, economic model constructions do provide a useful tool in understanding how economics works as well as a readymade "recipe" to solve economic problems. The task of "scenario building" has often been used in economic model construction as that would add an element of functionality into the model.

Economic model constructions are necessary as the use of assumptions, generalization and scenario-building serves the function of reducing otherwise complicated economic connections to a manageable setting so that analyses could be applied to handle specific economic aspects and problems. However, additional developments in both microeconomics and macroeconomics have indeed led to the development of new economic theories. At the same time, economic situations are changing rapidly due to new development in various aspects of human life. However, while there are new economic theories, there are also new economic problems. While some economic theories do offer theoretical solutions, they may not be taken up in solving economic problems. It would even be that the pace of increase in economic problems is faster than the number of newly developed economic theories, or faster than the speed in which existing economic theories could be used to solve economic problems. There is thus a "gap" between abstract economic theories and practical economic solutions, either due to the fact that theories are not practical, or not adopted or available.

One improvement is to apply a conceptual understanding to economic activities, events and outcomes. As economics is a passive discipline, the users of economic tools may not have a full knowledge of economics and therefore may not be aware of the full consequences, either intended or unintended. Decisions taken up by policymakers may be using economics as an instrument while the goal or eventual intention may not have anything to do with economics. Furthermore, economic outcomes take time to materialize. The consequence of what is done today may not be realized till much later, and the time lag so involved could be exploited by decision makers.

By examining the *ex-post* outcomes of economic activities, economic theories often focus on an individual or isolated aspect of an activity. The advantage of such an approach is it provides an in-depth analysis of the issue, but the disadvantage is that it may lack connectivity to other economic aspects, thereby rendering the theory and its subsequent analysis narrow, impractical and abstract. Conceptual analysis can be made useful to the understanding of economics by widening its analytical scope, linking various aspects and coming up with a comprehensive and complete framework of analysis. Conceptual Economics thus builds on economic theories and extends analysis to incorporate other aspects, either relating one economic aspect to another or relating the economic discipline to another discipline. In the process of conducting conceptual analysis, innovative and creative methods in understanding economics could emerge. For example, while economic theories relate mostly to *ex-post* situations, Conceptual Economics would include discussions on *ex-ante* factors. Hence, the understanding of *ex-post* economic outcomes would differ considerably once *ex-ante* factors are incorporated into the analysis. By adding new dimensions into economic analysis, Conceptual Economics shall bring to the study of economics a higher level of understanding intensively by relating and incorporating multiple economic aspects into consideration and extensively by connecting economics to other disciplines to generate a multidisciplinary approach to analyze economic development.

Analysis of Conceptual Economics does offer a new approach to the understanding of existing theories because concepts can be related to differences in time, scenarios and conditions. Conceptual Economics can attend more to contemporary economic issues and problems, which are constantly producing new scenarios. The dynamic analysis of contemporary issues would mean that the interpretation of economic concepts would have to be adjusted and revised according to current features. The same economic concept would need to be interpreted differently across time, space and incidents. Conceptual Economics does provide a more flexible approach in understanding the complexities of contemporary affairs using economic tools and theories. Conceptual Economics deals with real problems, and as such, few assumptions if at all can be incorporated. The strength in Conceptual Economics is its relevance to contemporary issues, and solutions could be timely, strategic and effective. Different economic criteria are used in conceptual analysis. One can argue that while theories occupy the surface of the analytical space, concepts are the more fundamental elements that go deeper than the surface in economic theory. Conceptual analysis must be issue-related as that could reflect the appropriateness of the concepts, and not mere assumptions that produce hypothetical scenarios. While many economic theories employ assumptions that could be unrealistic or unattainable, Conceptual Economics begins with the reality and search for solutions within the given scenario. Conceptual Economics gives a strategic approach in handling real-life and real-time problems and incorporates intuition in the analysis.

One can broadly elaborate on the two arms of Conceptual Economics analysis. Firstly, Conceptual Economics can be "intensive" in dealing with one economic problem, in that the discussion and analysis would "spiral down" deep into the origin of the problem, linking the problem that appears at the surface to the very root at the bottom of the problem. Indeed, superficial solutions are mostly window-dressings and can only be temporary, *ad hoc* and incomplete, and that the same problem would repeat itself after the effect of the superficial solution disappears. By "spiral down" along the line of investigation and elaboration, one can eventually expose the root cause of the problem to locate a sustainable and lasting solution. Such an intensive approach to conceptual analysis shall provide a sense of "depth" in economic analysis.

Secondly, Conceptual Economics analysis can be "extensive" in that one economic problem can be linked or related to another problem, and that merely considering economic solutions may not be effective without at the same time identifying the solution to related problems, so that a global solution that incorporates economic and other factors can be determined. Extensive analysis requires width and broadness in dealing with problems that may have multiple dimensions. Given that economic resources are powerful and useful tools for other social and human dimensions, a good understanding of economic concepts should therefore provide a more effective means for constructing solutions. Thus, incorporating an appropriate economic discussion should serve as a pivot in the search for an overall solution to problems.

Figure 1.1 provides a visual presentation of the two approaches. The "extensive" approach shown in Figure 1.1(a) allows connections to be made at two levels where the dotted lines show the connections within the economics discipline, while the solid line gives the connection with other related disciplines, which can be politics, psychology, history, religion and so on. The issue in question could be represented by Point A, and the two circuits starting from Point A indicate the two connections. On the contrary, the "intensive" approach is shown in Figure 1.1(b) where the downward spiral shows the deepness of the analysis, and merely considering the service may not be enough to find the root of the problem.

The "intensive and deep" versus the "extensive and wide" features in Conceptual Economics provide a powerful framework upon which human problems can be studied through the economic sphere intensively into the deeper root of the problem, as well as extensively by widely incorporating other social spheres in coming up with a lasting solution. However, there

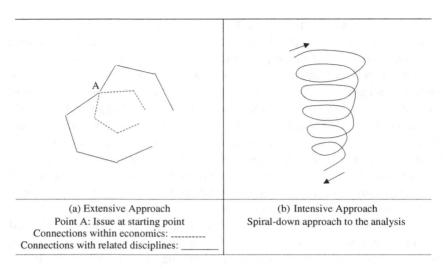

(a) Extensive Approach
Point A: Issue at starting point
Connections within economics: _____
Connections with related disciplines: _____

(b) Intensive Approach
Spiral-down approach to the analysis

Figure 1.1   Approaches to Conceptual Economics

is a saying that "things are easier said than done". Conceptual Economics should provide a step closer to the understanding of problems and identifying solutions, but nothing can be perfect. Even if solutions were available and adopted, new problems would emerge. More time would have to be involved, and decisions would be needed in understanding the problems and proposing the solutions. The way human problems are to be understood fully could be costly due to delays, lacking timely facts and reliable statistics, being subjected to different interpretations, and exposure of biasedness and vested interests. Equally, the process through which solutions are identified would not be "obstacle free".

One is not suggesting that Conceptual Economics can provide a solution to all problems, but its emphasis on intuitional reasoning can go far and provide an alternative mode of study. While economic theories provide analytical directions and predictions, Conceptual Economics serves as the thread that links up the various parts of the economy. As such, the minimum Conceptual Economics can achieve is to keep the economy in one piece, while the maximum could be an improvement in the overall economic trend, thereby strengthening the various aspects of the economy, making it more competitive, promoting jobs and welfare, and attaining a bigger "economic pie" for all to share. Conceptual Economics takes into consideration the human factor, which could either aid development through appropriate and effective policies or could be an obstacle in the development process as the adoption of inappropriate and wrongful policies adds to economic distortions, thereby burdening the economy and reducing the opportunities open to future generations.

In view of the growing global economic problems, though many of which are not originated in the discipline of economics itself, in view of the inadequacies in economic theories in solving economic problems and in view of the complexity of problems that are becoming multidisciplinary, the "intensive" and "extensive" nature of Conceptual Economics analysis could at least provide an alternative and powerful means to deliver solutions to global problems, and at most serve as a method through which individuals, businesses, politicians and world leaders could put economics as their top priority in their search for solutions.

IV The Nature of Tight Connectedness

All economic activities are related to one another as well as connected to activities in other non-economic spheres. When a consumer purchases a merchandize, it immediately relates to a chain of economic activities, such as retail, wholesale, delivery, invoicing and banking services, manufacturing, choice and use of material inputs in production, input supply chain and so on. Managerial work is also required at each level in the chain of economic relationships. The advantage of a free market economy is that the market through the "invisible hand" of price mechanism provides timely indicators and signals to businesses, manufacturers, designers, service providers, and consumers the needed goods and services. Economic resources are then appropriately utilized through these indicators and conditions. The voluntary nature in reacting to the market signal serves as the "driving force" in resource usage and allocation.

Production always associates with employment. Each chain in the economic relationship requires workers and jobs are then created. And jobs require different skills, knowledge and experience and are paid differently. Highly skilled jobs would earn more than low-skilled jobs, and jobs that require knowledge are paid differently. For the same job, pay may differ based on experience. Instead of using the term "income inequality" to symbolize the differences in earnings, differences in the "value added" among workers would be the more appropriate term. The function of education and training is to enhance individuals' "value added" so that they could be useful and can stand on their own economic feet. However, education and training produce differences in the "value added" content among individuals, and thus their earnings naturally would differ because some individuals have a higher "value added" content in their human capital than others. The economic intuition is that the society should ensure that all young individuals receive sufficient education and attain a certain ability to improve their "value added" than to criticize, lament and remorse on their earning differences.

Within economics, activities are intra-connected. Microeconomic activities have implications at the macroeconomic level. The manufacture of one product may not affect the activity at the firm level alone, because the production of one good would mean additional employment would be needed, and workers employed would mean less workers available for employment in other lines of production. The microeconomics of job creation in one production instantly affects the level of employment at the macroeconomic level. As employment rises, workers' spending would cumulate into the need for other lines of production, and as businesses boom, more bank loan provisions are required. The additional provision of bank loans would require changes in interest rate, which represents the cost of bank loans. Microeconomic activities can easily lead to changes at the macroeconomic level.

At the macroeconomic level, changes in policy variables could eventually work toward microeconomic activities. The increase in tax rate was meant to raise more tax revenue for the government, but the unintended consequence could be a fall in business incentives. Instead of looking for investment opportunities domestically, financial capital might be encouraged to leave the home market to look for a more market-friendly investment destination. Hence, financial capital so departed would enrich the host economy, while investment at home would be reduced. The fall in investment at home would mean loss of jobs, and wage would fall as unemployment rises. At the microeconomic level, a lower employment would mean a fall in consumption as people's take-home wage would be lower. The retail market would suffer because of a falling purchasing power and low sales. The shrinkage in one market could have a spillover effect on another market. A fall in employment in industries, for example, would mean a reduction in the demand for some personal services. Consequently, changes at the policy level would have microeconomic impact.

Numerous examples of the inter-connectedness between microeconomic and macroeconomic activities could be elaborated. However, these intra-connections would take place sequentially, though it would be impossible to track their impacts independently or individually. Thus, a rise in employment could be the result of numerous activities, and similarly a fall in purchasing power could be explained by different economic policy reactions. Such a difficulty in isolating the impact on one activity from another activity reflects the inter-connectedness feature of economic activities, as the work of one activity would create spillovers and shockwaves in other activities. The simple theory of "income multiplier" has been used to explain the chain of economic activities but fails to identify both the time span and directions of the impact needed in completing the chain of activities. A good sense of economic and conceptual intuitions would help in providing a more pragmatic understanding.

The power of Conceptual Economics is that one can effectively start with any example of economic activity, and the connecting nature of the economic discipline can widen the analysis to the macroeconomic level and at the same time narrow it down to the microeconomic level. While there exist macroeconomic and microeconomic theories, there are rare theories that attempt to provide crossover analyses. Conceptual Economics can help to fill up the intellectual gap and provide additional channel through which economic activities can be analyzed between microeconomics and macroeconomics. By making a comprehensive understanding of economic activities, analyses can cover a wider perspective and relate to multiple dimensions. This should produce a stronger and comprehensive understanding of economic activities across different dimensions. Armed with such an advantage, economic problems so identified or resulted could be dealt with more convincingly as more pragmatic solutions would be made available.

The "extensive — wide" feature in Conceptual Economics deals with cross-disciplinary analyses, typically with other humanity disciplines such as politics, sociology, welfare and culture, psychology, education and religion as well as disciplines in science and technology. As a passive subject, economic variables have been deployed extensively in the activities of other disciplines. All political elections make references to economic performances, though many of them are politically oriented. In sociology, social welfare provisions concern only and merely the spending side of the fiscal budget, ignoring the economic health of fiscal policy. Education is considered as a social investment in promoting human capital, and could be regarded as the root cause of "income inequality" as education trains individuals to take up different jobs which are paid differently. There is also the debate as to whether public provision or private provision of schools and learning institutions could be the better form of institutional setup.

In sports, the Olympic games are the modern and civilized form of "war" where countries send their athletes to compete. One advantage in many international and popular sports would be the "free" media coverage. There can be "rent seeking" and "free ride" as the names of sports persons are broadcasted along with the games. Indeed, other than news and weather, which other human activity is so widely and formally broadcast on a daily basis? In psychology, culture and religion, human behavior can have profound impact on economics. The drive to maintain one's appearance has given rise to the beauty industry that spans from clothing, cosmetics, surgery and pageant contests. Differences in cultural beliefs have also led to expansions in food industry and restaurant services, land usage and environmental issues. For example, flowers are popularly used on Valentine's Day, while "red pocket money" is given during lunar new year as a symbol of prosperity and luck. Different religions pursue different beliefs, such as while one religion is concerned about one's "next" life or life after death, another religion relates to one's "previous" life. Though most religious faiths advocate for peace and forgiving in one's life, at least one religion advocates for possible "holy war" that could be abused by dispirited followers who act with vested interests, resulting in potential violence and innocent deaths that go against the spirit of forgiveness and brotherhood. Religious faith does have implications on equality in humanity, economic openness and the way religious activities are financed and the economic activities so generated. For example, cash donations are made to temples and churches, but few would ever raise questions on the economics and the deployment of their donations.

In science and technology, the prime issue is financing the research activities, but how much newly developed science and technology can be applied to improve human life is another concern. There are clear debates as to whether the developments in technology, such as artificial intelligence and robots, could displace workers. Commercialization of technology has been a huge issue because it gives rise to new investments, developments in industry and consumption. A classic example of technology commercialization was Japan's "Walkman" in the 1970s that adopted an existing recording technology, turning it into a consumer product that one could carry about one's daily activities (Li, 2012, 2017a). The idea of such a handy product where everyone can conveniently own and carry one in their pockets has led to other developments in disk technology and usage, mobile phones, watches and cameras. These activities of technological commercialization have had further implications on, for example, the music and movie industry, knowledge dissemination and provision of various types of information.

All these discussions basically point to the argument that the economics discipline is linked with other disciplines, as both the input and output in other disciplines are expressed in economic terms or economic variables that have entered the decision-making process in these activities. The tight inter-connectedness feature of economics is such that despite being a "passive" discipline, economics is deployed in various other disciplines, linking it with politics, psychology, culture and religion, technology and scientific innovations. The linkages would be a "two-way" traffic: while economics is deployed in their activities, new developments in other disciplines also echo or radiate back to economics.

The "inter-relationship" refers to the cross-disciplinary connection between economics and other disciplines, while the "intra-relationship" shows the connections among economics spheres as in between microeconomics and macroeconomics. These two relationships can produce numerous consequences through multiple permutations, dimensions, incidents and connections in time and in various levels of decisions and policies made and adopted by individuals, businesses, institutions and governments. Economics serves as the engine to human growth in that while some societies and nations have made use of economics to benefit human welfare, some unfortunately deploy economics for unfruitful or even wrongful purposes, while others do not see the usefulness of economics in promoting their development and have remained primitive.

The art of economics rests not so much on the availability of resources, but the deployment of resources in enhancing their "value added", turning them to promote and improve competitiveness and serve humanity. Economics is not simply a daily subject because the various economic transactions reflect the surface's shallowness, while each aspect of economic activity can "spiral down" to much deeper implications as well as widen and connect to other human disciplines.

V Conclusion

There is no shortage of economic subjects, economic theories and economists advising on economic policies, and there is no shortage of economic problems either. One can argue that economics as a discipline in many ways has yet to be understood, partly because it is a passive subject, and experiments cannot be realistically conducted. As such, economic outcomes can be different. Moreover, many decision makers deciding on economic activities may not be fully aware of the consequences because outcomes take time to materialize. In addition, there is a need to distinguish between *ex-ante* and *ex-post* situations in economic activities.

The human factor is one of the key concerns. The economic problem could have been created by a single individual acting as the decision maker. The economic policy so decided can be executed by others, while the consequences can be tolerated by many others. The process from policy decision to policy execution could give rise to many issues. The principal–agent theory rightly argues that there may not be transparency in the interest of the decision maker (Fama and Jensen, 1983; Jensen, 1986; Holmstrom and Milgrom, 1991; Schneeweiss, 2003). Very often, the lack of transparency in the principal–agent relationship cannot be monitored and consequences may not be realized until much later when rescue efforts could not possibly be made. It could take another generation to revise and correct the unintended consequences of an inappropriate policy. Time would be lost, and the generated social cost would have imposed loss to others.

Conceptually seen like a globe, economic outcomes are always "relative" to each other because of their high degree of connectivity within economics and with related disciplines. Economic analyses that concentrate on one narrow issue could be easier for academic journal publication but would not have much practicalities. There is a need to change the mindset when analyzing economic problems as they are intertwined with other issues. One economic outcome can not only relate to banking decisions and job possibilities, but also has wider implications on religion, security and international relations.

Analysis must go beyond the "mono-dimension" nature of discussion, instead taking up a "multi-dimension" approach to examine problems. Conceptual Economics considers economic theories as the foundation, but interpretation should incorporate both the "intensive" and "extensive" nature of the issues. Extensity focuses on the width and shall relate to multiple dimensions within the economic discipline, typically crossing between microeconomics and macroeconomics, among different economic subjects. Intensity focuses on depth and the act of downward spiral in the line of thinking allows the analysis to go beyond the surface and locate the root cause of the problem, which may be originated in non-economic areas but have economic consequences.

Ultimately, economics is not a religion but an analytical framework upon which human problems can be analyzed and understood, and effective solutions can be brought forward to improve human welfare at the individual, societal and global levels. Conceptual Economics should, at the minimum, provide an additional tool to understand the complexity of human activities, and at the maximum, give an innovative approach to dissect and compartmentalize the complexities of many long-held human problems and provide manageable, lasting and applicable solutions. While human problems have different origins, using the economic tools would be an effective means to arrive at solutions. The advantage of using or relating to economic solutions is that costs and benefits can be quantified, seen, shared and allocated. Economics can become the commonality between conflicting parties and solutions shown in economic terms can be compared and evaluated. Furthermore, economic solutions are often futuristic and project a long-term result. The gains so obtained can have lasting implications to the individual and the society. Gains measured in economic terms can produce goodwill between otherwise conflicting parties, and the gains can be shown as signs of success in the negotiation process.

The pure use and application of economic theories has been projected as a simple method of dealing with worldly and contemporary human problems. Isolating the analysis to one single aspect of economics is inadequate and there is a need to widen the scope to include other issues in the same sphere and issues in other spheres or disciplines. Conceptual Economics pioneers the need to adopt a "multi-dimension and multi-level" approach to analysis. Similarly, there may not be one single solution, but solutions could be compartmentalized so that one solution or one aspect of the solution would at least help to untie one knot and other knots can then be untied eventually.

Chapter Two

The Liaison Role of Economics

I Introduction

This chapter provides some major concepts and their implications, and ventures further into new areas of analysis. Indeed, if understood and applied appropriately and correctly, economics can be a source of strength in promoting humanity and civilization. A better understanding of the role of economics and how it is related, used, expressed or exploited by other social science disciplines would be crucial to understanding how an economy can function properly, bearing in mind that many economic activities have been conducted for different social ends. Yet those decision makers who deliberately and knowingly abuse and distort economic activities would shamefully turn around and blame their poor performance on the economy. A major economic problem is the difficulty in distinguishing between the normal economic activities and the twisted economic activities as a result of weak or wrong policy decisions.

The conceptual discussions in this book can be condensed into several key areas. The first is the need to understand the *ex-ante* nature of economic endowment, while most economic analyses and policy decisions are based on the *ex-post* nature of economic outcomes. Second, in relation to other social science disciplines, the relationship between economics and politics has been often misunderstood or abused for political purposes. Economics is basically apolitical, but economic instruments and activities have been deployed for political ends, resulting in distortions and a lack of clarity between pure economic outcomes and politically oriented policy outcomes. Other than politics, the activities of other social disciplines are often expressed using economic instruments and activities.

The chapter completes by raising the possible potentials in the Conceptual Economics sphere and describing how it can become a new branch in economic analysis as it does fulfil some of the analytical gaps in understanding, knowing and practicing economics and making sound economic decisions. In a nutshell, Conceptual Economics aims to stimulate intuitive discussions and ideas that can lead to a greater and better understanding of the deployment of economic resources by all decision makers.

II Economics of Endowment

By its very nature, outcomes of economic activities are always "unequal" as they always differ from one another. This is because analysts and decision makers have mistakenly focused on the outcome end or the *ex-post* end of economic activities. The Gross Domestic Product (GDP) of an economy and its different components, such as consumption, investment and export, are the outcomes of previously performed economic activities. Households consume, but their ability to purchase depends on how much they earn, and this in turn depends on how marketable their personal endowments are, and such marketability depends on their knowledge, education, skill, innate ability and talent, family background and the way they were raised and so on. Thus, studying consumer behavior is the *ex-post* end of a chain of economic relationships.

The amount of investment is also an *ex-post* figure because how attractive the investment is depends on how competitive the economy is, and how market-friendly the policies are, and that in turn depends on other related performances, such as infrastructure provisions, public security and safety, banking facilities and effective financial institutions, as well as how much the public saves and the availability of loanable funds. Similarly, exports are *ex-post* figures, as they depend on the amount of "value added" in industrial production, level of technology advancement, availability and suitability of human capital, and the trustworthiness of the country's currency. All these prior *ex-ante* conditions are indeed the factors that lead to differences in outcomes among individuals, workers, businesses, industries and countries.

Differences in endowments are inevitable and cannot be avoided, and it is unfortunate if political activists politicize the economic outcomes by demonizing differences as "inequalities", thereby inserting political interpretations on economic outcomes. Indeed, economic growth is an *ex-post* situation, as it is the result of numerous economic activities mingling with each other through deployment of resources, time and different levels of decision-making on the one hand. And on the other hand, economic outcomes resulting from activities would vary according to the activity itself, which may involve a minimum amount of resource, or extensive use of technology, or take a longer time in generating results, or results may not even be measurable.

The "relative" nature of economic activities means that some activities move faster than others in time, some resources are more productive than others, some resources cost more than others and there could be huge differences in the decision-making when it comes to resource deployment. Economic outcomes are always different from one another because economic activities are always dynamic. Thus, the more relevant concern should be the various *ex-ante* conditions. How can *ex-ante* situations be improved, expanded and utilized effectively? There are loads of academic studies on economic outcomes, such as Gross National Product (GNP), investment, trade and exports and productivity, and few analysts have even considered the *ex-ante* factors that come before the results are generated. Lamenting on the differences in the *ex-post* results without making efforts to improve the *ex-ante* conditions can easily be politicized, as the difference in the *ex-post* results are visible and measurable, while conditions in the *ex-ante* situations are often invisible and intangible.

Policy makers must make efforts to attend to *ex-ante* conditions, ensuring that their improvements shall produce stronger *ex-post* results. By doing so, one probable consequence is the improvement, increase and reproduction of opportunities, letting the "opportunity multiplier" function to its greatest possible extent. As more opportunities arise, individuals and businesses with different endowments shall find new economic channels, and the improvement in people and business shall lead to improvement at the society or economy level, thereby leading to overall growth and development, as well as improvement in economic competitiveness. Hence, accepting differences should be the proper manner than criticizing the differences in outcomes as "inequality".

III Economics and Politics: Core Differences

Starting from the discussion on political economy, Conceptual Economics provides a powerful tool elaborating the essence and strength of economics as a means to enhance human development. Other than clarifying the fundamental inter-connectedness within the economic discipline, cross-disciplinary conceptual understanding between economics and other social science disciplines is equally important, particularly in the relationship between economics and politics, as politics often uses economics as its tool. The difference is that economics looks to progress, growth and mutual success, though economic rewards always differ among individuals. Politics capitalizes on differences, discrepancies, diversities and loopholes as a means to gain popularity, influence and power.

Differences in economic outcomes have for centuries been politicized by the leftist as income inequality, without knowing that income and economic differences arise due to the differences in endowments and the exposure and availability of opportunities among individuals. As the education system exists to inject knowledge into all young individuals, it at the same time sows the seeds of differences as the differences in educational attainments would mean differences in their economic attainment in future. Leftist advocates fell into a "chicken and egg" trap when on the one hand they urged the education system to perform, yet on the other hand politicized the outcome of education by capitalizing the resulting differences as "inequality". Such an approach to politicization cannot win because the law of economics is that there are always differences in economic outcomes.

One must understand that economic differences can only be dealt with within economics, and politicization would only worsen the issue. Economic differences arise due to differences in individual endowments. As such, the solution is to expand the opportunity set so that more jobs are created, and the rise in economic rewards shall lead to a rise in employment. However, even at a time of full employment, economic differences continue to exist. A proper attitude is to address the differences rather than politicizing and dichotomizing it as "inequality".

While all ambitious politicians want to win in elections, their political ideology when elected has immense impact on government policies as well as on the consequent economic outcomes. As such, economic performance could be more negatively affected by the inappropriate ideology and policy exercised by the political leaders than on the *per se* performance of the purely apolitical economic activities. This explains why electing pro-economic political leaders are important to the survival, expansion and growth of the economy and the country's development. Pro-growth political leaders would exercise their power and authority appropriately to improve the economic endowments of different economic entities in both the short run and long run. It is worth reiterating that what all voters want is a better and stronger economy so that their economic welfare can be improved, not a power-hungry administration that protects the interest of the cronies or that the entire economy's performance be directed by the politicians to gain votes in the elections. Politicians should win votes by producing effective deeds and measurable outcomes that benefit the entire economy.

Voters do have the role in electing their ruling leaders. As political elections are *ex-ante* activities because the actual performance of the elected leaders cannot be known before taking office, it would be safer to vote for politicians whose ideology and policies aim to promote the long-term economic competitiveness and not merely deal with short-term wealth redistribution, because this would be the only sure way to have the chance for the voters to enjoy the overall economic improvement rather than experiencing the consequent pain of a rising national debt and fiscal deficit where the overspending on the current generation would burden the economic capacity of the future generation. It is utterly unfair and unethical to the voters when the elected leaders end up *ex-post* with a huge debt and deficit that weakens the economy.

Among all social science disciplines, politics has formed a close relationship with economics. Politics is the distribution of power. Democracy allows political freedom in elections, provided all political parties and candidates adhere to the rules and laws governing elections. Any politically ambitious candidate can seek election, and most candidates are affiliated to either a right-wing or a left-wing political party. Thus, a rightist politician shall pledge for policies that align more with economic results, while a leftist candidate shall seek for dichotomies to stir up sentiments in an election. Nonetheless, candidates seeking for election may not be well educated in economics, and leftist candidates may put politics prior to economics. Although freedom is exercised in political democracy, how educated and informed the voters are can also lead to unpredictable results. Different voters may apply different criteria in selecting a candidate, depending on their interest and expectation from the candidate. Indeed, the most popular candidate may not be the most suitable or capable candidate, as elections are often based on the simple majority rule.

When elected, the politician shall become the leader who shall utilize and implement policies based on some political ideology. The passive nature of economic resources could provide a golden opportunity for the elected leader to deploy them based on ideological ends. Hence, a rightist political leader would create a suitable investment environment so that more opportunities can come forward to create jobs and promote economic welfare for all, while the needy households and individuals will be assisted through a welfare scheme. It is true that "supply-side" economics can be practiced and instituted into policies.

On the contrary, a leftist political leader tends to adopt "demand-side" policies by spending on instituting a larger government machinery. In the name of redistribution, high tax rates are the common instrument used by the leftist leaders, as they mistakenly believe that "inequality" was created by the rich, ignoring the entire understanding of differences in individual endowments. Economic disincentives usually result in a loss in competitiveness as investments would be driven away to more market-friendly destinations. The result is economic decline or stagnation, and the accumulation of the national debt would in turn haunt the welfare of the future generation. Thus, overspending on the current generation at the expense of the future generation would result in a much weaker and uncompetitive economy.

A loophole in political democracy is that democratically elected leaders are not responsible for the country's economic loss incurred as a result of the leaders decisions during the period of their rule. Hence, by building up huge fiscal deficit and national debt, these leftist political leaders could leave their office at the end of their political term without the need to worry about how the national debt and fiscal deficit would have to be paid, financed and rebalanced. In a business organization, the losses would have to be accounted for by the top management. Borrowers would be penalized if they are unable to repay their mortgage. Such business ethics produces a strong sense of morality and economic responsibility. But ethics and morality could be weaker among politicians as elected leaders do not need to be accountable for the debts and deficits they built up during their term of office. As such, political leaders, especially the leftist politicians, will effectively have an open cheque for them to spend to satisfy their ideological goal, while the economy would remain uncompetitive and the future generation would have to shoulder the debt burden.

This is the unjust aspect in a political democracy where it imposes unwanted and unintended results on the economy.

It is utterly unfair and unethical for any elected political leader to pile up the national debt which could hurt the future generation and minimize all possible economic opportunities. Experiences have shown that other than a few exceptions such as the need for a strong military, countries with rising national debts are usually controlled by pro-socialist or leftist political leaders, while pro-capitalist or rightist political leaders tend to concentrate on promoting a market-friendly economy in order to attract investments and expand economic opportunities, which in turn shall provide the governments the chance to reduce debts, and start accumulating national wealth and strengthen the country's currency. All individuals and businesses shall benefit from an expanding economy, regardless of their background and variation in endowments.

IV Social Sciences and Power Centers

While the study and understanding of economics is about resource allocation, the decision of resource deployment, however, rests with the decision makers. Economic resources do not have a life of their own unless and until they are deployed for different purposes by decision makers. Land can be made useful and productive only when construction is built. Capital is immobile unless and until investment decisions have been made. Labor can remain idle unless and until training is conducted and the worker can only become productive when employed. However, once construction has been conducted on a piece of land, such as the building of a university, that piece of land will serve the economy for a long time to come. Similarly, when invested, capital can produce numerous job opportunities and lead to various forms of production. And when trained and educated, the workers can be employed for decades.

One feature about economics is that once deployed, resources can provide a string of services and productivities that could last for a long period of time. Such infrastructure as railway or motorway can serve the public for many decades to come, thereby generating other opportunities and facilitating other economic services. Economic activities are therefore "relative" to each other: the deployment of one economic resource shall generate new activities which may last for a long time and will not deplete at the same time. And in the meantime, new resource deployment would occur, thereby expanding the quantity and magnitude of economic activities, which shall then mingle with each other. In the process, some activities are more productive than others, some resources deplete or depreciate faster than others, some additional activities would join the economic pool, and new resources are developed through science and technology to facilitate production.

Economic relativity shall generate differences in both input endowments and output results. All economic resources are different from each other at the endowment end. One piece of land would have a higher market value than another. One piece of machinery could be more productive than another. And one individual could be better educated and trained than another. Similarly, at the outcome end, one commodity could have a higher price than another. One industry could have a higher value-added component than another. Different prices are attached to different properties. Workers are paid differently due to age, experience, and the level of training and required qualification. As such, one can argue that because of differences in endowments, economic outcomes are unlikely to be similar. Students in the same class attend the same degree program, but their different career paths mean their earning abilities would differ after graduation.

One must accept the feature that economics is a discipline that deals with differences in endowments and produces differences in outcomes. The "relative" nature of economics is that differences occur in many dimensions: in the level of endowments, in the timing of deployment, in the level of resource deployment, in the period in which resources are depleted, in the level of productivity, in the level of value added, in the market price, in the usage of the final products, in the disposal of the products when used, in the payment of production factors, in the earnings made by investors, in the spending made by workers, in the saving behavior of households, in the way the government spends, in the need of the society, in the way economic growth and development proceed and so on. In short, difference is a core feature among economic activities and results.

In addition to the discipline of politics, all other social science disciplines will have to use economics as their tool in expressing their concerns or achieving their targets. In social welfare, it is crystal clear that any form of social welfare relates to the spending side of the fiscal budget. By its very nature, social welfare could hardly generate any earning for the government. Whether it is in the form of old-age pensions, unemployment benefits or health subsidies, they are expressed and calculated as transfer payments. Again, it depends whether "supply-side" policies that aim at generating employment or "demand-side" policies that produce generous welfare assistance are adopted by the government. Spending on welfare could also be made conditional on other criteria, such as whether the recipient had worked and paid tax previously, or retirement age can be prolonged so that more near-retirement workers can remain in employment in order to reduce government spending on the retired, or health spending can be instituted through an insurance scheme at an early age.

It is crucial to understand that welfare spending always relates to the expenditure side of the fiscal equation. The ability to earn has often been ignored by welfare advocates, while pro-welfare or leftist political leaders see raising tax as a solution to increase government earnings. These are in fact fallacies. A government's ability to make fiscal earnings is not by levying a higher tax but to have a more vibrant, competitive, market-friendly economy to attract investments which shall then generate employment opportunities, and as more workers are employed, there will be less people seeking welfare assistance, and at the same time more employed workers will pay income tax. This is how a government's fiscal earnings can be raised. Social workers and welfare advocates must bear in mind that welfare supports are pure spending to drain away the government's earnings. Indeed, the government's desire to spend shall depend on its ability to earn in the first instance.

The policy of a blanket provision on welfare is undesirable because recipients are diverse and may have different needs. A better solution to welfare is to ensure that welfare recipients can regain their financial independence within a short period of time and that there is an overall increase in job provisions so that they can stand on their own economic feet through employment and have better opportunities to earn and consume. The morality of economic welfare is not the amount one gets through government assistance, but the amount one earns through hard work and the ability to enjoy one's contribution to the society.

Politics, economics and social welfare considerations are the three areas of social sciences which have mingled closely with each other. Although it is a mistaken view, some shallow-minded advocates think that these three areas of analyses are not separable, as the discussion of one cannot deviate from the discussion of another. The conceptual discussion here does show the difference and the inter-connectedness among the three disciplines, and there can be a clear causality effect from one to the other.

The activities of other social disciplines, such as culture and psychology, are also expressed through economic tools. The richness in one culture is shown by the amount of economic activities associated with cultural ceremonies and festivals, the various means to express mutual respect and the social roles between individuals and generations. Cultural activities, festivals and event celebrations can also have an impact on the overall productivity, as the number of holidays would reduce the number of working days, though its impact could cancel out each other when all countries are having the same number of holidays. Nonetheless, holidays do serve the function of energizing the working population and the joyful time people have shall refresh them tremendously. To workers and their families, holidays are always a social good, and more is always preferred.

Gender differences can also be expressed through economic tools, typically in the kind of goods and services produced and consumed. Fashion and cosmetics are mainly geared to the purchasing power of the female consumer, so are the gifts people buy for different occasions. Parents buy different clothes and toys for their children of different genders. While sports are more popular with the male population, beauty contests and pageants are dominated by the females. Works that require physical strength are occupied more by the male workers, although there are exceptions and increasingly female workers are recruited to do similar strenuous jobs. Changes in the population structure and the changing social attitude have led to similar job recruitment for both genders.

Along with cultural and social activities, people's psychological behavior too varies in relation to economic activities. Some consumers believe that imported goods are of better quality and more reliable than locally produced products. Others believe in "brand-name" effects and are prepared to pay for a "brand-name" product which may have the same practical utility. The design of a certain product can appeal to the psychology of consumers, thereby helping producers improve consumer loyalty.

Nonetheless, economics performs as the commonality among all social science disciplines in arriving at their goals. Each of the social science disciplines cannot readily make itself explicit and active without the use of economic instruments and variables. Through economics, the work of other social science disciplines is brought to life. This shows a major difference between economics and other social sciences. Although there are numerous economic theories and analyses, the fact is that economic resources are passive entities and can only be activated by decision makers. And once activated, economic resources will perform differently. On the contrary, other social science disciplines need a vehicle through which their activities can be seen and materialized. Economics serves as the vehicle and becomes the essential component to other social science activities. In turn, the decisions made by social agents do reflect on the performance of the economy. This shows importantly the complementary or the serving nature of economics in relation to other social sciences, providing them with a visible and viable instrument to maneuver and at the same time, function as the receiving end of all their activities.

Taking a wider perspective, one can argue that there are many "power centers" in social sciences and humanities. Societies are organized in such a way that there are entities, corporations, associations and interest groups that hold on to a "power base", using it to control others and/or amass authority and gain influence on the followers, supporters and believers. The government is obviously a power center, through which policies are decided and individuals would be affected by the policies implemented by the various government departments and bureaus. Political parties which gather people with similar ideological viewpoints are power centers, and one of their functions is to propose members as candidates to compete in different levels of political elections. Religious institutions are power centers. Expressed in different forms of faith and spiritual desires, religious institutions can gather people for religious activities and influence others in the name of a certain faith. Religious activities appear in different manners and forms that mainly occupy the time and mind of the believers. Non-governmental organizations (NGOs) are power centers as they are meant not only to serve a humanitarian goal but they also exist as pressure groups to push and influence governments and individuals for their purposes. Professional organizations are power centers as they hold the key to certain professional practices, including the recruitment of memberships, professional training and the number of graduates fulfilling their professional qualifications. Such other public institutions as schools, universities, hospitals, labor unions and housing authorities are power centers which will exercise control and authority in their respective areas and disciplines. The media is a power center as the way they report the news could influence and steer the opinion of the viewers and readers.

In a civilized society, these power centers exist to provide services to different people, and due to the public nature of these power centers, checks and balances are instituted that monitor their work and performance, ensuring that their activities are professionally executed, fall within the rule of law and are implemented ethically and morally without imposing unnecessary harm to the society. One can argue that the "power centers" concept reflects the various institutions and organizations that exist or are established under different social spheres. The commonality among all power centers is that they need economics as the tool to express and achieve their goals, concerns and results. For example, many power centers seek funding support through donations, while professional organizations charge fees for memberships from those seeking professional qualifications. To some power centers, donation may be exempted from tax payment, and the lack of accountability could be abused by the leaders in charge of the power centers. Another example is that many NGOs and humanitarian institutions pay their workers a lower wage as they are considered as volunteers, as a contribution or will to share mutual believe and spiritual pursuit. In short, these non-economic power centers do apply explicit economic tools in their activities.

There are other economic power centers, such as the stock markets, banking institutions, multinational corporations, suppliers of raw materials such as oil and petroleum and global internet service providers, and numerous large and small business entities. In a sense, producers can already be considered as power centers as they decide on the production of goods and services, prices charged and what input materials to be used. Economic power centers, however, are meant to serve the production side of the goods and service markets, coordinating economic activities by deploying resources including investment and deciding on what and how goods and services are produced. Economic power centers serve as the engine of growth, through which economic welfare can be generated. There are established checks and balances, such as anti-competition law, property right laws and regulations on consumer products to protect those affected.

V Economics as a Vehicle

In relation to other social disciplines, the discipline of sociology, for example, especially in social work, deals with the interaction between institutions and groups of individuals and attends to the various social needs in the society (Urry, 2000; Gerth and Mills, 2009). How much would a family need, and how much welfare should be given to the needy families and individuals? How to classify different individuals into various groupings? Should one group of individuals be treated differently from another group, or would there be a possibility to bring harmony and consensus to different groups? Should one always look at the differences or look for means to eliminate the differences between groups of individuals? In short, human differences form the primary objective in many social studies. And due to human differences, the materials needed to satisfy the requirement of the diverse groups become the core discussion in the discipline.

One typical issue among many social studies is the intention and spending drive to satisfy the needs of individuals and households. The needy individuals and households are always at the taking end of the socio-economic equation. On the contrary, the ability to give has always been debatable and controversial. In the final analysis, the concern is whether individuals should fend for themselves, or depend on assistance. In social work and within the sociology discipline, the study of the social behavior of individual groups often requires the provision of economic assistance to some groups in the form of subsidies and welfare given to households and firms. Assistance given to the needy individuals would be measured, compared and shown in economic terms. Strictly speaking, policies on social assistance are being considered on the spending side of the budget equation, as to how much to give and spend on the recipients, and not how much to get back from welfare recipients.

The discipline of psychology brings the discussion of human behavior down to the personal level, as the psychological behavior of one person differs from another (Baumeister and Finkel, 2010; Wickens *et al.*, 2016). The psychological behavior from the same person may differ between one social aspect and another social aspect. Psychologically, different parents would treat their own children differently, and likewise, children may behave differently in front of their parents. The wish and desire through the feelings expressed by the individuals should crucially form the core discussion in the discipline of psychology. The adherence to human norms, the feeling expressed on individuals and the drive to gain certain kind of social satisfaction have resulted in many human activities being determined purely by individuals' psychological drive and desire.

Psychological activities are also expressed in economic terms. In cultural festivals, the feeling of the need to exchange gifts, or presenting gift to some persons are all conducted within the economic circles of production and consumption. The numerous personal wishes, desires and preferences formed in one's psychological spheres can all be reflected in various economic activities. For example, a more expensive gift would psychologically indicate the social status of either the giver or the recipient. Due to the social differences between family members, relatives, friends and colleagues, there are also psychological differences in the interactions among these different social groups. Thus, one would buy a different and probably more expensive gift for family members and relatives than for friends and colleagues. An individual's preference is often psychological, but it will eventually be reflected in the individual's economic activities.

The various aspects in the discipline of human and economic geography could also affect the geographical contours and features (Harvey, 1996; Henderson *et al.*, 2001). Urbanization, distances between population centers and tourism are confined by the physical aspects of human geography. The distance one needs to travel to work, the geographical attractiveness of one earthly destination, the need of land infrastructure in the process of urbanization and the use of land for development are discussions related to the physical environment in human sciences. Economic development surely differs among geographical zones.

The physical aspect of human geography can equally be reflected through economic activities and measures. Urban areas are more congested, and urban land would have a higher value than rural land. Housing would be more expensive in population centers because jobs could be clustered in built-up areas. The geographical requirement would be that societies situated in one tropical region in the world would require different survival needs and materials from another region, and that these differences would generate different forms of production and consumption. For example, a person living in a cold country would need clothing differently from another person living in a warm country. The human desire to deal with geographical differences has often been shown through economic activities, such as tourism, modes of transportation, delivery services and communications.

It is well known that among all the branches of social sciences, the disciplines of economics and politics are closely related to each other. Many unsophisticated analysts even consider the two disciplines as inseparable, and the discussion of one naturally implies the discussion of the other. The study of politics examines the overall direction the society is heading towards, especially in the distribution of power and authority between the leaders, the government and the public (Lefort, 1986; Lowe and Rüdig, 1986). Whether the leaders are chosen by a democratic election process or coercion through undemocratic means or through a system of inheritance shall be a concern in politics. Equally, the instruments and institutions through which the power of their leaders are monitored constitute part of the political process. In a non-civic society, political power would be concentrated in the hands of the few leaders.

In a civic society, politics is simply part of the civilized activity, and numerous civic institutions shall provide diverse and effective layers of authority that could monitor and guard against the decisions of the leaders. The more important political transition or transformation is whether a civic-oriented society would be promoted and nurtured, or the ruling leaders would practice coercion instead. In societies where civic establishments are lacking, the military or the religion could become an effective institution of control. In a civic society, professional institutions flourish to represent and promote the civic side of the society. The crucial element in politics is the balance of power and authority between the ruler and the ruled. For the political leaders to assert their authority and power, they will exercise various instruments through policy decisions, which often require the use of economic variables. For example, the use of taxation and the desire to balance the annual budget, the means to reduce national debts, and the policy on redistribution are all political decisions using economics as their tools and means.

One can extend the discussion to advancement in science and technology. Research and development activities are very much dependent on the availability of economic resources in the first instance. In medicine, for example, many new drugs have been tested for human consumption and the process in scientific development can be very costly. Space exploration surely consumes much economic resources while outcomes can only be cumulative and may not produce immediate results. Nonetheless, it is the outcome of research and development in science and technology that would lead to advancement in human life and civilization. A closely related issue in technology advancement is the commercialization of technology, which basically applies new and existing technology to household appliances for general consumption. Various examples of commercialization of technology can be made. The use of conveyor belt, for example, has aided industrialization and manufacturing in such technological products as motor vehicles. Since the 1960s, the design and production of Walkman in Japan commercialized tape recorder into a personal product, and its development was followed by other audio innovations. Mobile phones and robots are the more contemporary examples of technological commercialization.

The commonality among the various social science disciplines and science and technology advancement is that they are using economics as a tool or vehicle through which their desires, goals, intentions and ambitions can be satisfied. For example, politics does not have its own form, but it is often expressed using economic tools and measures. Social relationships can be expressed or made explicit using economic tools and comparisons. Psychological relationships are similarly the expressions of individual feelings and desires, but their physical parallels are shown using economic calculations, activities and transactions. Similarly, human geographical features, regional and geographical developments, infrastructural limitations and constraints are surely presented through economics.

Economics is the vehicle through which other disciplines in social sciences can be materialized. Economic tools, variables and policies have been adopted with the intention to satisfy the desire and goals targeted for different social disciplines. In other words, an economic decision may not be intended as an economic outcome as it could be used to serve other social goals and ends. One can thus argue that economics is a passive but powerful discipline as it holds the material key to other forms of social and human activities. Political science provides the societal path, social relationships concern the human needs, psychological relationships relate to human wish and desire, while human geography shows the physical capacity. But they all express themselves using economic tools, variables, activities and transactions.

Figure 2.1 summarizes and concentrates on the relationship between economics and the other four social science disciplines, though one can easily incorporate other aspects, such as law and science and technology, into Figure 2.1. While each of these social science disciplines has their own areas of concerns, the commonality is that they need economics as a vehicle through which their activities can be conducted. Although there are other connections among the four social science disciplines, they all use economics to deliver their policy outcomes. Thus, the economics discipline becomes the instrument for other social science disciplines in the calculation and measurement of policy outcomes. This superficially makes economics a powerful discipline. However, the danger is that the economic consequences resulting from the act of other social science disciplines may have a negative or undesirable impact on the economy itself. While economics serves other social science disciplines, there is also the "economic outcome" that one must attend to within the economic discipline itself.

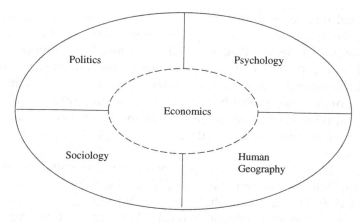

Figure 2.1   The Relationship Between Economics and Other Social Science Disciplines

In other words, the problem facing the economics discipline is that many "economic outcomes" are not meant to serve the economy itself but are used as instruments to achieve or satisfy other social goals. As such, the economic discipline could be "interfered" by the activities in other social relationships that could impose undesirable or unintended economic outcomes. And because these are outcomes expressed in economics, people often believe that these are economic performances and problems, and would begin to look for solutions within the economic sphere when the root of the problem has not originated from the economic discipline. These unintended economic outcomes and consequences would act as distortion to the functioning of a normal economic trend, thereby imposing further complications on the complex economy.

VI Think Outside the Box

"Think outside the box" has popularly been used as an approach or attitude in innovation and creativity. As an academic discipline, economic theories have been developed extensively and numerous quantitative approaches have been applied to analyze economic theories, and yet there are still numerous growing economic problems which appear not only periodically, but constantly or even daily. There are new economic problems emerging and many of the economic problems are not new and have existed for a long time. Thus, something must be missing in the established theories and analyses. The study of Conceptual Economics should take us one-step closer to providing solutions, or at least a better understanding of the so-called economic problems. New solutions would naturally come forward should there be a better understanding when economic problems are being dissected minutely to identify the origin of the problem, discovering probably that many economic problems are originated from other social science disciplines and the economic results are merely the receiving end and could even serve as the scapegoat in many problems.

By thinking outside the box, Conceptual Economics attempts to build a bridge in both "intra-disciplinary" and "inter-disciplinary" analyses. The "intra-disciplinary" analysis shall involve the linking of relationships within the economics discipline, typically between the two broad divisions of microeconomics and macroeconomics, and how the formation of the microeconomic parts shall impact on the macroeconomic aspects, and *vice versa*. In finance, for example, the study of the microstructure would concentrate on the details of financial transactions and products, while the macroeconomic aspect of finance shall examine risk, interest rate performance, banking and financial markets (Madhavan, 2000; Harris, 2003; Lehalle and Laruelle, 2013). It is true that academic studies tend to be focused, but these studies could become narrow as they would deviate from reality and practicality, making the studies redundant. Indeed, economic problems are often multi-dimensional, requiring a wider perspective in identifying and locating solutions. The depth of analyses would even be very technical, and the employment of assumptions would reduce the applicability of the analyses. Furthermore, the solution may involve trade-off and opportunity cost, and there is no "Pareto" optimum and "positive-sum" outcomes. There is thus a need for "intra-disciplinary" analyses within the different economic spheres to take a comprehensive approach to economic analyses.

The "inter-disciplinary" approach shall relate economics to other social science disciplines, typically politics, social welfare, culture, religion and psychology. As it has been argued and pointed out repeatedly, economics has been used as an instrument to fulfil goals and has become the explicit form of activities in other social sciences. As such, while certain economic outcomes may not be favorable, the original intention of the activity could be related to another social science discipline. Thus, the "spaghetti bowl" effect is that when different ingredients are mixed together, it may not be possible to distinguish between the real economic impact and the side-effect resulting from the activities originated in other social science disciplines. Nonetheless, it is a step forward in analyzing the "inter-disciplinary" relationship between economics and other social science disciplines. Economics does have a crucial role in the performance of all other social science disciplines.

The clarification between "*ex-ante*" and "*ex-post*" situations in all economic activities is another important concept because most economic analyses consider mainly the *ex-post* situations where economic results are quantified, measured and studied. Yet all economic outcomes and results are determined by the quality and viability of factor inputs, known as endowments. When there is a difference in the level of endowment, there shall be differences in the economic outcomes. Indeed, by exploring the possibility of different *ex-ante* performances, one can seek retrospective clarification and explanations for different *ex-post* outcomes. Economic results are relative to each other, and their differences can be due to several endowment factors. The appearance of differences in economic results is an innate feature in economics. Attempt to address the different outcomes can only be dealt with by improving the endowments. Politicizing economic differences in the form of "inequality" and dealing with "inequality" through redistributive policies based on political ideology could end up with undesirable consequences because the redistributive process itself would lead to economic distortions and disincentives.

Another economic concept worth emphasizing is the passive nature of economic resources, which can only be activated by decision makers. The "relativity" feature of economics is that once resources have been deployed, there are numerous multiplier effects and dimensions. The innate nature of difference is such that economic outcomes are relative to each other. Some resources deplete faster than others, while one production requires a higher level of endowment than another, and so on. Economic relativity appears when different agents are conducting different economic activities simultaneously, and one economic activity would have a different lifespan from another, and surely the impact on the economy would also vary from one another.

The lack of understanding in the innate feature of differences in economics has given rise to many misinterpretations, misconception, misuse and mistakes, especially when these differences have been capitalized by political opportunists who would exploit these differences for political ends. Indeed, if politics becomes effective in dealing with economic problems, many economic problems would vanish. Yet decades or even centuries old economic problems still exist or are still used by generations of radical politicians as instruments, means and causes in their political drive. Building a political platform which advocates the use of politics in solving economic problem usually end up with the continuation, or even deterioration, of the problem. Radical politicians come and go, but the problems remain. The loophole in political freedom is that the elected leaders are not responsible on how the economy has fiscally been depleted and weakened, resulting in a fall in competitiveness suffered by the businesses as well as the employees. Politicians and leaders must come up with a formula whereby elected leaders would be financially accountable for the consequences of their policies. It would indeed be unethical, unacceptable and wrong for any elected leader to pile up economic burden while they are in office and leave the financial burden to future leaders and generations to pay for the overspending made under their regime. The exercise of political freedom that results in electing a financially irresponsible leader could end up with a greater fiscal burden, a fall in economic competitiveness and lower output and productivity. That would not be a blessing to the economic freedom and welfare improvement for everyone.

VII Conclusion

Bold analyses can lead to two diverse outcomes. One possible outcome is that the ideas will be trashed. The other possible outcome is that it serves as a pioneer of a new school of thought in analyses. The novelty in putting forward the ideas in Conceptual Economics is that it takes a step back and asks why many persistent economic problems have not been solved, while the available and existing theories have not been able to deal with many of the global economic problems, such as inequality, poverty, crises, energy and environment, immigration and social cost. The question is whether there is a lack of appropriate economic analyses or that the problems and difficulties might not have originated from economics. But rather, the variation in economic outcomes, problems and difficulties, if any, could serve only as the dressing of other hidden and more profound social and political problems. As such, the solution should look beyond economic performances and outcomes. A fundamental feature in economics is that economic outcomes are always different from each other. This is because the different *ex-post* outcomes may be due to the different *ex-ante* endowments.

It is useful to summarize the various features in the discussion of Conceptual Economics. The first concept is that economic resources are scarce, but it is more important to be aware of the passive nature of economic resources, that economic resources cannot be made productive without decision makers activating the deployment of economic resources. The initiative, therefore, rests with the decision makers. The problem, however, is that decision makers may make erroneous decisions. Or economic decisions were made for non-economic purposes, while the consequences, however favorable or unfavorable, would fall within the economic sphere.

The discussion on economic relativity is that once deployed, economic resources are faced with different magnitudes and dimensions. Economic activities can vary in pace, space, speed, time and duration. Some resources last longer while others deplete faster than others. Resources would perform differently in the value-added chain, and thus command different prices and values. Thus, at any point in time, numerous economic activities mingle and mix with each other, producing an infinite multiplier effects, including some undesirable ones. While some economic activities are decided previously, new economic decisions continuously appear. As such, economic performances are always "relative" to each other, and outcomes from economic activities are always different from one another. There are numerous economic cycles coexisting with each other at any point in time. Individuals face employment cycles as some young workers join the labor market while others retire from the labor market. There are investment cycles as new investments of different style and magnitude emerge periodically. There are fiscal cycles where the government's political orientations may generate economic waves. There are business cycles where the economy fluctuates due to forces in supply and demand, changes in expectation and economic incidences that occur sequentially. All the activities in these various cycles occur along with each other, generating relativities.

Another relevant economic concept is the need to link economic outcomes to their origins, as a better understanding of the origins should produce a better understanding of the economic outcomes. There are two discussions on the "origins" of economic outcomes. One such discussion relates to the endowments possessed by individuals, institutions and economies. A high level of possessed and acquired endowments shall always produce a stronger economic outcome. But due to the differences in endowments, economic outcomes naturally are different from one another. It would be preferable, therefore, for one to focus on the improvement in economic endowments, rather than lamenting on the differences in economic outcomes.

The discussion on the "inter-disciplinary" study between economics and other social science disciplines should provide ample discussion on the "origins" of economic outcomes. The discipline of economics has been used as the instrument in other social science disciplines, typically in politics, social welfare, culture and psychology. Activities in these non-economic disciplines can only be made explicit and visible using economic activities and deploying economic variables. Thus, the economic outcome so arrived may relate to non-economic goals, but the economic outcome may also affect the economy, either favorably or unfavorably.

Politics has been closely associated with economics. It is because political decisions often use economics as the instrument for showing political results. As many economic policies are politically or ideologically oriented, the economic outcomes may be distortive and may not reflect the true economic situation. But the "spaghetti bowl" effect would make it difficult to distinguish between the actual performance, or if it was the result of poor policies adopted. Indeed, radical politicians often politicize economics in order to push forward their political goals. Typically, economic differences have been misinterpreted as "inequality", and political decisions were often conducted in vain using redistributive policies. The economic truth is that "inequality" can never be eradicated, but differences can be improved through increase in economic opportunities where individuals and businesses shall gain as the "economic pie" expands.

The argument in Conceptual Economics is that politicians and leaders should give economic performances higher priority than political ideologies. In a mature democracy, what voters gain would be the better economic results arising from pragmatic and effective economic policies, and the economy should not be held at ransom by politicians. It is the ability to make economic promotion that counts, and it would be unethical and irresponsible for political leaders to pile up the size of national debt, thereby committing overspending in the current generation at the expense of the future generations, resulting in an economic "vicious cycle" in the rise of debt. Coupled with rising tax and government spending, the consequence would be an increase in disincentive in investment and ultimately a fall in economic competitiveness, producing a weaker and burdensome economy for the future generations. Pro-economics or pro-growth political leaders should preferably be elected because they will care for the overall economic health of the country and economic sustainability and would ensure a strong economy for the future.

Economics is a thing that follows every individual for life. The economic life of any individual begins from the day the person was born. Economics comes into play in the way the child is raised and brought up by parents, the child's learned cultural behavior and living style, the child's education attainment and life opportunities to express one's innate ability and peer group activities. As an adult, economic activities are involved through one's employment and choice and ability in consumption and investment. The choice of raising a family has a lot to do with economics as individuals have to work out the available resources needed for raising a family. Economic decisions also appear in an individual's post-retirement life, as savings and financial assistance would be needed as the risk of not knowing when one's life ends would mean that resources must be put aside in preparation of one's retirement.

Economics is part of our lives, and no one can do away with economics. As such, individuals should make the best out of economics for their own benefits, maximizing gains, welfare and security as much as possible. While individuals can control their own economic activities, it is equally necessary to see to the effectiveness of economic policies to ensure a high degree of complementarity between individuals' economic decisions and policy outcomes. In other words, one's economic life must flow along with the macroeconomic atmosphere, but individuals also can influence policy decisions to ensure that economic policies are useful and helpful to their own economic advancement. In a democratic society, political elections are useful to elect leaders who hold pro-economics ideologies and aim at ensuring growth and development in their policy decisions and resource deployment. A "supply-side" economic approach is usually associated with policies that promote the endowments of individual economic agents and entities, to ensure continuous growth in the economic pie, though there could still be periodic difficulties and crises as the relative movement among economic activities may produce short-term difficulties.

Putting it in an analogy, economics to any individual is like the relationship between the person and the person's health. The person must keep himself or herself focused to stay healthy and avoid getting sick, but at the same time the person must ensure that the living environment will

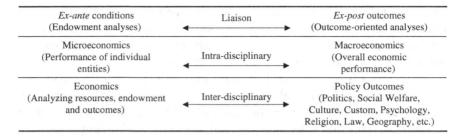

Ex-ante conditions (Endowment analyses)	Liaison	Ex-post outcomes (Outcome-oriented analyses)
Microeconomics (Performance of individual entities)	Intra-disciplinary	Macroeconomics (Overall economic performance)
Economics (Analyzing resources, endowment and outcomes)	Inter-disciplinary	Policy Outcomes (Politics, Social Welfare, Culture, Custom, Psychology, Religion, Law, Geography, etc.)

Figure 2.2   Summarizing Conceptual Economics

not bring unpleasantness and toxic conditions as to hurt the person's health. The study of economics is not "rocket science", far from it, rather economics relates to every aspect of life. Every individual is constantly and continuously conducting some sort of economic activity. Hence, an individual must nourish and nurture a mutually acceptable relationship with his or her own economic performance. And at the same time, work to ensure that his relationship with economics can only get better and is progressing, rather than bringing additional level of burden to the person's economic welfare. This requires the need to investigate the individual's economic performance at the personal level, as well as the suitability of economic environment at the societal level. The individual shall then seek economic improvement as much as possible in both personal and societal levels.

The discussion on Conceptual Economics has dealt with several economic issues, which have been summarized into three key aspects as shown in Figure 2.2. To begin with, Conceptual Economics raises the distinction between *ex-ante* situations that are concerned with the economics of endowments and the *ex-post* situations that show the outcomes of all economic activities. The second layer of discussion is the intra-connectivity between the need to understand microeconomics and the desire to relate it to macroeconomics, and *vice versa*. By combining these discussions, one can at least get a better intellectual understanding of the two arms of economics, while at most one can produce a better economic solution.

Another ingredient in Conceptual Economics is the extension to incorporate other social sciences, typically politics, social welfare, culture, psychology and others, such as human geography, law and technology. The conceptual strength in such an "inter-disciplinary" discussion is the reality that economics has been the commonality in all other social sciences, as they require the visible instrument in making explicit outcomes in their goals and policy outcomes. Economic instruments and variables thus enter the life and functioning of other social science disciplines. As such, policies that use economic variables could lead to results that may not be favorable to the overall performance of the economy, while it would not be possible to distinguish the effect of purely economic performance from the economic impact resulting from policies originated from other social science disciplines.

Section II

The Extensity Dimension

This section contains four chapters that examine the "extensity" dimension of economics. Within the economics discipline, the "intra-disciplinary" relationship discussed in Chapter Three shows how aspects in microeconomics can connect to macroeconomics. It would be appropriate conceptually to relate the two arms of economics simultaneously as that could produce a stronger framework for analysis. Hence, such concepts and theories as supply and demand, competition, comparative advantage and the difference between real and nominal economy are extensively discussed to show the "intra-disciplinary" relationships within the economics discipline.

The "inter-disciplinary" discussion begins with Chapter Four by examining the relationship between economics and politics, commonly known as political economy. The argument points out that economics is "passive" as economic resources can only be mobilized by decision makers. On the contrary, politics is "active" but may not have a form of its own. Hence, for political outcomes and results to be realized, politics needs economics as an instrument. A typical example is to interpret and politicize the different nature in economics as "inequality". Differences in earnings in economics are being politicized as "income inequality", and political decisions are then made on an economic issue.

Chapter Five extends the "economics–politics" relationship to include the role of the government and the deployment of fiscal policy. This chapter discusses some fundamental concepts and features of fiscal policy, focusing on the differences between "demand-side" policies and "supply-side" policies, and proposes an apolitical or "politics-free" fiscal model that puts economics as its prime purpose. The conceptual problem is that when economics is used for political objectives, it would be impossible to separate the impact from purely economic issues and politics-related impacts. The same can be true in other social science disciplines, as culture and customs, religion and social welfare are often expressed in economic terms, and their decisions may have different goals, but would have economic impacts, either favorably or unfavorably. Such a "interdisciplinary" relationship with other social disciplines is the theme of Chapter Six. Although the list of social disciplines discussed in this chapter could be expanded, it serves as a highlight in the discussion by relating economics to such key issues as culture, religion and psychology. Indeed, similar conceptual discussion can be extended to law, human geography, science and technology and many more.

Chapter Three

Intra-Connectedness among Economic Theories

I Introduction

While the discussion in the last section lays the conceptual foundation that incorporated several features in the discipline of economics, such as the difference between *ex-ante* and *ex-post* situations, and the tight connectedness among economic performances, this chapter aims to begin the content of Conceptual Economics first by examining and aligning the various dimensions within the broad discipline of economics, namely the intra-connections within economics and how issues within the two branches of microeconomics and macroeconomics can be integrated to provide a comprehensive analysis. This chapter looks at the "intra-disciplinary" relationship, while the remaining chapters in this section shall examine the "inter-disciplinary" connection between economics and other social science disciplines.

Microeconomics and macroeconomics form the two dimensions of economic analyses and they often are pivotal to other branches of economics studies. There are numerous theories in both microeconomics and macroeconomics, though analysts might have favored one against the other. Microeconomic studies touch on the analysis of individual person, firm or market, while macroeconomic studies consider the economy in its entirety and do not relate to any single individual person, firm or market. There are distinct favors in each of the two dimensions of economics analysis. Some advocates prefer microeconomics as it can concentrate on a single area that could be more effective and direct, others could argue that microeconomics is trivial, narrow and may have lacked understanding and implications on the entire economy.

On the contrary, macroeconomics does relate to more than one aspect in the entire economy, and implications can then be seen and discussed. Macroeconomics provides analysis on the path and direction as to where the economy shall proceed. Critics of macroeconomics, however, would argue that the analysis is too broad and unsure as implications and consequences would be difficult to identify, because the same macroeconomic variable can have different outcomes, and the same outcome could be the result of different instruments. The "cause–effect" relationship could be less clear in macroeconomics, thereby making the analysis mixed. Macroeconomics advocates that the outcome of macroeconomic analysis can filter into different microeconomic aspects through market mechanisms, economic behavior of individuals and firms in response to government policies. As such, the understanding of macroeconomics takes priority over microeconomics in that a proper understanding of macroeconomics would necessarily generate a good microeconomic order.

Such a debate is not meant to involve conflicts between the two dimensions of economic analysis, but to acknowledge the complexity of the economics discipline and the two dimensions should support each other to present a comprehensive understanding of the discipline. However, there have been discussions on the "micro-foundations" of macroeconomics, which basically focus on microeconomics as the fundamental aspect of economic analysis and argue that many aspects of macroeconomics can have their core and eventual analysis in microeconomics. While some analysis went further to argue that micro-foundations form the major discussions in post-Keynesian economics, others have applied the micro-foundation concept to different macroeconomic subjects, such as monetary and finance theory and economic sanctions (Clower, 1967; Weintraub, 1979; Nishimura, 1992; Forni and Lippi, 1997; Kirshner, 1997; Philip and Young, 2002; Bergh and Gowdy, 2003; Amendáriz and Labie, 2011).

The division of microeconomics and macroeconomics could be the two sides of the same coin. Microeconomics breaks down the analysis into the individual components of a macroeconomy, while macroeconomics connects and shows the global impact when all microeconomic activities are taken together, though there may not be a "one-to-one" relationship. Effectively, each microeconomic analysis can eventually link to a phenomenon in macroeconomics. Similarly, macroeconomic analysis can be dissected into different microeconomic components. The two dimensions of analyses serve more like complements, though there is much analytical work in each of the two dimensions. Thus, most academic analysts would concentrate on one aspect, as the academic state-of-the-art is to specialize in one aspect of the economics discipline. Such an academic practice may have its drawbacks because complicated economic problems may require multilevel and multi-dimensional analyses.

There are three core groups of microeconomic theories. The theory of consumer behavior comprises utility and preference functions that include income and substitution effects, purchasing power parity and externalities. The theory of production probably incorporates supply and demand theories, theory of the firm and competition, production cost and productivity, labor and human capital, Pareto-optimality and risk and uncertainty analysis. The theory of exchange includes principal–agent, rent seeking, asymmetric information, game theory and prisoner dilemma. These three broad groupings shall provide the fundamental list of microeconomic theories, which can be extended to other discussions. For example, the theories relevant to the discussion on Economics of the Environment are Pareto-optimality and externality.

There are two broad groupings of theories in macroeconomics. The group of theories that relate to the internal domestic economy shall include the monetary and fiscal policy and theory, theory on growth and development, demand-side versus supply-side economics, political economy and social economics. Macroeconomic theories that concern the external aspects of the economy include international trade, international finance and exchange rate, foreign direct investment, capital flight, globalization and international political economy. Within each broad grouping in macroeconomics, there can be sub-divisions and extensions. For example, interest rate, money supply and inflation shall come under monetary economics, while taxation and government spending shall come under fiscal policy. Exchange rate and international reserve shall appear under international trade and international finance.

In a nutshell, these five broad groupings of economic theories are not exhaustive because other specialized theories can either be incorporated into these broad theories or are the extension of these theory groups. Nonetheless, these five groupings are integrated with each other to form a comprehensive and complicated network of economic theories. Figure 3.1 summarizes the possible networks within the five groupings. The three groupings in microeconomics are related to each other in the

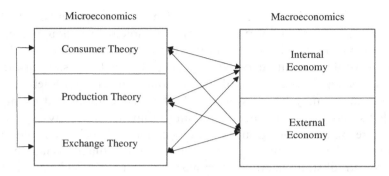

Figure 3.1   The Intra-Connectedness of Economic Theory Groups

first instance. For example, exchange theory is required when consumers deal with producers, or one producer is conducting exchange with another producer. All the three microeconomic groupings are related to both the internal and external aspects of macroeconomy. For example, the purchasing power of consumers would depend on the format of the fiscal policy, while producers engaged in exports would be involved with exchange rate movements.

Similarly, the two groups of macroeconomics can be connected to various aspects in microeconomics. Interest rate movements, for example, would impact consumers' preference as well as producers' choice of production. Industrial outputs can be exported to overseas countries, thereby making a close contact with exchange rate changes and international banking transactions. Similarly, the two divisions in macroeconomics can easily be connected. Trade and foreign direct investment would impact on domestic growth and development. Fiscal policies can impact on the external economy through international finance. Indeed, these economic groupings are knitted together showing their close connectedness in economic analysis.

II Supply and Demand: From Micro to Macro Analysis

The economic mechanics of supply and demand analysis using geometric presentations are the first lessons in microeconomics. At a more sophisticated level, algebraic tools using calculus methods are applied to show the supply and demand equations. The condition of supply and demand equilibrium can then be identified, geometrically and algebraically. The first lessons in the microeconomics of supply and demand analyses are useful as several concepts have wider implications on individuals' behavior and businesses. The discussion on "elasticity" is extremely useful in the pricing of products and the distinction between luxury and non-luxury goods. An "elastic" demand, for example, would suggest greater sale and higher revenue would be achieved at a lower price, and that obviously relates to ordinary or essential goods. An "inelastic" demand would contrarily mean greater sale and higher revenue could be maintained at a higher price, suggesting that it is a luxury good, or goods with high value-added content. Hence, it is the producers who must be clear in identifying if the good in question should be classified as a luxury good or an ordinary good. The "elasticity" concept can be a useful tool in understanding market demand and supply.

The demand and supply analysis goes further to make a distinction between change in demand with the change restricted to change in price and the shift in demand when the entire demand behavior is shifted, and demand can increase or decrease even when there is no change in price. When the consumer utility theory is included, the analysis on income effect and substitution effect provides further understanding and elaborations. The substitution effect is the change in consumption purely due to a change in relative price of a good. The income effect is the change in consumption purely due to a change in real income, relative price held constant.

All these are useful theories in understanding how the consumers and producers behave in the market. It is, however, more challenging when it comes to the assumptions employed. The economics of demand and supply shall generate an equilibrium price and equilibrium quantity demanded and supplied. It is argued that the market mechanism provides economic information to consumers and producers. In the real world, the producers may not know what the level of demand would be, and similarly, there could be uncertainty in setting the price. Similarly, what would be the equilibrium price and quantity, and when the equilibrium would be reached and how long it would stay. Or, the equilibrium concept is only a tool in understanding how the market functions.

Nonetheless, the theory of demand and supply has become a major pillar in microeconomics analysis as it has given rise to newer aspects of economic analyses in, for example, innovation, new product development and technological advancement. At the macro level, however, the analysis of "demand-side" and "supply-side" economic policies takes an entirely different level of analysis because it influences the direction of the economy's long-term path of growth and development, and it relates to the implications of government policies and the attractiveness of businesses. There are vast opposing differences in the outcome of "demand-side" and "supply-side" economics.

The key feature in demand-side economics is that it basically encourages spending as a force and source of economic growth. It is true that by consuming and spending, aggregate demand rises, and the economy looks prosperous as more spending and rising consumption would mean jobs would be forthcoming, allowing the income multiplier to expand. It follows that employment, so as wage, would rise, leading to an overall increase in economic growth. On the part of the government, demand-side or demand-driven economics would mean a larger fiscal spending to satisfy immediate demands, such as welfare and subsidies that would promote the purchasing power of the recipients, or subsidies to firms to sustain their production and employment. This fiscal spending does have short-term economic impact in that it raises the purchasing power of the recipients, who are likely to spend within a short time period. However, recipients of social welfare would experience a temporary improvement in their cost of living, while firms that receive government subsidy would have a temporary relief in their cost of production. The income multiplier does expand because of government spending on welfare and subsidy, but they are regarded as "terminal" expenditure as no further economic activities will be generated.

Fiscal spending on welfare and subsidy is particularly large in strong welfare-oriented and pro-subsidy governments. The economy of Greece as demonstrated in its debt crisis in 2014–2015, for example, has been a welfare-prone economy where large and continuous welfare is given to recipients, thereby accumulating huge national debts and resulting in a weak economy. The Chinese communist government has used subsidy as a fiscal means to pacify households and corporations to maintain employment and production, as in 2008 after the global financial crisis (Li, 2017a). For example, wage in China had been regarded as low to attract foreign investment, but in the iron-rice bowl scenario, the state would provide all kinds of welfare provisions. Thus, the low wage reflected only the "net" wage, as the state or the foreign investors would have to provide such essentials as housing to workers. In the end, the "gross" wage could certainly be much higher than the "net" wage. In short, demand-side economic policies are favored mostly in socialist countries or governments with strong welfare orientation.

A major problem in demand-side policy is its sustainability, as there are numerous related but unfavorable economic consequences and outcomes, especially in the lack of production and output as the rise in demand may not meet with rise in supply. To start with, rising aggregate demand while keeping aggregate supply constant would result in inflation, as the high purchasing power is not matched by rising output. Inflation soon eats into the households' purchasing power, and their real purchasing power remains unchanged. The positive impact of welfare spending would be canceled by the negative impact of inflation. Hence, even though it has been argued that welfare provision does facilitate income redistribution, its effect would only be nominal. Though there could be time lags between the two impacts, welfare and subsidy often provide a nominal or psychological advantage on redistribution.

In fact, some analysts even argue that provisions of welfare and subsidy would lead to inflation. The economic conceptual logic is that knowing that consumers who patronize their shops are the recipients of welfare, retails stores and producers would be reluctant to reduce their price or could even increase their price. Furthermore, inflation hurts the purchasing power of those not receiving welfare. Thus, while the welfare recipients benefit from the "free lunch", the non-recipients could face a higher cost of living because of the resulting inflation, however mild. It is true that inflation can arise from many causes, but retailers' response to the government policy could be one observed possibility. In short, while the political argument of welfare provision is to enhance the cost of living of the recipients and generate a sense of income equality through redistribution, there could be unintended consequences. One would be the pricing behavior of producers and retailers. Secondly, the fall in the economic welfare of non-recipients as a result of the rise in inflation. Another possibility could be the need to increase wage to compensate the rise in price inflation, thereby spreading the unfavorable consequence from price inflation to wage inflation. All these would eventually lead to an erosion in the economy's overall competitiveness as both price inflation and wage inflation complement each other.

Furthermore, concentrating on the spending side of the economy would mean a lower production capacity as welfare recipients are taking "free-rides" and would have less incentive to work. Other than inflation, the rise in demand could result in increase in imports, and the economy could soon experience trade deficit and a weaker currency. Unless the weak currency could aid physical export, which would depend on the economy's industrial capacity, the rise in imports and emergence of trade deficit would also lower the country's international reserve that officially backs up the value of the country's currency. A vicious cycle of "rising import → trade deficit → reduction in reserve → weak currency" could easily occur, thereby imposing unintended burden on the economy. Should trade deficit persist and together with a weak export base, the economy would soon face problems in international reserve and a decline in the value of the currency. As this happens, the price of import shall rise further should the currency remain weak, and the higher import price would further increase domestic inflation, and further reduce the purchasing power of domestic consumers.

Large and continuous welfare spending also poses fiscal burden on the government, especially if the business sector has slowed down and fiscal revenue is not forthcoming. To finance the welfare spending, the popular political step is to raise salary tax and corporate tax. Whether tax revenue rises because of high tax rate depends on the "tax elasticity" as shown by the Laffer Curve which states that the rising tax rate could reach a level beyond which tax revenue would decline (Laffer, 2004). The conceptual essence is that an excessively high or rising tax rate could lead to a lower fiscal revenue because the disincentive effect could be so high that both employment and businesses are discouraged. Business would slow down and that would have a pressure on corporate tax revenue. It is true that the government has the authority to impose the tax rate, the number of taxable items as well as the effectiveness in tax collection, but it does not have the power over the tax population, namely that the number of salaried workers and the number of businesses paying tax cannot be controlled by the government. Salaried workers and business corporations do respond to the tax environment they are faced with by changing or alternating their commitment to work or invest. On the contrary, it should be the duty of the government to ensure an increase in the number of salaried workers and number of tax-paying business corporates. This could be done by providing more incentives to workers and investors, and it is only through their effort that more government revenue could be collected.

Policies on demand-side economics through spending could only be short-lived, and fiscal spending in theory should be counter-cyclical to business cycles, spending more in economically weaker times, but withdrawing from spending when the economy is on a recovery path to avoid overheating, inflation and bubbles. The other potential danger of a prolonged policy on government spending is the accumulation of fiscal and national debt, as the increase in welfare or fiscal spending could occur at an economically tough time. Fiscal and welfare spending usually cannot be withdrawn once they are legislated, but economic cycles rise and fall. The committed welfare spending has to be satisfied even in a time of economic downturn. Thus, the fiscal deficit would soon accumulate to become a national debt, which in turn could weaken the economy further as pressure would be mounting on the level of the economy's international reserve, fiscal reserve and the value of the country's currency.

In fact, welfare spending would be decided more by politicians who would put political goals ahead of economic performance. One is not arguing for the elimination of welfare spending, but its appropriateness, size and sustainability should be given adequate thought, especially from the economics viewpoint because welfare provisions are always related to the spending side of the fiscal budget. At any moment in time, there are people faced with the problem of economic survival and financial assistances are needed. Welfare spending is regarded as "terminal" spending because they would only provide immediate benefit to the recipients, and spending would be made on retail goods and services. Thus, it does help the aggregate level of consumption, but it will neither generate further investment nor output for the economy. An economically sound welfare policy should consider avoiding unnecessary fiscal burdens generated. The three related questions are: (1) who the recipients are; (2) how much would be given to each recipient; (3) the viability and sustainability in the source of revenue.

Who should be the recipients? There are basically three types of welfare recipients. The group of recipients who require long-term welfare assistance would be the aged, the sick and the disabled. While welfare to the sick and the disabled cannot be avoided, one possibility to minimize the aging population could be to delay the retirement age so that the healthier workers can be given a chance to remain employed. Another possibility is to institute an economy-wide insurance policy so that workers can contribute to their post-retirement fund during their years of employment. The second group of recipients are the unemployed and single-parent families. Economic hardship arises when the "breadwinner" in the household becomes unemployed, or there are domestic issues that a family face. There are the social and psychological issues to be handled, but economically this group is regarded as temporary as employment could come forward once the economy recovers, a new skill is learned, or the children would have grown up and become independent in one-parent families. The third group would compose of the remaining needy recipients, such as the orphans and children coming from broken families, drug addicts who need medical treatment and so on. The time required for the welfare assistance could be longer as orphans may take years to become adults, while medical treatment provided to drug addicts would take time to heal. Nonetheless, the third group should form a minority in the recipient groups.

The more controversial issue is how much should be given to each recipient? Conceptually, many policies would advocate for an "adequate" amount of welfare. The problem arises in the interpretation of "adequate". For example, simple economic calculations would probably advocate for the minimum amount so that would maintain the recipients at the survival level to include living necessities. Pro-welfare advocates, on the contrary, would seek for a maximum amount so that the recipient can have a life equivalent to non-recipients, and that some non-necessities would be included. Their argument is to avoid social deprivation, especially teenage children as they are in the learning stage. Payment for piano classes for children in welfare-recipient families, for example, would have to be included in the welfare assistance. The concerns on the amount to be provided would relate to the extent of economic disincentives so generated and the amount of fiscal funds needed. While assistance is needed for the recipients, it makes no sense to turn the recipients to become dependent on welfare.

The source of financing welfare spending has often been overlooked. The misconception is that the government, especially the institution of a big government, is always powerful and can raise tax and other revenues to cover the welfare spending. Evidence has shown that every government has a limit in raising its revenue. Once committed, welfare spending will have to be continued year after year, but fiscal revenue is often constrained by several factors, including the business cycles, the degree of disincentives in the taxation system, investment climates and competitiveness of the economy when compared to neighboring economies. Many governments fail to equate the "spending side" with the "earning side" of the budget, resulting in fiscal deficit and national debts. High national debt would mean a weaker currency and a low level of international reserve. Consequently, the economy becomes vulnerable to shocks originated from foreign countries and becomes less competitive as the economy tends to become unattractive to foreign investment. The debt means that the current generation has overspent, and the future generation would have to suffer for debt repayment.

In conclusion, demand-side economics tends to provide an unstable and unviable economic path. On the contrary, policies that deploy supply-side economics can help to strengthen employment and long-term sustainable growth. Supply-side policies aim at improving the production side of the economic equation as increase in output can permit more earnings, and individuals could then look after their own economic welfare once economic security is achieved. Typically, physical investment and investment in research and development activities enhance production capacity and more jobs should be forthcoming. The rise in employment and income would generate positive multiplier effects. Investment leads to economic expansion, and growth allows greater economic security. To promote more investment, suitable incentives must be instituted, such as the adoption of market-friendly policies with low tax rates and minimum regulations to ensure flexibility.

Government budgetary policies can promote supply-side economics. Education and infrastructure development are the long-term instruments in securing supply-side economics. Education enriches human capital so that more able individuals are trained. Both formal education and vocational training aim to increase the supply of different professionals that support investment activities. Infrastructure is a social capital that enhances other economic activities. An underground railway system facilitates urban transport, a modern airport facilitates connections with overseas businesses. One usual argument against expansion in infrastructure is its cost, but it is equally true that the longer it waits, the more expensive the construction of key infrastructure becomes. Furthermore, once constructed, the service provided by the infrastructure would be immense and last for centuries. In short, the long-term benefit shall always exceed the short-term cost.

Another key to supply-side economics is the adoption of market-friendly policies, including a minimum tax to encourage business, least amount of regulations to enhance business efficiency and a pro-growth regime that promotes economic opportunities. Supply-side economic policies have proved to be successful as they allow economic expansions to take place and opportunities to arise. Investment activities will have positive multiplier effects in employment, income and eventually consumption. As investment leads to enlargement in output, more goods and services shall then be made available in the market for domestic demand or export to the foreign market. And the rise in export enhances the currency market as trade surplus should result in improvement in international reserve. Such a "thin end of the wedge" should eventually promote economic growth, especially if economic expansion is matched with appropriate expansion in infrastructural development, a market-friendly government and a civic society that cherishes privacy, stability and prosperity. Economic opportunities grow with supply-side policies.

There are related economic implications in the implementation of supply-side policies. As output rises and growth occurs, the rise in employment would mean less needy individuals would turn to welfare assistance, and in turn the government could minimize welfare spending for other purposes, typically in enriching economic capability so that income and output growth can be lengthened and sustained. The rise in supply shall lead eventually to rise in demand, but as output rises continuously, the purchasing power of individual households improves, especially when inflation stays low as production output rises with the rise in demand.

There are clear differences between demand-side and supply-side economic policies. Demand-side policies are based on spending that create a short-term effect in the rise in income and consumption, but such spending may not be sustainable as output may not rise in parallel. As such, the rise in demand could lead to inflation, rise in imports and disincentives to business should fiscal and national debt start to build up. In short, demand-side policies cannot promote output and growth, and could even end up with unsustainable "vicious economic cycles". Supply-side policies, on the contrary, tend to concentrate on the input end of the economy and aim at growth promotion as the source of strength. By taking care of the "supply-side" of the economic equation, improvement in the "demand-side" of the equation shall follow because investment and output expansion shall improve employment and income and eventually consumer demand through the rise in purchasing power. Supply-side economics thus creates lasting and sustainable "virtuous economic cycles" that shall benefit all.

While the microeconomics analysis of demand and supply has been the first lesson taught at the early stage in all academic courses, it has a much wider and different implication when the concept of demand and supply is lifted to the analysis at the macroeconomic level, because policy differences can produce vast outcome differences. It would not be adequate to consider only the microeconomic aspects of demand and supply because such analysis affects the economic welfare of individual households. The analysis in demand-side and supply-side economics opens another dimension in the understanding of the growth and development trend of an economy. By comparing the intricacies between demand-side economics and supply-side economics, analysts and policy decision makers can better judge which policy seems to be more suitable for long-term economic growth and development.

III Firm Competition versus Economic Competitiveness

The two nouns of competition and competitiveness sound similar but have vast differences and implications in economics. In the practical world, every individual competes. Young pupils compete in the classroom, students compete in the examination, youth compete to enter a higher educational institution, school leavers and graduates compete for jobs. Retail shops compete for customers, products compete with their substitutes, producers compete for market shares, politicians compete for votes, communities compete for funding, and countries compete for resources and technological advancement. To compete has become a "life normal". Whether it is an individual person or an individual economy, what concerns is how to become more competitive and look for opportunities where survival is easier in the competitive world.

The first lessons in the textbook treatment of microeconomics have provided many theories on competition in the theory of the firm. Beginning with perfect competition in which perfect information, many buyers and sellers who are price takers, free movement of resources, homogeneous products and perfect market knowledge are assumed, consumers and producers would settle in a market equilibrium with an equilibrium price and quantity sold and produced (Stigler, 1957; McNulty, 1967). The theory of perfect competition is powerful as a first step in understanding how consumers and producers interact through market forces. However, the assumptions may not hold in the real economic world. For example, market information causes delays and could produce differences in interpretation and expectation, while producers tend to produce differentiated products.

Short of perfect competition, theories on imperfect competition have been developed (Robinson, 1953). The other extreme of perfect competition is monopoly where the market is composed of only one producer or seller, who has control of the price and quantity produced, though the theory argues that the producer would also have to compete in the purchasing power of the consumers (Hicks, 1935). While many argue that monopoly with one supplier could lead to market manipulation and control, others argue that the monopolistic producer would have enough resources to finance research, development and innovation. There is also the case of "natural monopoly" when the market can only allow one firm to operate (Sharkey, 2009). Natural monopoly could arise due to the excessive cost of production, such as infrastructure development in transportation, or the market is so small that only one firm can survive.

Other imperfect competition models include duopoly (markets with two producers), oligopoly (markets composed of several producers) and monopolistic competition in which the market contains many producers with each producing differentiated products. Monopolistic competition seems to be the contemporary form of market competition, as it allows flexibility on the part of producers in designs and innovation, pricing and advertising. In addition, the contestable market theory incorporates the relationship between firms and the industrial structure, including discussion on efficient production, market size and production strategy (Spence, 1976; Dixit and Stiglitz, 1977; Baumol, 1986; Kierzkowski, 1989; Devereux *et al.*, 1996).

The theory of the firm and competition has given rise to numerous related microeconomic theories. The theory of externality has been the more conventional microeconomic theory that deals with "spillover" effects and negotiation of possible compensation (Coase, 1988; Cornes and Sandler, 1996). Between firms and consumers and among firms and given that managers in share-holding corporations are typically employees while the shareholders are the owners, the relevant theories include agency theory, asymmetric information, corporate governance and intellectual property rights (Jensen and Meckling, 1976; Akerlof, 1978; Cukierman and Meltzer, 1986; Jensen, 1986, 1994; Helpman, 1992; Hart, 1995; Gould and Gruben, 1996; Maskus, 2000; Chhotray and Stoker, 2009). While the agency theory deals with the relationship between managers and owners of the corporation, asymmetric information provides an analysis on the transaction between the seller and the buyer. Corporate governance discusses the effective management structure of the corporation, and technological and creative innovations are protected by intellectual property rights. The core analysis in these theories provides a discussion on improving efficient transactions among firms and between firms and consumers. There are antitrust laws established in many advanced countries to protect the market from being manipulated by monopolistic sellers or cartels either in the form of price rigging, market share collusion, supply agreements and barriers on market entry. There are numerous cases of mergers and acquisitions where one firm acquires another firm with the intention either to enlarge the market shares, secure the source of input supply, eliminate competitors or to diversify into another line of business (Posner, 2001; Hitt *et al.*, 2005; Viscusi *et al.*, 2005; Kaplow, 2013).

Several concepts of competition deserve some elaboration. Competition is a process that differs in time and between products and markets. A young market tends to be more competitive than a matured market, as market saturation may occur. Some products and markets are more competitive than others. Hence, different producers could face different degrees of competition in different markets. There is no uniformity in market competition because contemporary producers would try to differentiate their product through design, package, advertising or aim at competing in a market segment. The most essential element in competition is the market openness and freedom to market entry. However young or matured the market is, and however differentiated the products are, so long as entry is unrestricted, new producers and competitors should be allowed to enter the market. Very often, the restrict is not the extent of market openness, it is the amount of capital required for entry, as some businesses need huge set up capital before entering into the market. Because of product and market diversity, new producers would consider and calculate their market potentials and ability to survive. It turns out that competition is the driving force in modern business.

The discussion on the theory of the firm and competition relates primarily to the behavior and activities between firms and consumers. The discussion on competitiveness takes an economy-wide analysis and examines how one economy can successfully compete with another and how economic resources in each economy can be utilized to improve its competitiveness. There are few features in understanding economic competitiveness. Firstly, the availability of economic resources (land, labor, capital and entrepreneurship) are crucial, but their productivity and the extent of "value added" in the product's contents are important considerations. Competitiveness conveys the essence of doing or making the best at the lowest marginal cost of production given the existing resources so that the economy is doing its maximum possible in all potential lines of production, and the economy is performing stronger when compared to others. The third feature of competitiveness is sustainability in that not only the economy is doing its best possible but it is also gearing its resources in preparation for its future to stay competitive. The spirit of competitiveness concerns not only short-term economic survival but also long-term sustainability. Economic competitiveness serves as an engine that propels the economy to function effectively and maximizes the economy's potentials for its future generations.

The more conventional discussion on economic competitiveness concentrates mainly on developing countries and it is argued that improvement in their competitiveness could lead to greater development and growth in the less-developed countries (Wignaraja, 2003). The reasons for low growth in some developing countries include the extensive corruption among officials and the mounting national debt, despite the aid received from international organizations (Shabbir and Anwar, 2007; Olken and Pande, 2012). However, since the turn of the 21st century, there are increasing number of first and second-tier developed countries which are facing loss in competitiveness and falling economic prospects. Similarly, even advanced countries are feeling the need to improve their economic competitiveness so that they can compete with other advanced and emerging countries and would not be dragged behind as other countries progress.

Economic competitiveness is equally important when compared to the availability of resources. What counts is the productivity component in the use and deployment of resources. The availability and productivity of resources require an entirely different conceptual understanding. One can see in the "resource curse" argument that economies which are bestowed with natural resources could be poorer than economies constrained by resources (Deacon, 2011; John, 2011). While it is easier to quantify the availability of resources in one economy in terms of natural resources, human resources and capital resources, how the economic resources have been used to enhance productivity and growth depends very much on the "value added" component in the deployment of resources.

The economics of "value added" can contain a lengthy list of components that enhances the productivity of resources. In natural resources, it would be the extent of investment injected in turning them into usable products. In the case of human resources, the quality of education and training institutions are the primary component. In capital resources, the attributes include the reliability of financial institutions, the trust-worthiness of the currency, the market friendliness of government policies and overall political stability. The availability of physical and social infra-structures that provide effective mobility and civic security are the additional components. Economic literature often makes a distinction between advanced and less-developed countries, but the more interesting concern is why the less-developed countries remain underdeveloped for so many decades, even though economic aids from advanced countries and international institutions have been pouring funds into the developing countries. Yet one also finds that many less-developed countries are "resource rich". The answer is their low economic development must rest with the inability in raising the value-added content of their available resources. In short, the availability of economic "hardware" is vital, but the success rests with the extent of economic "software".

Economic competitiveness relates to nationwide issues and policies, and carries the message of long-term economic sustainability, survival and progress that involves multilevel dynamism, innovation and creativity. The textbook treatment of "comparative advantage" suggests that economies should produce where its marginal cost of production is lowest when compared to other economies, as that would minimize production cost and maximize output globally. This theory is useful in understanding how one economy can concentrate in some production lines, and reach its stage of "comparative advantage", and whether such comparative advantage could last is the most important concern. The dynamics is that while economies are enjoying certain comparative advantages, they also must prepare for new comparative advantages for long-term sustainability. To prepare for the comparative advantages of tomorrow, one must explore new production areas today, including new investment, and/or nurture a suitable production environment. This could mean the need to examine the "comparative disadvantage" today to explore "new comparative advantage" for tomorrow through market-friendly policies.

Economic dynamism and the desire to maintain competitiveness can be seen in theories such as product life cycle (Mullor-Sebastián, 1983; Klepper, 1996), where the production of some products could face various stages of development or their production could travel from one country to another over a period. In the case of textile production, for example, Li (2002, 2017a) argued that the manufacture of textile and clothing has travelled from Great Britain in the 1950s to East Asia in the 1970s and to Southeast Asia and China in the 1990s before all trade restrictions were lifted by the World Trade Organization in the early years of 2000. Examples of product life cycle can easily be found in electronic products, appliances and motor vehicles. The Walkman was popular as an electronic product based on the technology of cassette recording, but it soon developed into CDs and other pocket-size electronic devices. Mobile phones and internet online developments have incorporated several other functions, including camera and video recording. One generation of the product incorporates more functions than the previous generation of the product. Similar product life cycles can be found in motor car production as the new model precedes the old model to capture or regain a bigger market share or not to lose the market to competitors. In many ways, one can argue that it is the producers and manufacturers who are structuring the life cycle of their products, knowing that the life of any one technological product could only have a certain lifetime in the market before it is substituted by the next generation in production.

Although the product life cycle theory touches mainly on the dynamism of production at the firm level, it has economy-wide implications. To stay competitive, an economy must try all means to maximize the "value-added" component of all economic resources. In the meantime, while the economy is enjoying certain comparative advantages, there is also the need to explore new comparative advantages, as a new comparative advantage can replace a fading one. It is through the development of successive comparative advantages that one can maintain and sustain the overall competitiveness of the economy. Economic dynamism has further policy implications. For example, would the level of human capital be sufficiently strong in taking up the needed improvement in comparative advantage, or can the investment scenario provide a complement to the funds needed to expand new comparative advantages? In a nutshell, economic competitiveness is a much more dedicated issue that requires alignment among economic policies and strategies, and deployment of resources.

The discussion from the microeconomics of supply and demand to the macroeconomics of demand-side and supply-side economics shows a clear case of intra-connectivity between economic theories and concepts, in that microeconomics theories can be conceptualized into macroeconomic interpretations and implications, and *vice versa*. Such a fusion in the understanding of economic theories and concepts could help lift the economic discipline to a higher level of applicability in humanity studies. Indeed, taking a broad-minded approach in combining the theories in microeconomics and macroeconomics shall produce new insights in knowing how the economic discipline can be used to serve the global economy further, especially those political leaders who often make decisions using economics as their tool, but may not have given enough thought to the unintended economic consequences.

IV Intricacies between Consumer, Producer and Government Policy

Supporters of market economies advocate that with certain social awareness, legal limits and human constraints and conditions, individuals and businesses can be given a high degree of freedom to conduct their own affairs. The advantages of economic freedom include the choice and opportunity that individuals can maximize their own welfare while businesses can maximize production, and that both individuals and business would normally not rely on government welfare assistance and subsidy. In turn, with a reduced need for welfare spending, the government could produce a fiscal surplus, which could then be used for long-term development in infrastructure or in enhancing economic capability. Equally, with more individuals being employed and a booming business sector, more tax revenue would be collected as economic activities get expanded. Thus, economic prosperity would naturally promote a bigger economic pie where participants would have more to share. Economic prosperity allows individuals to take care of their own private welfare, while business optimism attracts additional investment. A minimal, market-friendly government should stay at the "back seat" and serve the economy by allowing the private sector to conduct its affairs through the "driver's seat".

Nonetheless, governments exist in all economies and their roles are to mediate between consumers and producers, between the needs of individuals, and monitor the behavior of businesses to ensure stability and a level-playing field for all, through ideally the pursuit of policies that should aim at equality in opportunity, openness and fairness. The government machinery collectively consists of political leaders, civil servants, administrative departments and related institutions. There are numerous economic theories that explain the relationship between individuals as consumers and as workers, businesses as producers and investors, government as the monitor and institutions as civic bodies that provide different layers and dimensions of public security. There is the judiciary body that promotes the rule of law and ensures equity under the law, and the infrastructure setup that facilitates the citizen's daily life.

The role of the government has been debated extensively, though often the debate has been politically oriented. The more conventional microeconomic theory of externality concerns the impact of the "spillover" effect in the activities between individuals where the act of one imposes cost on another, between producers and households where firms may pass on unwanted goods that affect the welfare of households, or between firms that have violated market morals and ethics. Externality cases are at times ignored as it is impossible to identify the party imposing the spillover and the other party facing a high legal cost. More often, however, there are numerous documented cases where legal procedures were followed to enable compensations to be made. In complicated cases, the government may have to get involved either because of its large impact or when public safety is involved.

Modern democratic countries will have their political leaders openly elected, while the government machinery often take instructions from the leaders in drafting economic policies. One unwanted consequence is the oscillation of policies when political leaders with opposing ideology are periodically elected. As such, economic outcomes tend to fluctuate and could face the problem of alignment from one political regime to another. Economic policies should best be apolitical, but economic variables are often used as instruments for political ends. In countries with low political ethics, political leaders together with top civil servants exploit their power and take advantage of the citizens by engaging in corruption and "power play". These leaders "rent seek" the country by taking advantage of their power through various means, such as embezzling public funds, engaging in cronyism and forming inner circles of influence which function like a private club (Rowley *et al.*, 1988; Tullock, 1989; Lockard and Tullock, 2001; Lambsdorff, 2002). In extreme situations when "rent seeking" activities are consolidated, the governing body can become invincible and abuse of power would be exercised to maintain control. It is only through a well-established transparent system of "checks and balances" that justice can be brought to rent seekers abusing their authority. The problem of "moral hazards" could be difficult to identify in political and administrative cases (Hölmstrom, 1979; Arnott and Stiglitz, 1991; Mirrlees, 1999).

On the contrary, there are pro-government advocates who believe that the government should have more power, especially in the distribution of resources and redistribution of income. The situation would equally be unfavorable when citizens take "free rides" from the generous welfare system, leading to overspending and deficits. A private firm normally takes up its cost of production and faces a loss when cost of production exceeds revenue income. An individual shall also take care of his or her own private cost of survival, and the household's earning should cover the cost of living and private welfare. However, there are incidents where private individuals, especially individuals with low endowment, are faced with their survival cost, and their earnings can hardly pay for their basic expenses. In other words, these residents are faced with difficulty in covering their private survival cost.

Welfare advocates believe that welfare assistance should be given to people whose earning cannot cover their private cost. This has often been considered more on humanitarian than on economic grounds. Simply put, when households pass on their private cost to the government, who in turn provides these households with welfare, such transactions mean that the government is taking up the private cost of the households, and transforming it into an increase in social cost. The government then would have to spend more on welfare as the size of social cost enlarges. The process of welfare provision does unavoidably pass on household's private cost to enlarge the government's social cost. The rise of social cost can have several consequences.

Firstly, the chance of the government facing a fiscal deficit and a national debt will be enlarged, especially in an economic downturn when revenues are not forthcoming. Secondly, household incentives would be reduced, as their economic survival becomes dependent on welfare. One can even argue that the rise in social cost serves as a means for the government to expand, because the government now must look after more and more welfare recipients who have become dependent on state assistance. Thirdly, as welfare recipients become dependent on the government, they may not be keen to return to the job market, thereby reducing the overall size of the employed labor force. The rate of unemployment would then be hidden among the welfare recipients. The political leaders would not mind raising the level of social cost because they will not be the one who must pay and be responsible for the large welfare spending. This is where the theories on rent seeking, moral hazard and asymmetric information become important. It is the tax payers who contribute to the government revenue, but it is the political leaders who have the power to spend the hard-earned revenues. In addition, elected political leaders may not need to be responsible for the government spending because their period of office would have completed by the time the government is faced with deficits and debts, which would then be passed on to the next generation of tax payers. In short, the enlargement of social cost is not a blessing to the economy, as it leads likely to debts and deficits, disincentives and high tax, while fiscal spending could instead have geared to promote the productive side of the economy, such as research in technology, industrial promotion and advancement in infrastructure.

Thus, while it is easy for political leaders to commit large welfare spending, it effectively is imposing economic burden on the fiscal policy. An increase in the size of social cost requires a larger government while the recipients would become dependent on government support. The larger the size of the welfare dependent population, the greater the need for a larger government bureaucracy. And that lowers business incentives as rising welfare, high tax and fiscal deficits are not market-friendly indicators to investors, and production and outcome could be constrained as a result, thereby lowering employment opportunities. The low employment possibility could even lead to a rise in the number of welfare recipients as businesses decline. As such, it will "self-fulfill" the hypothesis of economic dependency and big government at the expense of otherwise a productive economy. The large welfare recipients would politically be capitalized by the large government bureaucracy, while it is the tax payers who eventually would have to foot the welfare bill.

The economics of production cost at the firm level can be extended to understand and analyze the crucial difference between private cost and social cost. In project analysis, estimations of cost and benefit are made, especially projects concerning infrastructure development. When the concept of cost and benefit is extended to an analysis at the societal level, there can be differences between the party responsible for the cost and the recipient having to obtain the benefit. In welfare issues, there is a divergence in fiscal responsibility in that the policy makers decided their spending from the taxpayers, and the recipients do not need to foot the welfare spending. Namely, the political leaders decide, the taxpayers pay, and the welfare recipients benefit. The intermediator between the cost bearer and the benefit recipient is the government who will be influenced by its political stand and intention of the leaders and officials. Thus, while not all households can shoulder their private cost of economic survival, there is also a need to ensure that the social cost burden will not be excessive as to drag down the overall performance of the economy and produce unwanted consequences or being exploited by irresponsible leaders for their vested interest.

V Comprehensive Comparative Advantage

Modern industries and the process of industrialization probably began with the Industrial Revolution in early 19th century in the United Kingdom, and different European countries subsequently excelled in producing one good as compared to another, thereby giving rise to export and trade. The economic theory of comparative advantage preached that countries should specialize in producing goods with the lowest marginal cost, and trade for other good not produced. Thus, if the United Kingdom had the technology to produced guns, while Portugal excelled in agriculture and produced butter much more economically, there would be trade between the United Kingdom and Portugal for guns and butter. The textbook treatment of the theory of comparative advantage has formed a foundation in modern economics.

The theory of comparative advantage does give a strong analytical framework in understanding international trade and exchange. One problem with the comparative advantage analysis is the explicit discussion of value added in the production of goods. Typically, industrial and technological goods are more expensive than agricultural goods, and designs and innovation are the contemporary form of creating value added on top of technological advancement. Uneven trade transactions would arise when one country is exporting high value-added goods, while another country is exporting merely raw materials and agricultural goods. The result could be that the country exporting goods with high value-added contents would experience trade surplus, while countries exporting low value-added goods would experience trade deficit. This is known as the term of trade and it would have further implication on each country's growth, the value of their currency and the ability to trade.

Such a difference does highlight the importance of industrialization, as the various attributes of industrialization, such as technology advancement, design and innovation, research and development, automation, digitalization and mechanization would eventually lead to the rise in the value-added content of goods produced. Furthermore, the process of industrialization has helped to widen the base of comparative advantage, as more goods are able to gain comparative and competitive advantage. Indeed, competitive advantages due to product differentiation, for example, have given rise to both the import and export of the same products. One can argue that it is not the theory of comparative advantage that has lost it significance, it probably is the widening of comparative advantage overtime, as countries must rely more on additional comparative advantages.

Other than comparative advantage in the production of goods, comparative advantage in resources has also led to unintended results. Typically, countries endowed with capital differ drastically from countries endowed with labor. The explicit form of comparative advantage in resources appears in foreign direct investment, where capital-rich countries are seen investing in labor-abundant countries producing light manufacturing goods. Capital-rich countries typically experience high living standards and high wages, thereby making their light manufacturing sector costly and uncompetitive. The high cost serves as the "push" in their foreign direct investment. On the contrary, wages and cost of production in labor-abundant countries are low and becomes attractive to foreign investment. The low wage in labor-abundant countries serves as they "pull" in inward investment. Political stability and good infrastructure availability count a lot in attracting inward investment.

There are several visible advantages. Cross-border trade increases as the manufactured goods produced in labor-intensive countries have to be exported back to the investing countries. Thus, consumers in the capital-rich countries would have a higher purchasing power as the price of imported goods is cheaper than locally produced goods. Labor-intensive countries gain as the workers are employed, and the increase in job opportunity brings a better living standard to their families. The ability to export by the labor-intensive countries enables these countries in turn to import their needed goods. Economic welfare between the investing and trading countries improves, as one country gets the cheaper goods, while the other country obtains the needed capital for investment, thereby generating a "win–win" outcome.

However, there are unintended consequences. On the part of the capital-rich countries, one would be the loss of jobs as the light manufacturing jobs are "exported" to the labor-intensive countries, and there could be a time lag in redirecting these workers for other employment purposes. There has been the debate on protectionism (see, for example, Milner, 1988) which could appear in various forms. In the case of textile and clothing, there were trade restrictions in the form of quota, import duties, "country of origin" rule and voluntary restraint. The "sweat shop" argument has also been put forward by the leftist, arguing that foreign direct investments are exploiting the low-cost labor in the poor countries, and workers in the low-cost countries should be paid on an equal basis as compared to workers in the advanced countries. Such a leftist argument could not go far because it was exactly the cheap labor cost that attracted inward capital in the manufacturing sector (Emmelhainz and Adams, 1999; Wallach and Woodall, 2004). Through the Multi-Fiber Agreement (MFA) negotiated in much of the 1960s and 1970s, for example, export from Asian countries to Europe was restricted. Since the early 1980s, the "country of origin" rule has been applied to ensure that a certain portion in the production process must be conducted in the exporting country and not the "re-export" of the same good from the third country (Erzan *et al.*, 1989; Manchin and Pelkmans-Balaoing, 2007; Li, 1991, 2002, 2012).

On the part of the investment recipients, the growth in manufacturing industries led to economic growth and improvement in living standards. However, not all recipient countries improved along with advancement in physical infrastructure, social capital such as education and human development. For example, environmental decay leads to health hazards, while the consumption of luxurious imports results in trade deficits. In addition, weak governance gives rise to corruption and abuse of power by the officials. Experiences show that not all investment receiving countries benefit from inward investment, and many remain poor. In the final analysis, it depends very much on both economic and social changes in the domestic economy that would align with the advantages arising from inward investment. The economic success of East Asia has been shown as a "showcase" of economic development since the end of the Second World War, and several East Asian countries have caught up with the advanced countries, and in turn, they serve as supplier of capital to the neighboring countries (Li, 2002, 2017a).

Such a pattern of comparative advantage in resource deployment has led to the process of economic globalization where the crucial essential is the country's competitiveness. As more capital in the form of foreign direct investment has moved to low-cost countries, modern services and other tertiary industries have flourished in capital-exporting countries, thereby making the tertiary sector the dominant sector. Many modern services involve creativity and innovation and can produce a high value-added content. However, experiences show that there can be drawbacks in a heavy service-prone economy, especially in times of crisis. For example, many traditional services do not require much skill and might have a short "career-life" as younger and lower-cost workers would be employed to replace the aging workers. Many simple service jobs do not have a career-path and they are paid often on an hourly or on *ad hoc* basis. Since small skills are required in many service jobs and experience does not count, pay could remain low.

Many service jobs are often considered as "derived" jobs, in that these jobs are situated at the retail or consumption end of the economic process, and they are able to flourish only because households' income have risen and there is more to spend. Tourism, beauty business and personal services are based on a rise in income. Thus, a hazardous situation would occur to jobs in the service sector when the emerged financial crises are followed by severe economic downturn. The fall in income naturally restrict people's purchasing power, and the fall in the demand for personal services and tourism would produce a reverse multiplier effect on other service demands, resulting in job loss and rise in unemployment.

In other words, economies which depend heavily on services could become rigid should economic crisis occur as the economy's ability to absorb workers from other economic sectors remains weak. Displaced workers from services may not be able to find jobs in other industries, either because they do not possess enough skills for industrial jobs or the industrial sector has shrunk, and industrial jobs would no longer be forth-coming. Without the industrial sector to absorb the displaced labor from the fall in services, the economic crisis would take much longer time to heal and recover. In the meantime, the economy could remain uncom-petitive, while other more progressive economies could move up the competitiveness scale. Furthermore, many foreign investment recipients would have improved their economies considerably, and an expansion in their export would produce trade surplus and handsome international reserves, which would in turn "haunt" the capital-supplying countries as they need to import back the goods produced abroad. Hence, capital-suppling countries would lose on three fronts: investments that traveled abroad, loss of employment at home as investment was displaced, and cheaper imports resulting in trade deficit and a downward pressure on the exchange rate.

Globalization without political alignment has brought up several lessons in the debate between the need for manufacturing versus the development of services. Although technological advancement can bring new industries, the existence of low-skill workers in the capital-supplying countries still remains to be dealt with. There must be a better mixture between industries and services. While high technology industries generate high value added, light manufacturing jobs can absorb some low-skilled workers, thereby providing them with enough employment. Modern services do develop along the lines of creativity and innovation, but the presence of many service jobs is the result of production in manu-facturing industries, such as delivery, logistics, marketing and banking. Hence, a "comprehensive comparative advantage" strategy should include light manufacturing industries in addition to the development of high-tech and modern services.

A balanced industrial strategy would include both high-tech and low-tech manufacturing industries to provide job opportunities to workers with different skills. Furthermore, a light manufacturing sector can not only provide jobs but also the required skills can prolong the employment life of the workers, making them less reliant on government welfare. On the contrary, an absence of light manufacturing would mean that the low-skill workers cannot be employed, and they in turn would tend to seek for welfare assistance as their jobs have been displaced. This shall provide political opportunity for a pro-welfare government to raise tax and enlarge the government administration. However, one condition for the light manufacturing sector to re-emerge in advanced countries would be the need to restrict the rising production cost and the excessive minimum wage which kills the incentive of investors. Equally, an excessive welfare program could impose a certain degree of disincentive whereby workers would prefer to depend more on government support than to seek produc-tive employment.

The idea of a "comprehensive comparative advantage" strategy pro-vides several suggestions. One is that while the country is enjoying one aspect of comparative advantage, there is a need to explore new compara-tive advantage as the comparative advantage of tomorrow will replace the comparative advantage of today. Secondly, maintaining a balance in the economic sector among primary, secondary and tertiary sectors is pre-ferred. Typically, in emerging countries, the secondary sector dominates, followed by the tertiary sector, while the primary sector remains the smallest sector. In matured economies, and even though the tertiary sector is dominant, the economy preserves a relative high percentage of manu-facturing to absorb the low-skilled workers as well as to serve as an employment cushion should crisis break out. Unlike many services which are derived in nature, manufacturing industries create output and can be exported or reduce the need for similar imports.

The economic theories of comparative advantage, trade and development, and the division between industries and services are conceptually inter-connected in a web-like manner as the proper understanding of one theory could bring conceptual success when linked to another economic theory. Investment in manufacturing and physical industries belong to the supply-side in the economic process. An increase in industrial output and a balance between high technology industries and light manufacturing can provide ample employment opportunities for workers. Such a supply-side channel of development ensures workers' economic security, and their handsome employment possibility in turn would reduce dependence on government assistance.

Many services are "derived demand" jobs. Firstly, manufacturing industries give rise to various service businesses. Services are mainly demand oriented, and that the rise or fall of the service depend on the income level of the consumers. Hence, services, especially personal services, would be marginalized should economic hardship emerge, thereby adding a high degree of vulnerability to the service business. In many service businesses, the employment life of workers, who tend to be unskilled, may not last long as workers are aging. For example, sales ladies in fashion boutiques could be out of work once they reach a certain age as they are unable to compete with younger employees. Thus, low level of skills, lack of training, together with a relatively short employment life, would mean that these workers would become uncompetitive and experience a lower chance of employment, especially when these workers begin to age, and this results in the need for more government assistance.

In a nutshell, an unbalanced development between economic sectors would increase the vulnerability of workers, resulting in the need for greater reliance on government welfare, and together with a pro-welfare regime, the economy would easily end up taking "demand-side" policies. On the other hand, a balanced development between different economic sectors would provide a blanket of employment possibilities for workers with different skills. Hence, "supply-side" economic policies tend to be more stable and can provide a higher degree of economic security across sectors. An economy, therefore, should pursue different comparative advantages, and at the same time locate possibilities to develop new comparative advantage for future development to maintain and increase the economy's overall stability and competitiveness.

VI Nominal versus Real Economy

Having distinguished the importance between the share of manufacturing and service sectors in economic development, a similar parallel is the relevance between the nominal economy and real economy. This is because policy analysts, decision makers, pressure groups and groups with different vested interest often considered the superficial movements of economic variables. Typically for example, when aggregate wage is increased by 3%, and when price and inflation is also increased by the same percentage, the real economy shows no improvement, but the increase looks good to different stakeholders. Workers think their wage has increased, sellers assume they are getting more with the higher price, but they do not know that the increases would cancel out each other, and in real terms, both parties are not better off. The "deadweight" loss would be the economy as the higher inflation would make the economy less competitive, and goods would become more expensive; and as domestic export price becomes higher, less would be exported.

Many nominal economic activities would not have any effect on the real economy and could even hurt the aggregate economy eventually. But nominal activities have been popularized because different stakeholders think they would gain some economic result, or re-capture some loss. Very often, these decisions are made without knowing or anticipating the response from other stakeholders. Workers seek wage increase, thinking they would get more from the profit of the employers. When wage increase is successfully sought, workers might enjoy a brief period of increase in their purchasing power. But if business remains unchanged, the rise in wage would mean a lower profit or revenue received by the employers. In turn, employers would raise the price and pass the higher wage increase to the final consumers to retain the original level of revenue or profit. The rise in price reduces the overall purchasing power of the workers as their wages are fixed, thereby canceling out the economic effect of the previous rise in wage. Workers would then seek for a second round of wage increase, and such a sequence repeats itself. Eventually, such a sequence of economic activities could give rise to the rising cost of production, which would eventually find its way to the rise in price of the final product.

The sequence of events could equally have started from the employer's side. With the intention to gain a higher profit, the employer would sell at a higher price, which in turn reduces consumers' overall purchasing power, and as consumers, the workers' lower standard of living would lead them to seek for a rise in wage to compensate for their loss. When workers become successful in gaining a higher wage, employers would in turn raise their price. When these two sequences work together and repeatedly, it would be difficult to identify the origin of inflation. Nonetheless, the outcome would be a sequence of "wage-price" inflation spiral in the nominal economy, while total output could remain constant and may not increase in line with the rise in inflation.

In principle, wage increase must be reflected in the productivity of the worker, and the price increase should reflect either in an improvement in the quality or an increase in the value-added content of the product. However, such a theoretical connection has often been ignored or overlooked, and wage increase could be due to political reason, pressure from unions or administrative convenience. And the rise in wage in one economic sector would spillover to wage increase in another sector, while the rise in output would differ in different sectors. For example, some governments tend to increase the annual salary of the civil servants. To stay competitive, the private sector will have to raise the salary of the workers in line with the wage increase in the public sector. Hence, the nominal economy is controlled and influenced by the government administration more than the actual improvement in productivity.

Another aspect in the understanding of the nominal economy can be seen in the financial sector. Bank loans are provided to investors, and the increase in bank loans in the form of monetary expansion takes place before the subsequent rise in output. Unless there is an equivalent amount of monetary withdrawal at the same time, such as an increase in savings, provision of bank loans could be inflationary in the short run. In addition, not all bank loan provisions are used as a physical investment. In other words, the nominal economy in the form of monetary increase would be affected before there are changes in the real output in the form of increase in physical production. In extreme scenarios, these two types of economies would be functioning on their own at a separate pace which may not be in alignment with each other. Normally, the nominal economy moves at a much faster pace than the real economy.

Activities in the financial market also influence the nominal economy more than the real economy. When business corporates raise shares in the primary security market, the funds so raised are supposedly used for investment purposes. There is a direct measure between funds raised and investments made, though there might be time lags. Shareholders receive dividend returns from the corporate shares annually, and the size of dividends depends on the healthiness of the business. However, when investors sell their shares in the secondary market, namely the stock market, the price of the stocks fluctuates and the extent of fluctuation depends on the investment climate at the time. There is thus a possibility that the share price in the secondary market could be higher or lower than what the investor has paid in the primary market when the shares were initially raised. Although trading in the stock market is considered as an investment, stock trading activities are often speculative in nature.

There are also various financial products being traded in the financial market. Unlike shares issued in the primary market, financial derivatives are products built on other financial products and these financial derivatives may not have any parallel in the physical output. For example, financial companies would create various bonds and securities that are built on different stocks from different markets. Some of these bonds contain stocks from different markets across the world, others concentrate on one or two specific types of stocks in their portfolio. Hence, more financial products could then be created and traded openly. Such "investment" activities are simply different layers of stock trading, and they might present different degrees of riskiness to the "investors". In any case, the number of stocks in the primary market would remain unchanged, unless the issuing corporation decides to increase its issues. For example, the corporation can issue new shares as an alternative to paying out dividends. In other words, much financial trading activities are being constructed with no relationship to physical production. The nominal economy in the form of financial activities should expand much more rapidly than physical production. The creation of more financial products effectively means that new layers of financial activities so constructed are sold to different "investors" through packaging and branding.

The risk of financial products is usually clustered around each other. When one corporation, one product, one market, or one economy is doing well, the reduction in risk would then spread to other financial products, thereby giving a higher level of financial buoyancy. By the same token, the rise in risk or fall in expectation could spread like wildfire that could disrupt the financial sector easily. Thus, the fall in expectation in one financial product or in one financial market would spread instantly to other financial markets, trickling down to other international centers. Thus, the nominal economy could collapse much faster should crises occur or shocks that trigger downfalls in investment expectation.

Very often, the magnitude of financial collapse could severely affect the real economy as one type of financial activity could lead to collapse in another economic activity through speculation and downward expectation. Typically, a fall in the stock market would quickly affect the property market. Although the fall in the stock market would hurt investors and speculators, the effect of a fall in property market could result in fall in rents, leading to a fall in business expectation and purchasing power. Financial crises would quickly spread to other economic sectors, leading to rise in unemployment and closure of businesses. Next, if the rise in unemployment from the fall in financial and other services businesses could not be absorbed quickly in the real economy through employment in manufacturing, the economy would end up in recession and the slump could last for a longer period, especially if the economic structure is rigid and workers cannot easily be deployed to other economic sectors.

The nominal economy tends to fluctuate more than the real economy. The volatility in the financial market behaves cynically, rising when expectation is favorable but falling when shocks emerge. It has become normal for the stock market to fluctuate as that is the nature of all stock markets. As such, one shall not look too much into the movement of the stock market as an economic indicator because the frequent rise and fall in the stock market would become sequential, a period of fall would follow by a period of rise and the sequence repeats itself. On the contrary, the real economy concerns more of a long-term prospect, and a steady rise shall be preferable, and policies can be instituted to ensure that the real economy does not fall drastically to avoid severe economic hardship. For example, fiscal policy is theoretically used to smooth out economic activities, spending more during recession time to avoid hardship but saving more during economic booms to avoid overheating.

The conceptual message is that there should be a balance in the growth between nominal and real economic activities. The growth of financial activities in the nominal economy should not lead to a shrinkage in the real economy. While there is an expansion in the financial sector, there should equally be enough investment geared to physical production and manufacturing, as the rise of the former should not be at the expense of the latter. It is true that the windfall gain from financial activities could be larger than the profit gained from physical production, as the turnover of financial trading would be faster and easier than manufacturing activities. Many economies would like to have an international financial market, but in smaller economies especially when windfall gains from financial transactions were easier to come by, investment switching away from manufacturing could occur should investments or speculations in the financial market expand. When financial investment expands at the expense of manufacturing, the economic structure firstly becomes narrow, and secondly when financial crises occur, the collapse of the nominal economy cannot be supported by corresponding expansion in the real economy if the manufacturing sector has already diminished to a negligible proportion of GDP.

In a larger economy, the situation could be better as regional differences would allow growth and expansion in different economic sectors. While financial trading centers have been restricted to top commercial cities with efficient banking facilities, investment in manufacturing could spread to different regions either due to the source of materials, transportation facilities, human capital availability or technological clustering. Hence, it would be easier for larger economies to promote the real economy more effectively than smaller economies. Economic diversification is important to ensure a balance between the nominal economy and the real economy. It would be economically more sustainable especially for a smaller country to expand the real economy through industry production and manufacturing before indulging in massive expansion in the financial market. Or putting the discussion in reverse, there should be policy instruments to ensure that the expansion in the nominal economy would not be at the total expense of the real economy. In short and to follow up with the previous discussion, an economic balance is needed between manufacturing and services, as well as between development in nominal economy and real economy.

VII Conclusion

A new path in economic analysis is needed, a path that incorporates economic theories, different humanity studies and diversity in interpretations. In other words, an all-round or a comprehensive approach is required in dealing with contemporary economic issues, including the need to examine the *ex-ante* conditions in many economic issues. Toward this conceptual goal, this chapter starts by making inter-connections between and among different economic theories and analyses. The academic world in the economic discipline has divided economics into microeconomics and macroeconomics as if they can be separated, yet in realistic analysis, microeconomic ideas are needed in making macroeconomic analysis, and *vice versa*. When analyses are conducted at the professional level, one requires a good understanding of both microeconomics and macroeconomics, and their theories can be used interchangeably or can complement each other.

This chapter groups microeconomic and macroeconomic theories into five broad categories, with examples showing analyses that crossed theoretical boundaries. The simple theories of demand and supply analyses that examined individual behavior can be expanded to examine economy-wide situations between demand-side or supply-side economic policies, and their consequences, including both intended and unintended. Decision makers and policy analysts can have a clear "roadmap" in drafting economic policies, though vested political interests held by decision makers could have distorted policy directions and selections.

The interpretation of competition and competitiveness could be made clear by examining the economic analysis between business firms and economy-wide economic growth. There is a clear difference between competition in a market and competitiveness in an economy. Firms must compete in the market, while economies must stay competitive to ensure sustainability, not only for the benefit of the current generation but also more importantly for the future generation. Competition can only become more severe over time as new competitors emerge, and similarly, economic competitiveness can be eroded in two directions: the fall of its domestic economy and the comparative rise of a foreign economy.

The choice of economic theories discussed in the chapter aims to show that economic ideas can conceptually be connected. As such, a more comprehensive, relevant and powerful analysis can be presented, hopefully better solutions can be reached in dealing with contemporary issues. The theory of comparative advantage can also be used to connect how firms and industries in the microeconomy can be related to the macroeconomy through the deployment of resources, choice of exports and areas of industrial concentration. Comparative advantage is a powerful concept, but it must be seen dynamically, and the comparative advantage of today would mean the need to nurture new comparative advantage for tomorrow. The ideas in the discussion of competitiveness and "product life cycle" imply that comparative advantage could be a short-term phenomenon as new waves of comparative advantages emerge. A static application of comparative advantage could be detrimental to long-term economic sustainability as competitiveness could shift from one industry to another and from one economy to another. In short, when discussions are related to different theories and levels of analysis, the picture can become clearer, so as the understanding and consequently the recommendations and solutions. The remaining concern is whether the policy makers will choose the appropriate policy for genuine development or use the political process for other interest.

The discussion in the division between manufacturing and service provisions and between nominal and real economic activities carry a similar message of establishing economic balance between sectors. No economy can concentrate on any one sector, and a proper balance is needed for several reasons. Employment can be more stable among industries and businesses, and the rise of one sector will also lead to the rise of another, and not at the expense of another. Similarly, a fall in one economic sector should not bring economic collapse, but other sectors can come to its rescue in terms of employment absorption and avoiding economic recession.

A balance between manufacturing and services, and between exports and domestic consumption can secure the economy from external shocks, which are inevitable given the economic linkage in the global economy, but an adequate provision of domestic jobs can serve as a cushion to external economic shocks. Service jobs are needed, but solely depending on services can bring economic narrowness. Indeed, some service jobs are vulnerable to becoming marginalized once economic recession occurs, and the lack of skill requirement could shorten the employment life of the workers if age and physical appearance are the employment criteria. While industries are increasingly technology-related, light manufacturing can absorb some of the low-skilled workers, though the imposition of a high minimum wage would discourage investment in light manufacturing. The idea is to keep jobs so that more workers can stay in employment rather than imposing high tax and high minimum wage that could be a disincentive to investors, who could direct their capital and invest in a more market-friendly destination in a foreign country.

Economic competitiveness, sustainability and sectoral balances all point to the need to have a stronger real economy because it is where jobs can be created, it is where investment can be attracted, it is where exports can be created, and it is where rescue can occur should shock result in economic instability. It would be unwise if people merely look at the nominal side in economic calculations, thinking that will lead to economic improvement and development. Nominal economic calculations do create some short-term effects on the concerned groups, but the real effect will be balanced out once others make contrasting calculations. It is also discussed that gains to an individual in welfare provision at the micro-economic level could impose indirect cost to the society at the macro-economic level.

The expansion of the financial economy is highlighted in this chapter because its does create attraction for investments and speculative activities, but many financial products are derived from other financial products, and as they cluster together, the tragedy would be that they rise together, but also collapse together, thereby generating direct spillover and trickle-down effects to other economic sectors. While financial activities do have their own regulations and standards, financial market can best be expanded when the real economy measured in terms of manufacturing and export activities have grown to a secured level. The economy will become vulnerable should the expansion of financial economy take place at the expense of industrial activities; namely that speculation and investment in stocks and property occurred at the expense of industrial production.

By aligning several economic theories into a single body of analysis, this chapter shall serve as a "wake up" call that economic issues cannot be solved singly by looking at one economic theory, and that economic theories have to be analyzed dynamically to suit new and varying situations. After examining the theories of supply and demand, firm competition and economic competitiveness, static and dynamic comparative advantage, the impact of policy on consumers and producers, the division between manufacturing and service in economic sectors and the balance between nominal and real economic activities, the intention is to provide adequate analysis of how different economic theories can be connected to give a stronger analysis. The conceptual analysis serves only as a first but bold step in alerting analysts and researchers that contemporary economic issues can no longer be seen in a mono-dimensional manner but should be seen with an open mind to include various possible scenarios. As such, Conceptual Economics presents a more powerful analytical tool in dealing with complicated and multifaceted issues. In short, it is not the availability of theories that matters, it is the conceptual application and interpretation of economic theories that counts.

The "conceptual" discussion in this chapter considers the "intra-connectivity" between and among economic theories, crossing the different key divisions between microeconomics and macroeconomics. Indeed, one economic concept can have implication and relevance to both microeconomics and macroeconomics. The microeconomics of supply and demand can conceptually be extended to supply-driven and demand-driven economies. The cost of production can be extended to the concept of social cost at the macro level. Externality can be extended to trade and international economic relationships. The agency theory of the firm can be extended to the functioning of civil servants in delivering policies. A firm's production can be expanded to discuss resource allocation in an economy. Education and human capital can be discussed in the context of inequality, reduction in poverty and increase in opportunity. Investment can be conceptualized to include speculation and financial crises. The list of examples can go further.

There is indeed no shortage of economic theories. The restriction rests in the interpretation and usage arising from the conceptual fundamentals hidden in the theories. A fundamental understanding in Conceptual Economics should help analysts and policy makers to come to a better decision. The act of "intra-connectivity" aims to use economic concepts as an instrument in aligning different economic theories as that should add extra vigor to the economic theories. Concepts and theories can complement each other in delivering stronger analytical results.

Chapter Four

Economics Science versus Political Science

I Introduction

It is argued that social science disciplines are all related to each other as they take different dimensions to study human behavior. Indeed, there can be a close connectivity among the social science disciplines of economics, sociology, psychology, politics and geography. Of course, social science disciplines have their own individual areas of study and theories and have their own intellectual vigor that deserve in-depth understanding and analysis. It would be inappropriate to argue which discipline is more important or relevant than another in relation to studying human behavior and activities. One can surmise and make a simplistic argument on the connectivity among social science disciplines, as this can serve as a bait in highlighting the discussion on the inter-connectivity among social science disciplines (see, for example, Calhoun, 2002).

Such a discussion leads to the question as to the role of economics among these social science disciplines. The core concern is the way each of these social science disciplines expresses itself. This chapter uses the complexity between economics and politics as an illustration to show how the "passive" nature of economics was influenced, used or exploited and even distorted by the "active" nature of politics, because economic activities are often driven by other social and political desires, and the political decision makers may not need to be responsible for the economic outcomes, however favorable or unfavorable they are.

II Understanding Political Economy

A quick search through the internet on the definition of political economy shows a variety of definitions, and it carries different meanings in different historical epochs. According to Merriam Webster, political economy is "the theory or study of the role of public policy in influencing the economic and social welfare of a political unit". According to *Dictionary. com*, in the 17th and 18th centuries political economy would refer to "the art of management of communities, especially as affecting the wealth of a government", while in the 19th century, it was "a social science similar to modern economics but dealing chiefly with government policies". Yet the modern definition of political economy is "a social science dealing with political policies and economic processes, their interrelations, and their influence on social institutions".

A more comprehensive discussion on the definition of political economy can be found in *Encyclopedia Britannica* (EB), where the discussion written by Michael A. Veseth and David N. Balaam was grouped into Historical Development, Economics and Political Economy, National and Comparative Political Economy and International Political Economy. The broad definition of political economy is stated as a "branch of social science that studies the relationships between individuals and society and between markets and the state, using a diverse set of tools and methods drawn largely from economics, political science and sociology..... Political economy thus can be understood as the study of how a country ... is managed or governed, considering both political and economic factors".

A summary from the discussion in EB shall provide a basic understanding in the development and coverage of political economy. From the historical perspective, EB noted that over the centuries the analysis of political economy as a moral philosophy can be traced back to several European scholars and philosophers, but the intellectual inquiry on political economy appeared in the 18th century when the "mercantilist" school that discussed the role of the state in economic regulation was made prominent in the 1767 publication *Inquiry into the Principles of Political Economy* by James Steuart and the economic policies adopted by the French controller general, Jean-Baptiste Colbert. Reacting to mercantilism and the rising role of the state, other philosophers like François Quesnay, David Hume and Adam Smith made a systemic approach to the subject of political economy that cumulated to Adam Smith's monumental work in 1776 *An Inquiry into the Nature and Causes of the Wealth of Nations* which provided a comprehensive analysis on political economy. It was argued in EB that Adam Smith's ideas were also influenced by several other philosophers of the time.

The key ingredient in Adam Smith's 1776 publication was the emphasis on the role of individuals in making economic contributions to the society, as it was argued that state policies and intervention were often less effective in advancing social welfare than the self-interested acts of individuals. By repudiating the mercantilist school, Adam Smith's analogy of "invisible hand" basically cherished the usefulness of "individual-centered" economic policies and development over the "state-centered" form of economic control by the state. Recent studies argue that other non-European philosophers, such as Confucius, had advocated the virtue of individualism in economic development because an optimal economic state could be reached when all individuals could master their own economic and social welfare without the need of assistance from the state (Zhang, 2000; Li, 2017a).

According to EB, a similar development along with Adam Smith's "invisible hand" was David Ricardo's theory of comparative advantage that advocated for free trade, while utilitarianism was put forward by three other philosophers (Jeremy Bentham, James Mill and John Stuart Mill), but it was not until the work by Alfred Marshall in his celebrated *Principles of Economics* published in 1890 that economic science as an academic field was separated from political economy. However, while Adam Smith concentrated his analysis purely on economics, Karl Marx, who advocated the ideology of communism, introduced the idea of "class struggle" into the analysis of political economy in his treatise *Das Kapital* first published in 1867. To eliminate a "class-centered" economy, Marx inserted several political ideas for the effective functioning of economics and advocated the opposing and dichotomized interests between the capitalists, the bourgeoise or the employers on the one hand and the laborers, the proletariat or the working class on the other hand. Marx's communism believed in a "classless" society where all natural and human resources would come under the control of the state, and "equality" was achieved when every individual was allotted a certain material benefit by the state, and that economic exploitation by one social class over another social class would be eliminated entirely.

As Li (2017a) argued, communist countries tend to show a poorer performance than capitalist market economies as individual economic freedom is restricted. Under communism, economic benefits are collectively controlled by the state, while individual incentives are eliminated, and the so-called "economic equality" is substituted by a worse form of "political inequality" where individual freedom is robbed, and the various branches of the state machinery lack accountability and could abuse their power through corruption, patronage and cronyism. When communist party members are selectively recruited, the party member is privileged with power and authority, which could be translated into advantages of one type or another. With "political inequality", the favor received by the communist party member would result in economic gains that yield "economic inequality". Consequently, the elite groups in the socialist and communist countries do exercise both political and economic power.

Nonetheless, EB correctly noted that while the early historical phase of political economy took a "normative" path of study, economics analysis has increasingly become "objective and value free". The landmark publication in 1947 by Paul Samuelson in *Foundation of Economic Analysis* brought a complete "bifurcation of political economy and economics" because Samuelson pioneered the use of mathematical tools in studying economics, thereby making the analysis entirely positive, formal and precise. The debate on political economy was reiterated after the Great Depression in the early 1930s where the need for the state to intervene in the market was raised in the discussion on the "welfare state". The historic work by John Maynard Keynes in 1936 on *The General Theory of Employment, Interest and Money* advocated the usefulness of economic management through fiscal policy to ensure a balance between unemployment and inflation, the need to increase the government size relative to private sector economic activities and state intervention to generate growth and maintain sustainability. The Keynesian approach of economic management suggested that there could be an economic role of the government in domestic policies. Increasingly, some Western nations adopted interventionist policies, including nationalization of industries that resulted in severe and unsustainable losses as debt mounted.

The use of fiscal policy in economic management in the West came under challenge in the 1970s in the "stagflation" era when high unemployment coexisted with high inflation. Keynes's interventionist view was replaced by "classical liberalism" especially in the United States of America and in Great Britain. The dominant view held by Milton Friedman in the form of monetarism, where money supply was thought to be the more effective instrument than fiscal policy in economic promotion, had become the catchphrase. In his numerous publications, Milton Friedman advocated for the reduced role of the state, de-nationalization of industries and the return of the free market where the state could best be suited in the backseat and the private sector would be the main driving force in the economy. Friedman's monetarism aimed at promoting free market and there was a period of continued prosperity.

Despite the economic success brought about by monetarism and the "supply-side" policies adopted by the USA and Great Britain, there were new developments challenging the conventional understanding of political economy. In the domestic economy of many Western and European countries, political attention on the issue of inequality was raised once again, as different political parties had to work on their political platforms and inequality would always become a good political ticket. Some governments in the industrialized countries lean more to using welfare policies, but welfare spending is a "demand-side" economic strategy that would not promote growth as it mainly encourages consumption and possibly inflation. Coupled with the rise in government welfare spending is the increase in wages, and the inability of government in securing tax revenues, resulting in rising national debt and loss in economic competitiveness, especially when domestic capital flees to other investment-friendly countries.

III Economics and Politics: Lacking a Clear Cut?

To understand the interplay between economics and politics, one shall begin by looking at the nature and the ingredients of the two disciplines. Economics is the branch of social science that examines the deployment and distribution of resources and endowments. Individuals, households, societies and nations do hold various kinds of resources and endowments. While the hardware is the quantifiable amount of resources that is typically composed of natural resources, human resources and financial resources, the software looks at the various channels that promote the productivity of the resources, which shall depend on several factors. Typically, physical capital and human labor are the two conventional inputs to examine productivity performance, but other software factors include educational and technology levels, market friendliness, infrastructure provisions, reliable institutions, ethics and other social and cultural background factors.

The pure and simple economics equation is that differences in the inputs to the "economic engine" shall produce differences in outputs. Even if similar inputs are given, outputs can be different. Likewise, different inputs could produce similar outputs. No two individuals could be the same in their own endowment, due to innate ability, family background, educational attainment and training opportunities. All jobs are different, as training could be different, age and experience of the workers could be different, job priority in the production chain could be different, risk exposure could be different among jobs, and productivity among workers could be different. Similarly, no two entrepreneurs are the same. Every entrepreneur aims to conduct their businesses differently from others. Firms are different as production activities differ among firms and businesses. Firms engaged in physical production in the secondary sector would perform differently from firms engaged in services in the tertiary sector. Market possibilities would be different among firms in different economic sectors, among firms with different endowments and management strategies. The degree of competition is different among workers, among business firms and among markets. The extent of "value added" among workers in the production process is different, among firms in the same economic sector is different, and among markets in the same economy is different.

"Differences and diversity" are the key ingredients in all economic performances. At the output end, differences can be seen and carried in the price of goods and services, which can vary according to time and seasonal factors, consumer loyalty and specialty of the product, product quality and brand name effect, and the forces of market demand in general. At the input end, other than individuals' ability or the firm's management strategy, differences are created at the societal level. The society trains people to be different. The education system trains people with different qualifications, jobs and skills, people with different professions and abilities and consequently different employment possibilities, and wages are therefore paid differently among jobs, for the different employment opportunities and skill levels. Through the various institutional setups, the input side of the economic equation is exposed with diversities as required by the society.

In short, due to the required societal needs of professions and jobs, society is faced with differences at the input end of the economic equation. Typically, while there are pedagogical commonalities among schools at the primary and secondary educational level, there are different courses in the tertiary education that train students with different knowledge, exposures and thinking capabilities. Equally, students can choose their own education path through their interests and abilities. Hence, there are students graduating with scientific knowledge, artistic knowledge and knowledge on social sciences and humanities. Such differences in human capital that form the input end of the economic equation are needed because society has different job requirements, and as such, graduates will be paid differently not only at the start, their wage differences will persist due to differences in experiences over time, due to features such as risk exposure and timing and hours of work, due to geographical location of the employment, due to forces of demand in the market and possibly the "life cycle" of the product.

The proper mindset is that economic activities hardly produce similarities, and differences in inputs and subsequently in outcomes are obvious and unavoidable. Due to the extent of differences and diversity among individuals, households, firms and markets, there is no such thing as "equality" in economic outcomes. The fundamental idea in an "economic engine" is that given certain factor inputs, the market value of the generated outputs should be higher than the market value of the combined inputs because of the inclusion of the value-added content in the production process. The difference in the content of value added in the economic process forms the basis of economic growth. Economic growth is a natural outcome of positive economic activities, though some nations grow faster than others due to variations in their economic endowments and in their value-added content. Economic growth is a measure of economic outputs, but these outcomes are often influenced, affected and constrained by economic inputs. However, it is easier to measure a nation's economic outputs in the form of Gross National Product (GDP) than to measure its economic inputs because economic outputs are additive but economic inputs are often cumulative. Nonetheless, while the GDP shows the aggregate measure of national income based on consumption, there is also the production approach to measure national income.

However, due to the cumulative nature of the value-added content in economic inputs, the question is how to measure, for example, the contribution of the education system which produces graduates for various jobs in industries and businesses, or the health system that maintains a good hygiene for the public at large? Other examples include intangible inputs such as security, a peaceful and a market-friendly environment for the market to prosper, a reliable financial sector where business transactions could be conducted, and openness that provide equal opportunity to all.

Hence, a nation could face low economic outputs because of its low performance in economic inputs. Indeed, it is often the quality of economic inputs that count more than economic outputs in the production and growth process.

While it is too often that an economy's GDP has been used to measure growth, economic welfare, wage increase and so on, the true economic answer to promote growth and prosperity should rather be to examine the factors in the inputs' end of the economic equation. Although there could be innate differences among individuals, the more relevant concern is whether every individual, especially of the younger generation, is given the same opportunity to receive education, and whether every graduate is given the same opportunity in job search and whether every worker is given the same opportunity in employment performance in the market, considering biological, social and cultural factors.

There is a need to focus on studying how economic inputs can be improved. Other than some measurable items, such as expenses on research and development, advancement in technology, the number of registered patents showing the progress in innovation and creativity, the lack of openness and equality in opportunity could be a crucial factor in promoting economic inputs. In a rare but pioneering empirical study on economic opportunity, Li (2014) used global economic data to show that there are extensive and intensive factors that influence economic opportunities. Extensive factors reflect the broadness of factors, such as the extent of foreign direct investment and availability of bank loans, while the intensive factors are mostly the input factors that show how far the extensive factors can go in creating economic opportunity. Empirically, economic freedom, peace and sustainability, and market friendliness are the examples of intensive factors. The study concludes that the intensive factors are more important than the extensive factors in promoting economic opportunity. In other words, while economies are having such resources as financial capital from banks, capital raised from stock markets or foreign investment, what counts, more importantly, would be such institutional factors as personal freedom, reliable civic system, market friendliness, rule of law and infrastructural support.

By their very nature, economic resources are passive and can produce results only when resources are being actively deployed by decision makers. On the contrary, political ideas often appear in a vacuum which need to be activated to produce visible results. Political activation requires instruments to bring about visible political results. There are controversial political arguments and ideologies, but since there are few pure and deployable political instruments, economics has inevitably and extensively been used as an instrument in political maneuvers and decisions. The subject of political economy studies the way in which economics has been incorporated in political decisions, thereby producing results which could be more oriented to politics than to economics. Hence, while the intention to produce political results was the primary goal, the economic outcomes could become the residuals only, implying that the economic outcomes may possibly be unfavorable to the economy or could even produce negative results. For example, political decisions aim often at short-term results, while economic activities need a longer time for results to materialize.

Thus, when political decisions are not intended to produce long-term favorable economic results, the unintended short-term consequences could be distortive, leading to unintended results. As such, it could be the political interference in economics that produces layers of economic problems, distortions, crises and recessions. It is not possible to separate the economic performances that are the result of pure economic activities from the result of economic activities geared for political purposes. And yet, when the economic outcomes are unexpected, people tend to complain about the deficient economic performance, without realizing that the economic problems can originate from political decisions. In other words, while the original intention was political, the final judgment has often been placed on the unexpected, unintended or unfavorable economic outcomes. This is the unfair part in political economy when economics has been executed for political purposes.

The way economics is being used for political purposes depends on the ideology of the political party and its leaders. In a democratic election, politicians may not be well informed about how the deployment of economic variables would result. Likewise, voters may not be knowledgeable about economics. Even though political leaders have their own ideology, how well political leaders know about economics could be an issue. Furthermore, would the political leaders be surrounded by educated economists or cronies who are just political opportunists dependent on how the political leader selects his or her own cabinet? Hence, even though the political election process is democratic, the elected political leader would have total authority in selecting his or her aids in executing policies. This explains the *ex-ante* nature of political election, and the work of the elected political leader could only be known after taking political office. Political results are therefore *ex-post* in nature.

Capitalism and communism are the two extreme forms of political ideologies, and there are cases where elements of one ideology have been mixed with another that form a "mid-way" between the two extreme forms of ideologies. While each of the two ideologies has distinctive features and advocacies, the two ideologies exploit, apply and incorporate economics differently. The key ideological difference between capitalism and communism is the concentration of the political and economic power. While capitalism believes in disbursing power in the private hands so that the government and the state see only to the needs and construction of essential infrastructure and ensure the keeping of a certain societal and civic standard, communism preaches collectivism and concentration of power in the state. State ownership of resources and the powerful government are responsible for distributing material consumables to citizens. The "equality" aspect is that all citizens receive the same material needs, but the "inequality" aspect is the presence of political privileges and advantages. It would therefore be naïve to argue that people are equal under communism.

The capitalist ideology provides ample room for the private sector because it puts the well-being of individuals as the top priority, and individuals are free to conduct their economic activities. Armed with such institutional infrastructure as the rule of law, business ethics, property rights, freedom in market entry, individuals are given the incentives to perform their best and their achievement would not be restricted and would be protected under the law. Classical economics advocates that what is legally and ethically good for the individual shall be good for the society, and the combined results and outcomes of the economic activities of all individuals shall produce the final output for an economy. The private sector shall take the driver's seat, while the government shall serve as the monitor or "firefighter" in ensuring the rule of law, national security, provision of infrastructure, exercising prudent monetary and fiscal policy and rescuing the economy only when needed. The capitalist ideology adheres closer to the natural outcomes of economic activities, and economics activities shall not be interfered, manipulated or abused by the desire and ambitions of political opportunists. Capitalism believes that with economic growth and prosperity, all individuals shall benefit from the expanding economic pie, but due to the differences in endowments, economic rewards may differ among individuals. In contemporary societies, it has been accepted that certain level of social security will be needed to ensure some minimum standard of economic survival, which would be provided to the needy and endowment-low individuals. Social assistance is regarded necessary as some individuals may face temporary economic hardships.

The analysis becomes complicated when political, social and cultural ideals and arguments are forced or imposed on economic activities, gearing economic outcomes to non-economic ends. Typically, the ideology of socialism or communism imposes political advocacy on economic performances and activities. Instead of addressing the complementarity between resources holders, typically the investors and employees in the production process, a "class society" has been polarized and dichotomized into two extremes of bourgeois and the proletariat, into capitalists and peasants, into rich and poor, and class struggle is advocated as a political means to reduce the "economic power" of one type of resource holder. Such an analysis becomes divisive as the two groups of resource holders are placed opposite to each other and assume that their activities produce only "zero-sum" games, where the gain of one party occurs at the expense of the other party.

Communism went further to argue the elimination of the bourgeois class and the domination of the proletariat through state ownership of all resources and in turn the state would conduct production plans and allocate materials and consumables. Communism mistakenly assumed that given the power to the state, the state will act consistently in treating all citizens, and the party officials would serve the nation selflessly. This assumption has practically been violated from the beginning, as the concentration of power in the hands of party leaders and government officials results in the abuse of power as argued by the theories on agency, asymmetric information and rent seeking, and since political power is unevenly distributed, a situation of uneven access to resources is developed between party officials and the public. Allocation of materials could be biased, especially in times of shortages, leading to corruption and rent-seeking activities. Political inequality would be more severe and detrimental than economic inequality, as unequal political treatment could become permanent and fatal, and the disadvantaged would not be given opportunity to improve their daily life activities. The practice of communism has turned out to be the opposite of what was preached and advocated, and in the end, the state became most powerful as all resources are "owned" by the state in the hands of the few party leaders, individual freedom is removed, and individuals permanently survive at the mercy of state officials in the provision and allocation of daily materials. The desires of individuals are not entertained, and double standards often exist in the treatment between different sectors of the population.

The essence in communism and socialism was the politicization of economics, arguing that instead of economic complementarity among resources, the economy was polarized into an opposing state between the various groups of resources holders. A state of division or divisiveness had constantly been instituted and instead of building trust and harmony and creation of opportunity, coercion and directives were exercised by the powerful state. Political inequality became extreme and lifelong. Instead of protecting and promoting the "proletariat" class from "exploitation", the proletariats under a communist regime were in fact controlled and exploited by the state as their life depended on material allocation and their freedom to seek employment or start a business were controlled or even eliminated. In a capitalist regime, the "proletariats" would still own their resources and could make improvements when the demand for their resources increased. In a communist regime, the "proletariats" would not be given any opportunity and their way of life was effectively frozen and kept at a static standard. In preaching communism, a state of polarization had to be created by the politicians because a dichotomy allowed opposition, which could then be exploited for political purpose. And economic differences served as a golden opportunity for communist-minded politicians in creating polarization between diverse groups of resource holders.

The political instrument of polarization and dichotomy has been used by communist-minded politicians even in modern days. For example, the polarization argument has been extended to differences in gender, in race based on the color of the skin, in religious faith as some religions adhere to a variety of discriminatory practices, and in citizenship where sanctuary states accept and treat illegal immigrants the same as domestic residents thereby creating social discontent among the indigenous residents. The strategy could simply be that by polarizing an issue, a problem would then be created, and actions would then be needed to deal with the "problem". Thus, by creating a polarization, the leftist politician could always benefit by capitalizing on the problem. In short, so long as differences exist in human affairs, polarization could always be created and capitalized by leftist politicians.

There can be a "clear-cut" difference between economics and politics, in that economic performances depend on differences in the inputs and outputs in the production process. Differences and diversity are embedded in the very nature of economic activities. Capitalism exhibits itself in the form and practice of an open market that allows individuals to exercise their own incentive in creativity and promoting productivity. Differences in outcomes are acceptable and may not be detrimental provided that the economy is growing, and employment opportunities are created for individuals to improve their economic welfare. Economic resource holders should complement each other, as investors need materials, employers need workers, and workers need jobs. Producers need consumers to purchase their finished products and consumers need producers to produce goods for them to consume.

It is true that jobs are rewarded differently, but this is due to differences in endowments, productivity and the market conditions. What is more important is not the differences in rewards, but the opportunities where workers can get a higher reward through endowment enhancement in the form of training, accumulation of experience, and most important of all, continued investment to create jobs and promote economic growth. Economic freedom further allows individuals to become mobile in their activities and choice should be available to resource holders in deploying the unrestricted use of their resources. Market friendliness and improvement in competitiveness are the key ingredients in economic prosperity. Economic activities should be apolitical, and the "law of economics" that governs the behavior of resource inputs and commodity outputs through the production process and market mechanism where individuals could participate would produce differences in outcomes.

However, the explicit nature of politics is such that political activities often use economic instruments in materializing and exercising political power and authority to produce political attention and results. When a politician aiming to attract votes in an election makes a remark to expand nursing jobs, for example, there can be numerous economic implications that the politician might not have calculated. Would the education institutions be effective in producing more nurses within a short period of time? Such a political decision would have impact on several areas, including the sufficient availability of nurse teachers, the funding and the opportunity cost to the fiscal budget and the existing medical institutions that can provide employment to new supply of nurses. When a political decision is made using economic tools, it is very likely that the politician may not have full knowledge on the economic consequences of the political decision but would not be bothered if it is meant to be a political decision. Similarly, voters may also not be fully aware of the economic implications of the political decision. There is thus an economic cost of every political decision.

Political promises are often made in economic terms, but the actual economics could turn out to be very different or there could be severe unintended consequences that produce long-term economic burdens. It would be impossible to make clear-cut distinctions between the aspect of economic consequences that are the result of political decisions versus the aspect of economic consequences that are the pure operation of economic activities. However, political economic decisions are often judged by economic performances. And the worse could be that the unintended and unfavorable economic consequences could further lead to more political decisions on the economy. Eventually, economic activities can constantly be affected by the different waves of political economy decisions.

IV Economic Differences or Economic Inequality?

The best example of politics intruding into economics is the political argument on economic or income inequality. Given the input differences in the "economic engine", differences in economic outputs and outcomes are unavoidably "unequal" among individual workers, investment projects, firms, markets and nations. It could also be true that the differences could be huge, depending on the extent of the value-added content, nature of demand and market size. Equally, it is unfortunate that many analysts examined the lighter side of the economic equation and focused on the differences in economic outcomes but did not see to the differences in such economic inputs as human capital, opportunity and size of investment, openness and reliability of institutions and social fabrics, advancement in technology and infrastructure, and so on. The economic answer to differences in outcome should be the improvement in the input end, for example, by raising the educational quality and training possibilities of workers, by instituting market-friendly policies to secure and attract more investment, by improving the social fabric and infrastructure to improve productivity and efficiency, by permitting more market freedom to promote creativity and innovation and by ensuring the appointment of a responsible and selfless government whose officials and leaders would look to the overall improvement of the economy as their top priority.

Improvements in the input side of the economic equation shall lead to greater and better outputs, but economic differences or "inequality" still exist. The difference could be that the income gap would be made narrower, and the existence of economic opportunity could allow employment to rise and wages to increase as productivity improves. In short, while inequality is the unavoidable outcome in the "law of economics", the economic solution shall be an ongoing process of improvement in the input end of the economic equation. The formation of a reliable, open and effective economic and civic system that nurtures, protects and promotes the quality at the input end of the economic equation is the answer to fair and equal opportunity applicable to all individuals, businesses and markets, thereby eradicating or minimizing manipulation, rent seeking, biasedness, corruption and cronyism. The ultimate objective is to reduce human errors to the lowest possible in mishandling economic activities so that a more equal and open society can be established. A society is said to have achieved equality and fairness when individuals and businesses are given the chance to perform their best within the viable legal framework, apolitically.

Differences in the input end of the economic equation are inevitably unavoidable. Social and economic policies create differences through the education process as some young people receive more education than others, thereby leading to differences in their productivity and ultimately the income they receive. One simple answer would be to look at the percentage of young people receiving higher education. The percentage could be as low as 15–20% in poor countries though illiteracy has been removed. In advanced countries, the percentage could be as high as 40–50%. How can a society achieve income equality when only a minority of young people is receiving higher education? The university graduates would forever have a wage or earning power higher than those without higher education. Through education, the society itself created "inequality" as individuals' personal endowments would consequently become different. In political terms when it comes to the number of voters, it would mean that there are more endowment-low voters than endowment-high voters.

Similarly, investment projects differ from one another in the capital requirement and the market in which the investments operate and the time length required in the maturity of investments, and all these factors would produce differences in outcomes and returns to the investors. Individual creativity and advancement of applied technology in the production of consumer products also differ in scale and magnitude. People with innate talent could earn much more than those with professional jobs. Creativity and innovation also generate differences in the input process. These differences in economic inputs and outputs are the acts within the law of economics and should be treated apolitically and not carry any ideological content.

However, the very fact of economic differences means that there are people with low individual endowments, and may face survival problems due to sickness, family hardship and other non-economic reasons. The development of a matured civic society would have a social assistance system in which needy households and individuals faced with economic hardship would be aided through a public scheme. To avoid excessive fiscal burden and a large government administration, social assistance should best be provided on a monitored and standardized basis. The provision of assistance in the redistribution policy should best be effective and not be an instrument for the development of a huge government machinery, or a source of debt accumulation that would burden the taxpayers and the future generation. Social assistance should be considered on the need basis and not on grounds of political manipulation.

Economic differences, or unequal economic outcomes, should be considered as an incentive or driving force for individuals and businesses to progress. A "prepare for the rainy day" attitude, instead of complacency or waiting for assistance, should best be adopted by individuals in moving forward as a means to conquer economic risk and uncertainty. It is only through economic progress that a higher social ladder can be reached by individuals. Differences should coexist with opportunities and growth. Outcome differences in the form of inequality shall not be static, but the availability of opportunity produces a dynamic picture where differences can be narrowed, or the pace of progress can see some overtake others given the changing market conditions. Opportunities are provided to individuals and can be multiplicative as the creation of one opportunity leads to the rise of another opportunity. Economic differences should not be considered as inequality as the economic gap can vary among individuals and activities, in time and pace. A pro-active and enterprising individual shall not be threatened by differences as the availability of chances and opportunities would be the better alternative.

The more relevant question is how to ensure equality in its greatest possible extent. It is true that civic and non-civic institutions have been established in many societies as a means to regulate and at the same time exercise control. However, some established institutions can be a hazard to equality promotion. Practices in some religion, for example, would discriminate one gender against another, thereby robbing the opportunity of the disadvantaged gender. Racial differences and discrimination are artificial acts which could be instituted and enforced, thereby enabling one race to have a clear advantage over another race. In undemocratic societies, certain political parties have the monopoly on the political agenda, and by becoming a member of the political party, the person would automatically be advantaged and can gain access to the source of power. Indeed, the undemocratic political system through the work of the government administration could already be the basis of inequality. Self-centered leaders manipulate the political scene for their own benefits through cronyism, selection bias, corruption and coercion. The corrupted leaders progress through the embezzlement of funds and enrich themselves, while the rest of the society stays stagnant.

One commonality among such inequality as gender, race, class and religion is the permanent nature of these instituted inequalities. In a gender-biased state, for example, one gender will permanently be disadvantaged against the other gender. Such inequality will become "lifelong" as the disadvantaged gender will never have any opportunity to progress. In turn, the survival of the disadvantaged gender would have to depend on the advantaged gender for support. On the contrary, although economic outcomes in a capitalist economy are different and unequal, individuals do have their freedom and choice to make progress through training, job mobility, taking up a second job, starting their own business or migrating to a more market-friendly region. Thus, forces of inequality and outcome differences will not be static but can be dynamic and economic improvement can be made as opportunity arises and depends on how enterprising individuals are.

Hence, seen in an absolute term between the different lifetimes of an individual, and not relatively when inequality would be compared between individuals, the economic welfare of an individual shall absolutely improve overtime. Indeed, it is a typical employment pattern that young and inexperienced workers receive a lower pay than experienced workers. But as one worker gains more experience, rewards would increase accordingly. Hence, in absolute terms, the point of comparison is within the individual overtime. However, when politics enters the economic process, the situation changes considerably. Income inequality can become an "evergreen" topic in politics, as perfect equality can never be achieved. Thus, capitalizing on income inequality has been a popular political instrument to appeal to the voters. Income differences can easily be polarized and dichotomized into rich versus poor, high income versus low income earners, white collar professionals versus blue collar factory workers, experienced senior versus inexperienced junior workers, investors and capital holders versus laborers and so on.

Many of these terms are part of the political jargon, though in economics, they are considered as the diverse types of resource holders. The very act of such polarization allows politicians to capitalize on it, mobilizing it to become an issue to be tackled politically. And economic instruments are used in fulfilling the political goals. When a political criterion is imposed on the different economic outcomes, the so-called "income inequality", the usual chains of political economy decisions include policies on redistribution, welfare provisions and "care" that extends welfare expenses to areas of assistance which are otherwise private spending decisions. Political instruments include the establishment of labor unions, minimum wage legislation, and nationalization of industries, all of which aim to exercise the transfer of political power from the workers to the union leaders.

So long as there is the existence of government, there is a need to impose taxes to provide revenues to fund the expense of the government machinery. And it should be acceptable for the high-income earners to pay more tax than low-income earners, and similarly, businesses with higher profits should pay more than low-profit businesses. This is based on the principle of ability to pay. Able individuals and businesses are making higher earnings, and in turn they are more able to contribute revenue to the government. However, the economic effect of a political decision to redistribute income would primarily mean that wage payment and earnings might no longer be singly determined by the economic aspects of work, namely productivity, but by the political desire of the leaders. If political leaders prefer to follow "supply-side" strategies, there could be an improvement in the input side of the economic equation through promotion and enhancement in the endowment of individuals, through education to produce high quality human capital, investment to produce more jobs and employment possibilities, improvement in public infrastructure to enhance long-term competitiveness, and pursue market-friendly policies to enable more businesses to succeed. Such a policy that works on "redistribution" at the input end effectively enriches the potentials of individuals and businesses. The result shall be an enlargement of economic opportunities such that both individuals and businesses benefit, and as overall income and profit increase, the government in turn gains through the rise in tax revenue.

Unfortunately, redistribution has been conducted using "demand-side" strategies by imposing a heavier tax on the high-earning and endow-ment-high individuals and businesses. With the political desire to redistribute individual earnings from endowment-high to endowment-low individuals, a welfare scheme would usually be established by a socialist-oriented government to spend on endowment-low individuals. The "demand-side" strategy aims to expand the consumption ability of the recipients without themselves having to earn for it. Conceptually, the government through welfare spending is effectively absorbing the "private cost" of individuals in their inability to survive economically and transform them into the "social cost" to be shouldered by the taxpayers. The size of "social cost" will then be decided by government officials and political leaders whose decisions could be based on a political agenda dressed up in the form of social need and care rather than long-term economic progress and competitiveness.

Welfare spending is regarded as "demand-side" policies as such spending singly aims at enlarging the spending power of the recipients, and such welfare spending would not be geared to production activities. Hence, while the level of aggregate demand rises, the level of production remains the same. In the short-term, welfare spending tends to be infla-tionary if the spending is not matched with the increase in production or leads to rise in imports if welfare recipients spend on imported goods, thereby adding pressure on the balance of payment in international trade. Furthermore, since all welfare spending would not be taxed, the govern-ment could face fiscal imbalance, resulting in likely deficit and debt, especially in tough economic times when revenues are short.

By comparison, the "demand-side" economic approach to income inequality would consider only the spending side of the economic equa-tion. On the contrary, "supply-side" economics would go further to con-sider the input side of the equation and look for policies that increase income and job possibilities. With rising opportunity and investment, the rise in employment should lead to rise in income, thereby lifting the over-all level of income to a higher level in absolute terms, even though there is still inequality on a relative measure. The two-folded advantage of a "supply-side" economic approach includes a rising income and thereby a rising tax revenue on the one hand, and on the other hand as the number of low-income recipients would have more employment opportunities, the government would need less to spend on welfare assistance, and the retained fiscal revenue could be used to promote other "supply-side" economics, such as training and education, and research and development to improve the economy's competitiveness.

Other political instruments in dealing with income inequality typically include the formation of labor unions in large corporations, legislation of minimum wages and nationalization of industries. However, studies have shown that many large labor unions have become powerful institutions and are capable of imposing political influence and demand from the government, political parties and corporations (Robertson, 2004; Botero *et al.*, 2004). While labor unions are meant to act on behalf of their members, their policies could be protectionist in restricting new entry of non-unionized workers, thereby limiting the growth of the labor force and job opportunities. Politically, labor unions support labor movements with the ultimate intention to accumulate power, promote pro-labor political candidates, win political elections and probably run a leftist government. It could be true that working conditions can be improved, but the political power of the unions might impose potential damages to the economic side of businesses when political interest and ambition become their prime objective.

There are numerous economic implications of labor unions' activities (Hirsch, 1991; Nickell and Layard, 1999). Collective bargaining would relate the wages paid to workers more in line with political desire than to workers' actual productivity. The resulting higher wages paid would lead to a higher cost of production, thereby making the economy less competitive. Secondly, as the labor unions are constantly seeking higher wages, at times regardless of other macro-economic conditions, employers would be unwilling to raise wages knowing that the labor unions would come forward with their wage demands anyway. Political desire imposed by labor unions would result in economic distortion in the wage sector. The pattern of businesses could also change as the political power of the labor unions evolves.

When the high labor cost is passed on to the consumers through the rise in prices, the workers eventually face a high inflation. Thus, the "higher wage" would only produce a nominal result as the consequent "higher inflation" would eat into the workers' purchasing power, causing their real wages to remain constant. In economics, wage increase should reflect the rise in productivity. The rise in wages resulting from labor union bargaining would provide an opportunity for the retail sector to raise the price of the final product, thereby making it difficult to identify if the inflation is "cost push" or "demand pull". Nonetheless, a high inflation rate hurts the economy as the purchasing power is lowered. In turn, employees and labor unions could further exercise their political power to seek compensation for the loss in purchasing power, thereby giving rise to another round of wage negotiation, leading eventually to a "wage–price" inflationary spiral. Thirdly, there is also the foreign trade effect as import rises. All these activities would point to the result that the economy would become less competitive, either due to rising inflation or a deteriorating balance of trade.

The establishment of a minimum wage should produce a similar result, that wage payment is found more on political grounds than on grounds of economic productivity. The simple economic analysis of a minimum wage is that a minimum wage could be effective when it is set above the equilibrium market wage. At a higher than market wage, those remaining in employment would benefit from the high minimum wage, but the overall employment could be lower than the equilibrium level of employment. In an efficient market, it is possible that the unemployed could undercut the minimum wage and offer to work at a lower market wage. Furthermore, it has been argued that minimum wage can only be effective in non-professional jobs, where wages are probably paid on hourly basis. In a period of economic growth where demand for labor rises, it is likely that the minimum wage would be ineffective as employers would be prepared to pay higher wages to attract and retain workers.

A major problem in a minimum wage legislation is its "blanket coverage" and that it does not make distinctions among different types of low-skilled jobs and does not take into consideration workers' experience. There are different kinds of hourly paid jobs, while some are more physically demanding, others may require duty shifts, may suit a certain gender or different age group of workers. Thus, to have a similar "minimum" wage applicable to all hourly paid jobs may not be relevant and certainly cannot motivate workers to switch between jobs to allow job mobility. Disregarding experience is inappropriate, as a less-experienced worker could be paid less than an experienced worker. Thus, having received the same level of hourly wage cannot provide incentive to workers to perform better, as experience and strong performance would not be counted and rewarded as the wage does not distinguish workers' quality performance.

Li (2012) and Li *et al.* (2016) argued for a "starting wage" in each kind of hourly paid job, so that experience can be included in the wage payment, and as different jobs provide a different "starting wage", workers can have the opportunity and freedom to select and choose their kind of jobs depending on their experience, expertise and location. The "starting wage" shall differ between jobs, and the possible increase in wage should serve as a market indicator and allow market mobility among the workers. Thus, it is argued that the "minimum wage" could turn out to be the "maximum wage" as employers would be unwilling to pay more than the minimum wage, and there is equally no incentive for the workers to look for jobs with differences in earning and job prospects. The political desire of the minimum wage legislation is to provide a higher-than-market wage to hourly paid workers, but such "security" has costed the workers the incentive to look for jobs and to improve their skill for a better employment prospect, and equally, employers have no incentive to see to the improved performance of the workers. Such an economic consequence would mean that the workers would have a narrower exposure to other employment and no opportunity to maximize their work potential. Such a result could be severe especially to the younger workers who would have a long working life. Politically, these workers would probably remain and be restricted to work on hourly paid jobs and not able to make a career out of their employment. In the long-run, these workers' welfare would be worse off, showing a typical case of a political desire leading to a poorer economic outcome.

All these discussions point to the fact that economics has been used for political intentions, and the resulting distortions or consequences may not be favorable to the economy but may have satisfied the desires of political leaders and politically oriented decision makers. The commonality among all these politics-driven decisions is the mistaken view that politics can be used to correct economic performances, and that "differences" are being politicized as "inequalities". And yet, after decades of leftist policies to correct "inequalities", economic or income inequality still exists, proving that it is the "difference" that one should conceptually look at and not the exaggerated "inequality" aspect. Unfortunately, such a mistaken view has still been adopted by leftist politicians in the hope of gaining votes in elections.

"Economic inequality is the best form of inequality" is definitely a challenging statement, but it is true because "difference" is a feature that is present in all economic activities. "Inequality" thus is not an economic term, but it is a political term imposed on an economic outcome by leftist politicians. Economic activities should be apolitical, but efforts must be made to improve economic performances. As compared to other forms of humanistic inequalities, such as gender, race, religious with regional prejudices, which could be lifelong and institutionally determined with individuals not given the chance to improve, "income inequality" can always be improved if given individual freedom and availability of opportunities so that "differences" can be narrowed or varied. When individuals and households are given the chance to determine their own economic life, differences in outcomes are expected, but what counts is that individuals can achieve their own welfare. It is a mistaken view altogether that the leftists politicized such a "difference" in economic outcome as "inequality".

V Reinterpreting Political Economy

The study of economics is no rocket science, it needs to be understood within the mindset of the discipline itself and not be intervened by incorporating political desires. Similarly, economic or income difference is not that much of a devil or the "end of the world", it needs to be understood between the input side and output side of the economic equation. It would be mistaken to impose a certain political desire in economic outcome and then complain about such an economic outcome without understanding the endowment variation in the input side of the economic process. While the study of political economy mixed political decisions with economic activities, and since political behavior is the more active discipline than economics, it has often been mistaken that economic problems are outcomes of poor economic decisions, as they could be politically motivated from the very beginning. Thus, while political decisions lead to short-term political outcomes, the "deadweight loss" could be that the economy may suffer in the long term in the form of distortion, stagnation, weak performance and low growth, which in turn would result in loss in economic competitiveness when compared to neighboring nations which pursue a more progressive economic path. The lesson is that one should first consider if the low or inappropriate economic performances were constrained by the ill-decided political acts. As such, it would be proper to first address the need to make appropriate and sound political changes that could supplement economic policies and not the reverse.

A simple economic understanding is that differences appear in all economic activities, and it is exactly such differences that drive all enterprising individuals and businesses to perform better and stronger in their economic activities. Economic differences are unavoidable, but they can be accommodated provided all economic participants have or are given the freedom and right to perform within the legal framework. Checks and balances should be instituted through the presence of the rule of law and all law enforcement agencies, establishment of civic institutions that provide standards, acceptable ethical practices and sound regulations, and apolitical policies that eliminate biasedness, corruption and cronyism. Though there are differences in outcomes, legal and ethical economic activities are not meant to harm individuals. In turn, it should be the individuals who would make the best out of the free economic system to maximize their private welfare. Societies are composed of individuals, and societies can progress only when every individual is given the chance, opportunity and possibility to perform their best unrestricted within the rule of law.

In short, economic performance would be stronger with a pro-growth political regime that considers the importance of "supply-side" economics and policies are geared to promote the input side of the economic equation by ensuring ample education facilities, provision of sound and appropriate physical and societal infrastructure, and adoption of market-friendly policies to encourage investment and enlargement of job opportunities. However, one must admit that there are needy individuals and households who are faced with difficulty in economic and social survival. There is also the need for law enforcement and policing of communities. There is the border that nations need to protect from foreign invasion. There is the need for the government to engage in international affairs, ensuring economic and global competitiveness. There is a need to look, think and act forward to ensure that the future generation will be better off than the current generation and not the reverse.

To assist those individuals and households who are faced with problems of economic survival, a program of economic welfare shall be instituted by a responsible government to ensure that a certain degree of "economic transfer" can be carried out to provide temporary assistance to the needy. The unemployed youth and workers and many single-parent households need temporary economic assistance to help them to overcome their tough times until jobs are forthcoming. The sick, the elderly and the disabled will need a longer period of assistance and medical provisions shall be needed in addition to economic assistance. However, the more controversial debate is how far and to what extent should economic welfare be provided to the needy individuals. It could be economically suicidal if economic welfare decisions were made purely on political grounds as the decision makers might not be aware of such economic consequences as fiscal deficit and debt accumulated.

It may be useful to relate or link the provision of economic welfare to some economic criteria, and not purely on political grounds. There can be several useful and applicable economic criteria in the provision of economic assistance. For the unemployed, the criteria would include if the individual had ever paid income tax, the length of time the unemployed had been employed, the economic condition of his or her spouse, or if the person seeking economic assistance owned any property or invested in assets. For the unemployed youth, the economic criteria could be whether the youth is living with parents, whether the parents pay taxes, whether the youth has taken up any temporary employment or voluntary work previously in schools, or whether the youth is prepared to take up further vocational training to acquire a marketable skill. When it comes to an entire household with two or more members, the amount of economic assistance would be higher. But equivalent criteria would have to be imposed to avoid abuse and misuse that generate disincentive on the part of the breadwinner in the household. Social assistance would have to be instituted, especially young children in need of education to avoid cross-generational poverty. The most important criterion applied to assistance provision is its temporary nature, and conditions are applied when changes in the economic position of the household occur.

The economic aspect should come before the political aspect in making political economy analyses and decisions because the impacted economic activities could have long-term implications, either favorable or unfavorable, that would remain even after the political impact or results were materialized. The more effective and long-lasting aspect in political economy should be the adoption and exercise of "supply-side" policies that aim in improving the input end of the economic and social equation, while leaving the output end to the free market forces with equality in participations by all individuals freely within the rule of law.

The problem in socialism or communism is the bias in looking at the outcome end of the economic equation. And to "equalize" the outcome end of the economic equation, the input end must be controlled by the state, thereby taking away individuals' freedom. Capitalism on the contrary treasures the contribution by individuals, notes the endowment difference in the input end of the economic equation, and opts for "supply-side" economic policies to enhance the richness of individual endowments through education, provision of infrastructure, health support and so on. It promotes equality in opportunity and openness to individuals by instituting civic organizations that serve to check and balance the potential harmful mistakes made by the government. The establishment of a civic society should produce numerous layers of protection individuals can rely on, in addition to the existing government machinery and political establishments. Individuals are in control and in command but acknowledge the differences in the outcome of economic activities. In short, enriching the input end of the economic equation is the preferable policy goal than to examine singly and politically the outcome end of the economic equation.

It would be naïve and unproductive to deal with the differences in the outcome aspects while knowing that the differences arise from the endowment variations in the input end of the economic equation. Indeed, could "economic inequality" be solved, it would have been solved given the current state of civilization the world faces. There are so many studies, arguments and policies instituted to deal with economic inequality, yet it still exists and can get worse at times (see, for example, Li and Zhou, 2010, 2013; Zhou and Li, 2011; Li *et al.*, 2016). One must accept that economic inequality cannot be solved but at best can be reduced and narrowed through instituting productive and effective policies that enhance the quality of input factors, typically enhancement in human capital, expansion in viable financial investment, promotion of productive industries and businesses, and ensuring ample infrastructure support and market friendliness. Armed with strong and high-quality factors in the input end of the economic equation, the outcome end will still produce differences but for sure individuals will get better and their economic welfare would only improve continuously.

It is the absolute comparison in income inequality that looks at the same individual over his or her working life that matters more than relative comparison that looks at different individuals' income performance at any time on a "snapshot" basis, because it would be unfair, unwise and unproductive to gather all working individuals on an income scale regardless of their age, profession or type of jobs, and years of experience. Indeed, relative comparison can never come to any solution because differences always exist. It is a tautology to complain about economic inequality on the one hand but creating differences on the other hand through the education system that nurtures the different abilities of individuals. It is only the politicians who exploit the issue of economic inequality for political end, while the presence of economic differences should be apolitical and can best be dealt with within the economic arena itself.

VI Political Spillovers

Economics is a "relative" game, often with "positive-sum" outcomes where all parties gain, though the rewards would differ among parties. By contrast, politics is an "absolute" game where a political election shall only result in one winner, while other competitors will loose and have to wait for the next round of elections. Politics is a "zero-sum" game where there is only one winning party, all other competitors become losers. Such a conceptual difference between economics and politics can generate numerous results, either favorable or unfavorable to economics.

Political freedom in the form of democracy has been accepted as a normal institution in civilized nations. As written in the constitution of many nations, political leaders are elected through an open process for a fixed term to head the government. In matured democratic nations, the same political leader can have a fixed term of office in a successful re-election. However, the intention to limit the number of terms a politician could run for leadership is to avoid the same person occupying the leadership for too long and that others can have an equal chance in the democratic system. Political parties are formed to promote certain political ideologies and serve as machineries in choosing candidates for elections. There are rules, laws and regulations instituted to govern the conduct of elections and voting to ensure fairness, representation, openness and eliminate wrongdoings and abuse so that all candidates are in the same level-playing field, while voters are given equal chance to vote for their candidates. Democracy allows the citizens to choose or replace their political leaders periodically, and unpopular leaders can be voted out of office. The democratic system is meant to allow citizens to choose the able and suitable leader to head the government.

In a matured civic society, politics is just one of the various means for citizens to air their opinions, and the political system is one of the numerous channels through which citizens communicate with their leaders and the government. Other than the government administrative departments and bureaus, civic institutions are meant to empower the citizens and provide another layer of communication and protection. Such civic institutions as professional associations, social organizations, media, banking and financial institutions, community and neighborhood units have been established to provide additional layers of public protection. Thus, any individual person in a civic society may not necessarily need to engage actively in politics, other than to fulfil the voter's role in an election, but safety and social protection can be secured through the presence and work of civic institutions.

However, while political freedom through democracy does allow individuals to join the election for the leadership position, there are two conceptual problems in political elections. Firstly, Dahl (2006) raised the question of political equality or inequality. Political candidates and voters are "equal" before the election as it is open and free for individuals to join the election game. After the election and the leader is elected, political inequality starts as the leader now becomes the ruler, while all voters become the ruled. Political power would then shift to the elected leader, who will have the authority to run the government, choose his/her cabinet members and ministers in the government departments and bureaus, and decide on policies that the leader thinks fit. Political election produces an absolute outcome in inequality.

Secondly, Li (2017a) pointed out that political elections are "*ex-ante*" activities as the candidate contesting for election could elaborate on his/her policies, but whether the results can be delivered become "*ex-post*". The promise made on the *ex-ante* situation may not be delivered on the *ex-post* situation. Hence, there is no guarantee that the elected leader would do the job for the good and benefit of the voters and the people at large. This is exactly the risk that the agency theory advocates, as the elected leader, given the absolute political inequality, could have a different agenda once elected. In a democratic system, the elected leader could serve the official term before contesting for another election, and if the "political report card" was not favorable, the voters can vote out the leader. But the damage done, if any, by an ineffective elected leader, could last for years before it could be corrected.

The reality in political elections can appear differently. To start with, it is costly to run an election in the contemporary world, and any candidate will have to have ample financial support before considering contesting because the person could face losses if not elected. Thus, candidates must be quite "well-off" financially, though sponsorships and fundraising could be possible, but they would also be restricted by the law in seeking financial support to avoid "insider deals" or corruption. Nonetheless, there are always loopholes or indirect means for candidates to seek financial support. Secondly, even though the leader is elected, the members of the cabinet and other top civil servants are not. Given that the absolute authority rests with the elected leader, the leader has the freedom to choose his/her administration. In a politically matured society where there shall be channels through which government administration and policies could be monitored, the extent of political transparency should be high. Otherwise, it would not be possible to ensure checks and balances on what the administration has achieved or failed to achieve.

One other aspect in case the elected leader has served for more than one term of office or for a long time is that the entire administration and top civil servants would gradually be instituted to ensure similarity in political views and ideologies. However, should there be possible differences in ideologies with the next incoming elected leader, problems may arise because many of the key positions in the government administration would remain, as the crash of ideology and policy would impose intangible difficulty to the incoming leader. It could take some time before the newly elected leader could replace the top administration with his/her own members. In other words, political succession could involve delay and possibly a period of ineffective governance when the newly elected incoming leaders and the administration personnel from the previous regime hold different political ideologies.

Ultimately, what counts is whether the elected political leader chooses to adopt policies that are oriented to promote the economy, or the leader is purely a political animal and uses economics as a political tool without any regard to the overall economic consequences. How knowledgeable in economics the leader and the leader's advisers are, is an important consideration in the economic outcome of the political process. Bearing in mind that economic activities produce chain relationships, one activity could lead to another, possibly with unintended consequences. For example, as Li (2013, 2017a, 2017b) pointed out, a prolonged period of ultra-low interest rate could theoretically help to lower investment cost. This could look favorable politically as borrowers are faced with a lower investment cost, but the economic consequence would be that the low cost of borrowing can stimulate unproductive investment and speculations. And the consequence of a rapid rise in real-estate prices would equally penalize potential buyers who would then be faced with a speculative property market. On the contrary, the utility function of buyers in the users' market could be higher when faced with a higher interest rate but a lower and steady property price.

Most importantly, a prolonged period of low interest rate leads to a fall in the value of money, thereby imposing new difficulty on the monetary policy as the value of money shrinks. And when the ultra-low interest rate becomes a "new normal", reversing the low interest rate policy would be politically unpopular. Consequently, distortions arising from prolonged period of an ultra-low interest rate policy would continue. When the property price becomes overheated as a result of speculation, and instead of reversing the ultra-low interest rate, more restrictive but often short-term policies are introduced by the government on the housing market. However, such restrictive policies could be seen more as a political capital to show a "caring" government, but it also results in more government interference. Furthermore, property speculation would return once the short-term impact is over, leading to another wave of property speculation, and the buyers in the users' market would continue to suffer. Many other examples could be found in cases where economic activities were deployed for political goals, but the relative nature of economic outcome is such that one economic activity would produce a chain-like relationship and result in other economic consequences, often unintended but distortive, and further correctional actions would then be required.

Another issue is the personality of the elected politician in relation to his or her ethical standard and intentions. On an *ex-ante* basis, it would be difficult to know if the politician aims at serving the people by effectively and appropriately deploying the leadership authority or uses the gained authority to favor his/her own vested interests through amassing wealth and power surrounded by cronies. Since political election is an *ex-ante* exercise, the aspiring politician would certainly put up convincing arguments to win the election, but there could be gaps between what was said *ex-ante* and what was done *ex-post*. A principled politician shall show strong ethics and implement policies for the sake of the citizens. On the contrary, an ill-intended politician would abuse the power and authority to gain benefits from the leadership position. As political power is absolute, corruption and advantage gained through cronyism and improper relationships could easily follow, especially when there is a lack of monitoring schemes and an absence of a transparent machinery strong enough to deter political abuse in a timely manner. When elected, the leader could be so self-centered as to amend the rule of law or even the nation's constitution to suit his or her political desire and ambition.

Even though the voters can examine the background, the personal and professional history of the political candidate, ethics is a personality issue and voters will not know how the elected politician would behave until after the elected candidate is in office. In addition to ethics, the political ideology of the politician shall provide the path on how the elected leader would execute his ideological goals through policies. Let us consider two extreme cases of possible policy events when a socialist or leftist politician is elected into office, and this will be contrasted with a capitalist politician voted into office. The differences in political ideological would generate vast differences in the economic policies and outcomes. To start with, it is likely that the political platform between a socialist candidate will be entirely different from a candidate believing in capitalist principles.

The political platform of a socialist candidate would popularly choose such issues as inequality and poverty because by nature, in all economies, there is always inequality and poverty. Furthermore, the psychology of politics is that it is the poor, the weak and the underprivileged who are treated unfairly. In economics terms, these are considered as "endowment-low" individuals who would be delighted to see some sort of "revenge" or take advantage of the rich as that could please them psychologically and at the same time would obtain some advantage in the form of increased assistance and subsidy should a socialist candidate be elected. As such, it is believed that life would be easier if the elected politician was on their side. When elected, a socialist leader would increase government aid and assistance to the poor.

Consider the economic results of the different stakeholders when a socialist politician is elected. The subsidy and welfare recipients would achieve a higher personal utility as "free lunches" will be provided. It is true that the needy individuals when faced with survival problems should be assisted, but the large and prolonged provision of subsidies would discourage their incentive to earn, or the willingness to learn a skill or pick up the experience of a trade. The benefits received from the welfare would delay their urge to look for jobs or seek employment, even when the economy is recovering or booming. After some period of time, these recipients would remain as they were when subsidies and welfare were first given. The difference is that these people would continue to remain uncompetitive and lack marketability in the job market. It is unlikely that these people would find jobs as their knowledge and skill remains unimproved. Simply put, these recipients would be "frozen" in their welfare-receiving status and could forever rely and become dependent on government assistance as their marketability stays shrunk.

To the leftist politician, it would even be better to have more welfare seekers because these are the group of people who would become dependent on the government, and that should justify the need for more government spending on welfare and ultimately the need to build up a bigger government administration. As such, the politician's power would then be further consolidated, because the political "report card" would show that there are more people needing assistance and the politician is attending to their needs by spending more fiscal resources to aid the welfare recipients. Under the socialist political leadership, the poor remain not only poor but also "frozen" as their marketability stays shrunk. On the contrary, the political leader does gain by capitalizing on the issue of poverty and building up a bigger government administration. In short, the poor would not get better under a socialist leader, but their life would remain static in a state of poverty.

In fact, the size of the poor population may even become larger under a leftist political leader. As government spending on welfare explodes, it would soon result in a fiscal deficit. Do not forget that welfare assistance does not come from the leader's income, it comes from the tax revenue of the taxpayers. As fiscal deficit rises, it is likely that a higher tax would have to be imposed as the political psychology is that the rich individuals and businesses should pay more or even be penalized for the fact that they are the "endowment-high" individuals or prospective businesses employing workers. Next, should the government deficit persist, the alternative is to raise government borrowing in the form of bonds which would have to be repaid in the future. Thus, the economy becomes debt prone as the level of deficit increases.

The rising taxes and national debts would have other negative economic implications. Typically, "endowment-high" professionals and prospective businesses would look for alternatives by seeking employment in foreign countries, the so-called "brain drain", or investing in market-friendly destinations overseas. A situation is known as a "capital flight" when financial resources leave the country before problems erupt at home. This could be seen by the way citizens and officials are sending their money, capital and family out of the country in the first instance.

The mounting national debt coupled with an unattractive investment environment would mean the country is becoming poorer and weaker. Furthermore, if imports exceed exports over a prolonged period, the country's currency would be faced with the pressure of devaluation as its reserve becomes low. All these trends point to economic decline and rise in unemployment as jobs are lost due to the fall in competitiveness. The rise in unemployment would mean a larger pool of the poor population, and more welfare and subsidies would then have to be provided. A "vicious economic circle" would develop that began with rising welfare and excessive taxes to assist the poor, the appearance of "brain drain" coupled with "capital flight" as fiscal deficit and national debt mount, the fall in investment would mean the rise of unemployment, and the poor population would increase, thereby adding more pressure on welfare spending. With the rising debt and unemployment, the younger generation, even if they are educated, may not have a promising future partly because of the high taxes, high debts, lacking investment opportunities and limited job possibilities.

A socialist leader gains most from the expansion of the poor population as it would provide the socialist leader with more political capital. And instead of changing the policy, the same ideology would persist, and the leader would further promote a bigger government by opening more administrative units to cater for the needy poor, to check on the tax population, to seek for aids to cover the debt and deficits and look for assistance from ideologically friendly countries abroad. In the meantime, the economy remains weak and uncompetitive as the level of international reserve drops significantly, and the government must look for means to rescue the economy. The effort to rescue the economy would prove in vain when the nation itself has run out of assets. Socialist policies will not work because they are aimed at sustaining poverty and generate "vicious economic circles", and the weaker the economy would become, the more political capital the socialist leader would have. The more dependent the population is on welfare and government assistance, the less likely the economic opportunities that would be forthcoming. And that further reinforces the political capital of the socialist leader, who would become even more powerful as more and more people needed assistance from the government. In short, the more dependent the population is, the more powerful the socialist leader becomes. Thus, to become a strong and powerful socialist leader, the task of political capitalization would be to reduce the ability of the people, turn up the size of the poor population and promote a weaker economy to ensure insecurity.

The chain of economics reactions such that by adopting "demand-driven" policies which focus mainly on spending and not on producing, the economy would be weakened by the resources geared more to spending than to production. The high taxes and rising debts would discourage investment, leading to a fall in productivity and economic competitiveness, and subsequently a fall in job availability and low employment potentials. As income subsequently falls, more people would be expected to rely on government support, and rising debt and deficit would weaken the economy further.

Socialist politicians often look for conflicting issues that generate dichotomy and extremism in society. Poverty, inequality, race and gender differences are the popular examples used and capitalized by socialist politicians in many nations. And their ideological "solution" would be to introduce and implement more government and administrative interferences so that they make the voters believe that they are dealing with the problems. Yet, a bigger government and additional administrative units could only lead to more government spending, and with a weak economy, debts and deficits would further increase. The political problem is that these socialist political leaders could get away with it as they are not financially responsible for paying the debts and deficits. It is the citizens in general, especially the able taxpayers, who suffer for the political decisions of the socialist leaders. The poor also suffer as job opportunities are not forthcoming, and they will remain poor and face no improvement in their livelihood.

On the contrary, let us consider the economic path and consequence if the elected political leader adheres more to capitalist principles of economic development. Normally, job promotion and reduction of government spending would be the policy goal. The only means to achieve job promotion is to nurture a market-friendly investment climate typically through a reduction in taxes. When investors consider new business potentials, the rise in investment shall lead to greater economic opportunities. As more jobs become available, coupled with a lower tax, workers' consumption power shall rise, which should promote greater private spending and a positive multiplier could emerge, leading to more positive spillover effects on the economy, including probably the rise in wages and earnings as unemployment falls.

As the overall economic competitiveness improves, investments become more attractive, especially physical investment that enhances productivity and an expansion in production capability. With the rise in profits, large corporates can use the additional resources for research and development that enhances technology and improves the work environment, including the provision of bonuses. In short, investment in the private sector shall take its own pace in economic growth. The government would have more resources, resulting possibly in fiscal surplus, as the expansion of prospective businesses as well as the rising wages shall contribute more tax revenue to the government. On the contrary, the rise in employment would mean fewer poor people and a fall in the need for social welfare. The combined result is that the government shall end up with more fiscal resources, which shall then be deployed to promote long-term economic competitiveness, through stronger infrastructure provisions, greater enhancement in technology development, and increased engagement in education to strengthen the overall level of human capital. These shall surely help to promote the country's long-term economic capability, generating more opportunities for the future generation, while a healthy fiscal position shall generate positive results in the country's reserve and exchange rate.

Thus, a "virtuous economic circle" is created through capitalist economic policies in the following sequences. With a fall in overall taxes and the nurturing of a favorable investment climate, industries shall be revitalized and expanded, and new businesses would be encouraged, thereby leading to rise in employment and job opportunities. The rise in earnings and income allows households to have a greater personal purchasing power and results in a larger income multiplier. The government in turn shall experience a stronger and healthier fiscal position, which could then be used to improve the economy's overall competitiveness and generate a positive performance in external trade and strengthen the country's exchange rate position in the global economy.

Capitalist economic policies are meant to enhance people's marketability and the economy's production capacity, so that workers in all walks of life can make use of the market-friendly environment to do their best for their own private welfare. Capitalist economic policies are ultimately welfare, wealth and capacity enhancing, creating more opportunities, choices and markets for all economic participants. The government adheres to economic freedom supported by the rule of law and good ethics and serves as a "monitor" of the economy, fine-toning economic policies when needed, and supporting the needy individuals and households through a functional assistance scheme should they face temporary economic hardship.

Through the deployment of capitalist policies, the economy shall focus on "supply-driven" strategies that: (i) expand and promote the quality of factor inputs to promote competitiveness; (ii) pursue market-friendly investment conditions to promote jobs; (iii) ensure a low income tax regime to encourage employment; and (iv) deploy fiscal resources to enhance future productivity and capability. Opponents of capitalist economic policies focus on only one issue, namely the earning gap and economic difference so generated because investors and workers are rewarded differently in the economic process. But these opponents also fail to understand that rewards are governed by the differences in their endowments in the first instance. What is more important is that even though economic gaps exist, all economic participants, be they the investors or workers, are better off and can enjoy their own economic welfare so earned and achieved.

Politically, capitalist economic policies are meant to allow individuals to perform their possible best, while the government's power would be confined to the "back seat", leaving the private sector as the economic driver. Capitalist-oriented political leaders should adopt economic policies to enhance growth. And the growth of economic welfare in the private sector has positive spillover effects socially as individuals would be busily occupied with their peaceful economic activities and that social stability and security would be enhanced as crimes and violence are minimized. While socialist-oriented political leaders tend to capitalize on differences, divisions, dichotomies, discrepancies and conflicts to build up a political platform to gain support and generate a political battle, capitalist-oriented political leaders tend to look for harmonies, promote opportunities, identify means to contribute and incorporate differences to ensure fair shares based on endowments and are prepared to accept and provide assistance to those in need. Capitalist policies believe that every participant will have a role in the economic process, including "endowment-low" individuals who shall be given opportunity for improvements and training to enhance their marketability.

There are numerous examples and evidence from the performance of different world economies when their leaders pursued socialist-oriented versus capitalist-oriented economic policies. Indeed, most socialist-oriented economies tend to remain weaker than capitalist-oriented economies. In addition, leaders pursuing leftist policies tend to blame their failure and weakness on something else. For example, many former colonies accused imperialism for their weakness, despite having gained political independence many decades ago. The leftist in the USA blamed the slavery history for the disadvantages faced by the black Americans, despite knowing that slavery had been abandoned for a long time. The question is whether these political leaders are using the sad chapter of history as a psychological shield to gain votes through stirring up the voters' emotion? Political leaders should positively encourage voters to move ahead and create a brighter future through the orientation of a more enterprising attitude and behavior.

Reasons like imperialism, slavery, gender, immigration and minority rights and employer–employee relationships have often been the contemporary examples used, adopted and capitalized by leftist politicians to gain attention, votes and ultimately power in political elections. It could be due to the psychology of socialist ideology that one's weakness or disadvantage has always been imposed by another person or a historical event, while the psychology or attitude in the capitalist ideology is to work one's way up through creativity and ingenuity. Success can only be achieved through one's own hands, and there is no "free lunch". People with capitalist attitude shall hold an enterprising approach and behavior in conducting their economic activities, exploring opportunities and possibilities rather than waiting for assistance, acting energetically and progressively with an innovative mind rather than looking for sympathy.

VII Inserting Economic Criteria into Politics?

There are many popular sayings, idioms and folklores. For example, "wherever there are people, there is politics", or "even if you do not get involved with politics, politics will get you involved, like it or not". The successes of humans in different societies are often built on visible and symbolized materials, such as monuments, historical sites and landmarks. However, societal "successes" not only positively reflect people's hard work collectively but could also imply people's ambitions on power, control, influence and ownership. And people's ambitions can be ambivalent seeing that they could benefit some people but hurt others. Politics could often be the vehicle through which human ambitions are expressed.

Politics is a "zero-sum" game with absolute outcomes, and the opportunists engaged in politics have the same psychological desire to win. A common feature in politics is that a player in politics must look for differences or differentiations, as that shall provide them with an issue or platform to speak on. Differences in opinions and in treatment of people and affairs would always be the starting point. Politicization would mean the need to expose, expand and even exaggerate the differences to attract attention and support, with the goal to win in the political fight. Race, gender, ethnical groups, the elderly, low-income earners, the underprivileged, language barriers, territorial disputes, the haves and have nots, and heritages and royalties are the sources of differences which have popularly been exploited by political opportunists.

Fighting for differences often ends up with prolonging, deepening or dichotomizing the differences, making the issue more difficult in reaching a compromise or harmony, because once differences have been established politically, the issue would become dichotomized and no one side would surrender easily. There are, on the contrary, broadminded politicians who work for all, and instead of dichotomizing extremes, they pull together differences to form a common goal, making sacrifices. Thus, instead of looking for differences to divide humans, it would be great if politicians look beyond differences and work toward a common good so that individual differences can be buried under the resulting benefits for all to enjoy and share. Thus, there can be a sharp contrast in the direction an ambitious politician pursues, namely whether to look for differences that divide people or bury the differences and fight for a common goal.

In a democratic political system where a common individual can be elected to become the leader of a country, it could indeed be difficult for the voters to know the intention of the candidate seeking success in a political election. Would the person be a leader that looked for personal vested interest and benefits or a leader aimed to serve the people and to create common good for all? A political leader, whether elected or otherwise, would face pressures from his or her own vested interest, the supporters from his or her constituency, the voters from the larger public, and the people surrounding the elected politicians. These human pressures would produce physical and psychological demands that could complicate the original intention of the election. A leader could do a lot with the acquired power through success in an election, and it would be difficult to judge and assess if the acquired power was exercised effectively. It often would be too late to make corrections when power is abused, and harm is done, though a transparent legal system would somewhat alleviate the abuse of power by the elected leaders.

The issue in democratic election is that it would be difficult to hold the elected leaders accountable if corrupted practices and abuse of power were adopted clandestinely by the elected leader for personal selfish gains, especially in countries where the rule of law is weak, and the leader is protected by his or her cronies and reliable civic institutions are largely absent. A democratic system allows free political participation, but there is no guarantee that the elected leader would serve the country selflessly and with broadmindedness. As political election results are *ex-post*, both the good and bad things done by the elected leader would be known and assessed only after the leader has taken up office. The typical example is that a leader chooses to engage in huge fiscal spending, but the same elected leader would not be personally responsible for the accumulated debt. And after the term of the elected leader is over, the leader would leave the office, but the accumulated debt would have to be shouldered by the voters and the taxpayers.

There is thus a gap between the *ex-ante* situation and *ex-post* result. Indeed, most elected leaders would amass wealth during and after their term of office. An elected leader in the contemporary world can gain both power and wealth at the same time. The question is, how can an elected leader be held responsible for his or her successes and mistakes? The democratic system only allows voters to vote the leader out of office, but the leader would still walk away freely with the amassed wealth, while the economy would have to suffer for the mistakes made, such as the huge national debt which would have made the economy uncompetitive and resulted in a lower rate of growth. This is particularly true in countries with mainly two opposing political parties. The left-leaning political party would tend to overspend and allow debt to accumulate, while the right-wing political party would try to rescue the economy and generate as much growth as possible so that people could become self-reliant and businesses flourish. With the swing between the two political parties in elections, the economy would also suffer as different economic policies could produce distortions, unwanted and unintended consequences.

Despite the presence of democracy that permits political freedom, there is no way that the elected political leaders can be held accountable economically or financially should debts have been created during the leader's political regime. In other words, there should be a system such that the elected leader's own economic status would also be affected should the voters think that the elected leader had performed poorly. For example, in case the elected leader's policy has led to national debt accumulation while the leader was in office, the elected leader's earning, physical assets or pecuniary wealth would be penalized and reduced. This can be done either by holding up the elected leader's earning till the end of term, or the leader would deposit his or her asset as a kind of guarantee at the time of taking up office. These economic assets would be returned to the elected leader after the end of the term of office, but there would be a test before the elected leader would get the asset back. Various impartial criteria can be instituted in such a test. For example, a minimum threshold in the rate of economic growth and a maximum level of fiscal spending the elected leader could exercise in his or her office term. Penalty would set in if the conditions are abused, and debts are accumulated.

In other words, economic cost and benefit would also be applied to political elections, and the elected leader would go through an economically oriented mean test. For example, if national debts were accumulated and economic growth performance reached a certain low threshold, the elected leader would also be penalized through receiving a lower earning or a certain percentage of the asset deposited would be taxed or annihilated. Such an economic test would ensure that while the elected leader would exercise his or her political power, the elected leader would not hold the economy at ransom, and the economic performance would not deteriorate or deviate too much within the elected leader's term of office. As such, economic performance would become a built-in process within the political arena. To promote impartiality, these economic conditions and criteria can be instituted through the country's legislative process to become laws for all future political leaders to follow and adopt. In turn, the voters would feel more comfortable because the elected leader would also be economically responsible, and that the elected leader's political ambition would not spillover to do harm to the economy. Both the voters, the public and the economy could then be secured in political elections as elected leaders come and go.

Such an insertion of economic criteria into political elections should not be a science fiction. Economic instruments and activities have often been used or exploited by elected politicians, rightly or wrongly. The elected leader would only be interested in political outcomes but may not be responsible for the economic performances, positively or negatively. As elected leaders are political in nature, any political activities should not spillover negatively to the economy. Political decisions often require short-term results, but economic activities tend to be long term and the consequences when they emerged would have long passed the political decision-making process. As such, the elected politician may get away with the economic consequences from the chosen political policy. Furthermore, political consequences are often non-economic in their appearance. At best, there could be media reports and discussions in internet channels, demonstrations and rallies from supporters and critics involving disciplinary action from law enforcement officers, but that would not replenish the direct economic loss.

By instituting economic criteria on political performance, economic activities could partially be shielded and secured from unnecessary cynical movements and influence from political cycles. In turn, elected political leaders would have to show more concern in their economic policies, in addition to achieving their political ambitions and goals. If instituted properly, supported by the rule of law and a high degree of civic acceptance, economic performance would be stabilized and not disturbed, disrupted and distorted by political acts. In other words, there will be another monitoring layer on the elected politicians, in addition to voting the politician out of office. However, it is "easier said than done" in implementing such a layer of monitoring because there is the need to have a truly independent monitor.

VIII Conclusion

While the function of economics is the allocation of resources, the function of politics is the allocation of power and authority. Many non-specialists often argue naïvely that economics and politics are one inseparable discipline. Such a view reflects squarely the need for more conceptual elaborations between economics and politics. As discussed, politics is an active discipline which cannot be realized without the use of instruments taken from the economic arena. Taxation, free-trade agreements, investment policies and exchange rates are economic variables that are dictated by political orientations. Economics is a passive discipline as economic results are often used to serve other purposes.

Economic instruments have been applied by decision makers with different ideologies, but economic outcomes differ between ideologies. As such, economic distortions can arise from the adopting of politically oriented policies, and one unintended distortion could lead to another distortion, resulting in a chain-like relationship. The worst is that people consider the economic distortions as economic mistakes, rather than the inappropriate choice of political decisions. For example, an extremely high tax rate has been charged on high income earners. The redistributive argument is that the rich should shoulder more taxes. On the contrary, the correct concept could be to look for ways to promote more able individuals, who can then pay more taxes. The conceptual difference is politically oriented. The proper economic concept would be to promote opportunities so that more individuals can become able and earn a higher income.

The discussion in this chapter shows that the two disciplines have been intertwined, and there is a need to show a clearer conceptual understanding of how political activities have impacted on economics. Decisions that range from political ideologies, political elections and political parties to political acts can all come under the spotlight when a clear conceptual analysis is made on the distinction between political and economic decisions.

It is true that there are numerous political discussions outlining the differences between the two ideologies of capitalism and socialism or communism. This chapter conceptually uses economic ideas to discuss the outcomes of the two ideologies when elected politicians adopt one ideology against another. By including the economic discussion on political ideologies, the economic outcomes become dichotomized into two distinct trends, and one can easily compare the economic outcomes between the two ideologies. Such concepts as the *ex-ante* and *ex-post* situations in political elections, and the ethics and ideology orientation of the political candidate, can generate vast differences in their economic policies.

The question of inequality has also been discussed politically when economic analyses are applied. The so-called "income inequality" would not be the end of the world as it merely reflects differences in economic outcomes. It is ultimately the availability of opportunity that shall promote welfare and individuals' absolute inequality would be narrowed, while relative inequality could be tolerated so long as the overall welfare of individuals increases through growth and employment. The issue of economic inequality should not be politically exaggerated, because economic differences can be dealt with within the economic sphere. Indeed, it could even be more effective to improve equality through economic means rather than through political fights, because engaging in a "positive-sum" game is always preferred to a "zero-sum" game. On the contrary, policies based on political differences could end up with a "negative-sum" game where all parties lose. In economic jargon, a "Pareto-improvement" is preferred and occurs when an activity that would lead to at least one person's gain is better than another activity where no one can gain.

Despite a high degree of political freedom in the form of democracy, there is still a possible gap between what was said in an election (*ex-ante*) and what was done during the political term (*ex-post*), especially in economic policies where the elected leader could walk away with the economic harm done and mistakes made. Once elected and power has been acquired, the exercise of power cannot be checked effectively, especially if there is a lack of institutional support and monitoring and assessing the policies of the elected leader could be difficult. While political outcomes could have spillover effects on the economy in the form of rising national debt and deficit, weak output growth and an uncompetitive economy would be the more visible answer.

The idea to improve the relationship between political election and economic performance is the probable proposal of an "economically tied election", where the earnings and assets of the elected leader would be withheld until the political term ends, and criteria would be instituted such that a poor economic performance would carry an "asset penalty" on the part of the elected leader. This should not sound unreal as the ultimate intention is for the elected leader to work to improve the economy, rather than squander economic resources for political ends. There has to be a way to test the ingenuity of the elected political leader.

Chapter Five

Economic Considerations in Government Policies

I Introduction

The focus of the discussion in the last chapter has been the relationship between economics and politics, and how political ideologies can impact economic outcomes either favorably or unfavorably. Ideologies aside, politics always involves the role of the government. Therefore, it would equally be important to examine the process of government policies. Ideological goals are reflected in government policies, but the implementation of economic policies can also lead to unexpected or unintended results due to misunderstanding of economics, the lack of statistics data, time lag between decision and implementation, appearance of shocks in the implementation process, change of government resulting from new elections and the extent or lack of complementarity among different policies.

Since all policies require funding and the government's expenses and revenues are shown in the annual budget, the nation's fiscal policy becomes the most important policy for all contemporary governments, as it provides a clear picture or an "X-ray" of the way the government is handling the economy: Whether the government is overspending resulting in deficits and growth in debt, whether the government is focusing only on short-term issues or aiming at promoting long-term competitiveness, whether the government has miscalculated the extent of revenue income, whether the government has exercised fairness and equity to all sectors of the economy, and most importantly whether the government is balancing spending between "demand-side" items such as welfare and subsidies and "supply-side" items such as infrastructure and education. While it is the economic activities in the private sector that drive the economy, the government's annual fiscal policy should aim at nurturing a "virtuous economic cycle" to ensure steady and sustainable growth.

Thus, the performance of the fiscal policy in every nation plays a pivotal role in reflecting the economic health of the nation as well as paving the path for future development. While every item in the fiscal budget shall affect different sectors of the economy, there are economic theories that provide analyses on the sustainability of fiscal policy, but then again, political desires by leaders and decision makers would generate distortion in the functioning of the budget. The first task in this chapter is to outline the basic economic theories on fiscal policy and explain how each fiscal component shall play its role in the healthy functioning of the budget. The discussion shall then expand to situations that could result in the malfunctioning of the budget and the various undesirable consequences, eventually leading the government and the economy to experience losses and decline in competitiveness. It is intended to show that on its own, a successful fiscal policy can serve the economy appropriately, and could lead the economy from strength to strength, thereby benefitting both the current and future generations.

II Some Fiscal Features

There has been much debate and analysis on the economic role of the government. In a capitalist economy where there is economic freedom and ownership and transaction rights are clearly defined, economic resources are owned by private individuals and businesses. The government shall not own any resources but act as an intermediary in dealing with affairs among the citizens, creating a suitable economic environment for businesses and investments to progress, balancing the growth path of different sectors and ensuring stability including the execution of an assistance scheme that is ready to help needy individuals facing economic difficulties.

The first economic principle is that fiscal policy should be balanced, though this may sound naïve as fluctuations in economic activities may result in unpredictable fiscal movements. The more acceptable concept is to have a balanced budget over the business cycle, typically in a period of three to five years. The idea is that to have a budget balance over the business cycle, the government will have to find ways to make corrections during the business cycle and not delay actions that may disfavor the fiscal situation in the next business cycle. It should give a strong fiscal signal of a healthy government to both investors and workers, especially if surpluses are created while deficits are eliminated within a business cycle.

Secondly, the proper performance of a fiscal policy must be anti-cyclical, meaning that it moves inversely with the business cycles, expanding in economically unfavorable times to avoid severe hardship but contracting in times of economic booms to avoid excessive inflation and overheating. Given the government's goal is the pursuit of economic stability and attempts are made to avoid severe fluctuations, it makes sense to reduce fiscal spending during the periods of economic recovery and booms, as the rise in investments and job opportunities in their own pace shall lead to a rise in wage earnings and consumers' purchasing power. The overall unemployment shall fall, and economic hardship shall be reduced. In other words, the economy can take its own economic expansion path, and additional government spending, especially spending which produces only short-term results, should be stopped, or else it could lead to economic overheating. In such a situation, it is likely that fiscal surpluses can be generated, and the government can start saving and increasing its fiscal reserve, which is always a sign of a healthy government.

The availability of a fiscal surplus has various advantages, in addition to the increase in reserve and government savings. Fiscal surplus allows the healthy economy to think and move ahead in creative activities that would promote long-term competitiveness and production capability, such as promotion in technology and human capital advancement. Since economic shocks cannot be predicted, such as natural disasters, financial crises and accidents, their occurrence would usually be sudden and sharp, requiring immediate actions and deployment of funds. To get prepared for such "rainy days", the government should then set aside some fiscal surplus and can establish funds which can be geared specifically to tackle the emergence of a crisis. An "earthquake fund", for example, can be set aside that takes care of victims in those earthquake-prone countries. Other funds can be established, tailoring to such needs arising from financial crises or international aid for natural disasters. These funds shall form part of the fiscal wealth but may not be counted as surpluses as they are geared to special needs. Furthermore, these funds can be incorporated as bonds in the financial market. With these establishments that take care of the fiscal surpluses, the government shall then estimate the budget without worrying about the sudden occurrence of crises. As such, the fiscal policy shall be used to cater for the normal and regular items as the risky element would be taken care of by the establishment of the special funds. Fiscal stability can further be enhanced.

In economic challenging time, the reverse shall take place. The government shall "dissave" to reduce its fiscal reserve to have extra spending to rescue the economy, either through a policy of employment promotion, welfare provision, or look for ways to encourage investment to maintain jobs. Government spending in tough economic times serves as a "cushion" and would probably be "demand-driven" in spending with the aim to reduce extreme hardship. "Employ one person to dig a hole, and another to fill up the hole" is the crisis mentality expressed by Keynes (2016) in his celebrated work first published in 1937 as an advice to the government in recession times. Though there would be no short-term increase in productivity, government spending in rescuing the economy would be the last resort in avoiding severe economic hardship. It is likely that the government shall face a fiscal deficit by running down its reserve, but hopefully the duration of the recession is short. In running down the fiscal reserve, the concern then is how low the fiscal reserve can go before the government has to face a fiscal crisis. There have been debates as to how large or small the government reserve should be, especially in small and open economies. In the case of the Hong Kong economy, for example, Li (2006, 2012) argued that a fiscal reserve equivalent to 24 months of government spending shall serve as a comfortable cushion. Of course, if funds geared to cater for crisis events are already available, the economy could then be rescued through the deployment of the previously established funds. The funds shall provide financial comfort to the affected individuals, and at the same time would not impose a burden on the normal functioning of the fiscal policy.

Although every budget should be balanced and anti-cyclical, one should not expect perfection in fiscal policy as there are numerous complications. The existence of time lag could be critical in implementing and executing fiscal policies. Situations change faster than people expect, and information delay could further be aggregated by administrative delay in decision-making. It is possible, for example, that by the time economic rescue arrives, the situation would have recovered, thereby adding extra oscillations to the fiscal fluctuation, or the situations have deteriorated faster than the arrival of the rescue, resulting in the further demand for rescue funding. Nonetheless, an effective and efficient fiscal administration through the availability of effective data and practical experiences should be able to minimize delays and time lags.

Every budget consists of numerous spending items, and the government needs to balance the various spending items as they affect diverse groups of individuals and economic sectors. Typically, items that concern short-term spending are regarded as "demand-driven" policies, such as welfare and housing expenditures, while items which are related more to long-term situations are mainly "supply-driven" policies, such as education, health, infrastructure and technological developments. One simple theoretical approach to balance these two broad categories would depend on the stage of the economic cycle because the spending that is allocated to one category would mean less for the other category. In economically tough times, for example, the focus should be more on the "demand-driven" items. On the contrary, the emphasis should be on "supply-driven" policies in times of economic recovery and boom. Hence, the proportion between the spending on the two categories is crucial not only in affecting the amount recipients received but also serves as an economic indicator to investors, foreign corporations and international economic organizations. Such a proportion or spending split can be derived through practice or can follow a more theoretical percentage, such as 65:35 or even 70:30 in favor of "supply-driven" policy items. The government should set clear priorities on fiscal spending, laying out ultimate economic goals.

However, there can be various requirements and dimensions in fiscal spending. For example, military spending could be high and specific as it is meant to defend the nation or to maintain peace in the global context, and thus its requirement might not be proportional to the economy as military protection would depend more on needs. Other fiscal items could produce "chain-like" relationships and their impacts could oppose each other with different results. Bear in mind that economic activities are not a "one-to-one" affair but could have secondary impacts. And with the presence of time lags and delays, secondary impacts might require additional policy actions. Spending priorities should examine fiscal consistency to avoid distortions and conflicts. As a result, economic policies can also be linked to each other, with one policy trying to deal with one issue, while another policy could be needed to handle the consequence of a previous policy. Typically, should the government be prepared to provide welfare support, there should be another policy aimed at generating jobs so that the welfare recipients would not be entirely reliant and dependent on welfare, especially if the recipients are young and hold an enterprising mentality that seeking a job is preferred to relying on welfare aid.

As most nations participate in the globalization process, international organizations such as the International Monetary Fund (IMF) are rested with the responsibility to check if the fiscal framework of individual nations is up to standard requirements, or there are loopholes that must be amended. A nation's fiscal performance is considered within the context of numerous economic risk factors, including performances in monetary policy and financial market stability, inflationary factors, trade and currency fluctuations and their sustainability. Deviations from the international norms will be warned so that troubled economies would address their problems without delay, though there are cases where the government was not cooperative with the policy recommendations from the IMF.

One effective possibility is for every government to have a dedicated, politics-free team that examines the economic impacts of the policies. While governments are mostly politically oriented, it may not be appropriate and adequate simply to impose political desires on economic policies. Furthermore, political leaders may not be aware of macroeconomic relationships. It therefore may be desirable to have a section within the administration to examine the economics of every government policy; at least the political leaders will then be warned and informed about the probable economic consequences. Having a better understanding of the economic outcomes could even help the leaders to come up with more desirable and stronger policies. In other words, it will be highly desirable if proper economic considerations are given the top priority in the list of political decisions.

III The Tax Population

As most governments in market economies typically do not own resources, the source of government revenue comes mainly from tax collection. The theoretical argument is that a transparent and responsible government must "earn its way" before it has resources to spend, and therefore, every spending item must be accounted for. Taxation is the usual source of revenue. The two major sources of direct taxation include income tax levied from wage earners and corporate tax levied from business entities. It follows that in a booming economy when wages are rising, and businesses are making handsome profits, government revenue through taxation should rise, and *vice versa*. There are also various indirect taxes levied by the government and items such as tax on alcohol and liquors, gaming in casinos and other consumables fall under the indirect tax category.

A tax structure, as Li (2006, 2012) pointed out, is composed of four elements: tax rate, tax items, tax efficiency and tax population. The tax rate is simply the percentage of earnings that the government decides to impose on various tax items. The tax items are the number of items that are being taxed especially in the indirect tax category. Tax efficiency shows how effective the government is in collecting tax revenues. There are various possibilities where the tax efficiency is low: tax avoidance, informal economic activities, use of cash in transactions, underreporting, delay in tax payment and cheating. Tax population is the pool of workers, businesses and consumers that are affected by the tax rates and taxable items.

There is a crucial difference in the performance among these four elements in the tax structure. The tax rate, tax items and tax efficiency all come under the control of the government. The government decides on the percentage of tax to be levied, what to tax and how effective the collection can be, but the government cannot control the tax population. There is thus the possibility of divergence in behavior. Indeed, the tax population usually reacts to the government's decision, especially on the direct tax rate, and decides their next moves. Typically, given the existing size of the tax population, a rise in the direct tax rate should put pressure on the tax population, leading to its possible shrinkage as workers and businesses would look for alternatives, such as putting their wealth in offshore accounts. Similarly, a rise in indirect tax would discourage consumers as their purchasing power will be limited by the rise in indirect tax. Hence, tax rate movements could behave inversely with the tax population.

Such an inverse relationship would mean that there are constraints on the tax rate, and that a higher tax rate does not automatically lead to a higher tax revenue. The "Laffer curve" (Laffer, 2004) argued that when the tax rate is low, a rise in the tax rate would result in a rise in tax revenue. On the contrary, when the tax rate is already high, a further rise will result in a fall in tax revenue. The explanation behind this argument is exactly due to the changes in the tax population. At a low direct tax rate, workers and businesses would consider the increase in tax rate as their duty to provide the needed revenue to the government. On the contrary, when the direct tax rate is at the high end already, a further rise would discourage the tax payers, who in turn would start to look for alternatives.

Professionals can migrate to a more tax-friendly country, or they will reduce their work as their additional pay would be taxed heavily on the extra work done. The high indirect tax should also discourage consumers, and consumers may think of alternatives of avoiding tax through transactions in the informal economy where economic activities are not recorded. The work of a "handyman" or business transactions conducted by hawkers, for example, are considered as informal economic activities as their work will probably not be registered and reported to the tax office. Therefore, it is a myth to think that a higher tax rate will lead to higher tax revenue.

This effectively means that there is an "optimal" tax rate, below which more revenue could be collected when the tax rate is raised, above which less revenue could be collected when the tax rate is raised. The implication is that there is the optimal rate that shall keep the revenue income at its highest possible level. Empirically, the optimal rate can be located for different economies, using tax revenue data when a higher or lower tax is imposed, considering the different stage of the business cycles. There will not be a single optimal rate across countries but shall differ among countries and at different economic times. In the case of Hong Kong, for example, Li (2006, 2012) found that the range between 15% and 16% should be the optimal direct tax rate which should yield the highest possible level of direct tax revenue.

The concept of the optimal tax rate provides several economic implications. Firstly, the government is not all powerful in deciding on taxation because the tax population will not be controlled by the government. Indeed, the reaction of the tax population shall be the answer to how unpopular the rise in tax rate is. Another implication is that the taxation may not be the only instrument in raising revenue. A low tax rate but an enlarging tax population could also bring a rise in revenue. This is known as "tax elasticity", meaning that a low tax with a larger tax-paying population could equally allow the government to raise enough tax revenue. The challenge then is for the government to deliver policies that would improve and enlarge the tax population, which basically means that both income and profit are rising so that more direct tax revenue is collected.

The condition for the tax population to expand is the presence of a prospective economy where growth is generating economic advantages, such as employment enlargement, favorable investment returns and a positive businesses atmosphere. It would probably be true to argue that a decrease in the tax rate could favorably change the economic climate considerably, bringing incentives to workers and businesses, which in turn would generate a multiplier effect on consumption, and rising demand should lead to more production and growth in industrial output. For these economic environments to occur, it is necessary for the government to pursue a "supply-driven" economic strategy, where improvement is focused at the "input end" of the economic equation with incentive provision given to investment, technology and human capital enhancement. In short, growth in economic capability and capacity should be the answer in enlarging the tax population, as that should lead to more tax-paying individuals and businesses, and that each of these entities will be paying more tax as their earnings and profits rise. To work on bringing a larger size of the tax-paying population should surely be more effective than simply raising the tax rate.

IV When Fiscal Policy is Politicized

Understanding the idea of the tax-paying population may not be easy, as some socialist-oriented political leaders are talking about putting heavy tax on the 1% of the richest. What could happen when the fiscal policy is totally politicized and has been used as instrument for a political goal? The simple calculation is that would it be more revenue worthy by heavily taxing the 1% richest or engaging in policies that should enlarge the tax-paying population so that there will be more able people paying tax? Or, it is a political gimmick to isolate the richest minority of 1% as the target of victimization? This simply shows that fiscal policy can easily be politicized, and that fiscal problems and situations of prolonged fiscal deficits could be more of a political problem dressed up in economic terms than the invalidity or inability of the policy itself in rescuing the deficit. As such, it is the wrong ideology that the political leaders hold should be responsible for the deficit and not the economic outcome resulting from the deficit. Statistically, there is always the top 1% however the income is measured. Even if the income of the highest earners is reduced, the second highest group of income earners would statistically become the top 1%. Such a political move reflected a lack of knowledge in simple statistics.

A politicized fiscal policy can have several features, including the analyses predicted by the "agency theory" and the performance gap before and after being elected as advocated in the difference between *ex-ante* and *ex-post* acts of the political leaders. The elected political leaders acted as the agents of the people and engaged in decision-making, but they do not need to be personally and financially committed to the consequences of their decisions. If there is fiscal surplus, the surplus will not financially be pocketed by the agent. If there is a fiscal deficit, the deficit will not financially be paid out by the agent. In other words, one may not know how "*bona fide*" the agents are in their policy decisions, which could be based on political grounds and ambitions, leaving the economic consequences as secondary importance. Unfortunately, due to the absolute nature of political power in the hands of the elected leaders, the extent of "*bona fide*" behavior of the elected leaders can only be realized *ex-post*, when it could be too late to introduce changes or make corrections.

In many ways, all fiscal policies have been politicized as the fiscal policy forms part of the political instrument exercised by the elected leaders and their government. It is also true to argue that governments are faced with demand and pressures from different institutions and organizations. Different pressure groups, for example, would exert their influence on the government in satisfying their demands and often demands are in the form of financial support, imposing different degrees of pressures on the annual budget. Indeed, it is extremely rare for the reverse to occur that pressure groups are helping the government's fiscal policy in seeking less funding or paying back the funds previously received. Fiscal spending is always a "one-way street". This is particularly true among pressure and pro-welfare groups which are constantly seeking for more welfare support, regardless of the state of the economy. It is always the argument that more welfare spending is better, and to the recipients and welfare advocates, welfare support can never be "enough", as more welfare support given to each item is better and more welfare items are always preferred. One never hears from the welfare advocates on issues such as how to rescue the fiscal deficit.

Again, knowing that the leader will not be financially responsible personally, a socialist political leader would always advocate for more welfare support in the name of rescuing the poor or reducing inequality. Experiences show, however, that economies with strong welfare policies tend to face a high tax rate, but the high tax rate may not bring higher revenue, resulting in increases in deficit and debt. Hence, an unpleasant economic situation of "high tax rates — high welfare spending — high national debt" developed over time, and the worst is that there is no sign of these economies recovering because as one economic distortion breeds another distortion, the economy is becoming problem prone and it is impossible to disentangle the chain of economic distortion unless there is a reversal in political attitude and orientation.

There could be a lack of knowledge on the economic consequence of a higher tax regime. The socialist political leaders probably thought of a positive relationship between high tax rate and high tax revenue so that the government would have more to spend on welfare and subsidy. The economic logic is that the high tax rates coupled with high welfare spending produce disincentives on the part of investors, and the fall in investment would mean less employment opportunities and this in turn produces a fall in tax revenue as the tax population shrinks. This simply would result in the decline in economic competitiveness, and the fall in production would mean a rise in imports, leading to the appearance of a "twin deficit" — fiscal deficit and trade deficit. Politically, such a scenario could be capitalized by the socialist leader as the situation would call for a bigger government in dealing with the deficits. Economically, the situation is suicidal as the rise in unemployment would mean a rise in the economic hardship of many more workers and their families, and no one could see the "light at the end of the tunnel". As employment opportunities decline, the poor shall remain poor, or even the pool of poverty would increase, resulting in a rise in economic hardship or a decline in the overall living standards.

In a nutshell, a "high tax, high debt" situation leads only to economic stagnation and decline. The fall in economic competitiveness has a high price to pay, especially in the unfavorable prospect faced by the younger generation, as they would realize the absence of job opportunities when they search for employment, while the high tax discourages them already as their earning will be heavily taxed, making them think that taking welfare from the government could be a more comfortable economic alternative than to seek employment. The psychological dilemma is that "why bother to work when being a welfare recipient is equally comfortable?" As such, the enterprising attitude of the younger generation could be worn out even before they join the employment market, turning them to become dependent on the government for assistance. A socialist political leader would manipulate and steer the country's fiscal policy to the extent of making the economy uncompetitive and more people turning up for assistance and eventually an expansion in government administration. The result is prolonged poverty as the welfare recipients do not have prospective employment opportunities. Unfortunately, such an outcome would even be capitalized by the socialist leader for more intervention when the economy is already starved of investment and jobs. Political decisions are not the answer to economic problems.

Other alternatives open to the socialist leader are to seek international assistance from other pro-socialist countries or withdraw commitments from international organizations. Such a political move does not lead to any economic improvement domestically, as it merely uses the political instrument to cover and delay the economic ills. The country will then be at the mercy of the international organizations and neighboring countries, and the negotiations usually would involve what benefits the donating host countries could receive, such as trade preferential treatment, exchange rate advantage, investment migration and absorption of skilled labor. The aid or donation from foreign countries or international organization could give the political leaders some breathing space, but the fundamental conditions remain unchanged. At the international level, the IMF would impose pre-conditions for providing economic aid to debt-prone countries, but changes must be introduced to improve the domestic economy. For example, there will be a time schedule when domestic deficit could be reduced through cutting government spending and how the fall in government spending will proceed so that debts will be lowered. The core argument is that economic ills cannot be solved by political maneuvers but would require a genuine and determined reversal in economic policies that would lead to the unsustainable situations. And, the period of economic correction could often be harsh, depending on the depth of the trouble and how effectively the political leaders are prepared to introduce changes and whether most of the citizen would "bite the bullet" and agree to face the hardship.

Such analysis is not an exaggeration in economic decline because a politicized fiscal policy can have detrimental consequences. Unlike in total socialist and communist countries where the state under the communist party is all powerful and controls all economic resources, in democratic countries where elections are periodically held, pro-socialist political leaders would usually be voted out when the economy experiences difficulties resulting from the adoption of inappropriate policies and the growing economic weakness can be seen from the rising national debt and deficit. However, when non-socialist political leaders are subsequently elected, there would usually be a reversal of policies, with the aim to improve the economy through expansion in investment, employment and production capability and reverse the fiscal trend away from deficits. National debts shall then be reduced, bringing improvement in competitiveness. These successes, however, would in turn be criticized by the socialist politicians, as they would capitalize on the divergent performance in income and inequality would again be used as a political instrument in a new round of political attack. It would be up to the wisdom of the voters to understand that could income equality be achieved, it would have been achieved a long time ago. It is because economics always generates uneven outcomes, and "income equality" is more of a political jargon than an economic possibility. The political leaders should therefore concentrate on how to generate more economic outcomes and not restrict the "able" sector of the population and businesses from performing their best to serve the economy.

On the contrary, a non-politicized fiscal policy would mean that economic policies are introduced, decided and conducted based purely on economic performances, means and outcomes. The starting point is the intention and attempt to show a balanced budget, meaning that government's spending must fall within the ability to earn. The political focus is then switched to the ability to earn, rather than the desire to spend. The ability to earn does not mean imposing a higher tax or increasing the taxable items but taking up "supply-driven" economic policies to enlarge the economic capability and capacity, and through a bigger tax population and a more prosperous economy, more tax revenue will automatically be collected. It is the size and quality of the tax population that counts more importantly than the imposed tax rate. A larger tax population shall lead to higher tax revenue. A better qualified and trained tax population would mean a higher income received by the tax population, and a high income would lead to higher tax revenue.

The approach to promotion of profit tax is similar, and that more businesses and bigger profit in each business enterprise shall lead to high revenue from profit tax, regardless of the profit tax rate. Hence, the government policy should be aimed at enlarging the tax population among both income earners and businesses. Indeed, a more market-friendly tax rate should be attractive to investment which would result in a larger production capacity, advancement in technology or application of technology, and rise in employment as more workers are needed to fill up the new jobs from additional investments. Business expansion shall produce a greater number of tax-paying businesses. The newly needed job opportunities shall generate new employment, and a higher wage would probably be needed, though some jobs would be paid higher than others. As technology advances, additional skilled jobs are needed, and additional training would be provided to the employed. Improvement in skills and technology advancement shall mean a rise in earning by the workers. The improvement on the side of human capital that results in high wage earning should produce an increase in the salary tax revenue. In short, all these policies eventually would enlarge the tax population from salaried workers and businesses.

There are thus vast differences in the economic outcome between a politicized fiscal policy and a fiscal policy putting economics as its prime consideration. The ideology of the elected political leaders could influence the direction of the fiscal policy considerably. It is true that given the complexity of the fiscal policy and the need to attend to so many spending units, the political leaders would be faced with tremendous amount of pressure from the stakeholders, opposition party, pressure groups and non-governmental organizations, foreign governments, business communities, labor organizations and so on. Since organizations represent diverse groups of individuals and professions, it is likely that their demands are for their self-interest, while the government will attend to the bigger picture in gearing the direction of the fiscal policy.

Running and administering the government machinery is a complicated task, as it requires the establishment of suitable departments and bureaus, and the sufficient availability of skillful staff serving as top administrators. In party politics, top administrators would likely have to come from the same party, and that limits the choice and availability as skillful administrators with different political affiliation would not be considered. In a small economy, the pool of human capital that produces skillful administrators would be relatively small, and that would constraint the performance of fiscal policy when second-best administrators are recruited. Indeed, the appointment of top government administrators is often made on professional as well as on political grounds. As such, it is possible that the appointed administrator may have a strong political affiliation but a weak knowledge of the relevant affairs. Again, the appointment of a top government administrator is *ex-ante*, but the outcome of the administrator's performance is *ex-post*. In a straight two-party political system, for example, and assuming knowledgeable administrators are equally divided in their political ideology, this would mean that the elected party could only make the selection from the pool of the available administrators with the same ideological viewpoints. This may limit the chance of allowing the most able professional administrators to be recruited.

In many ways, the political leader may not be able to oversee the entire fiscal policy as numerous officials and administrators are involved. However, the leader's personal and mental integrity is very important as it should be a major criterion that any elected leader should have. Whether the elected political leader aims to seek benefits from the elected office and whether the leader is surrounded by a group of cronies or there is bias in the appointment of the top government ministers and administrators form part of the influence on the economy's fiscal policy. It is the ideology that the elected political leader holds that shall form the ultimate direction, trend and path of the government policy. Indeed, experiences from global economies show that those economies led by socialist leaders tend to be weaker, stagnant and are faced with constant economic difficulties and hardship and there is little sign of economic improvement, even though the nation is blessed with plenty of natural resources. In the name of removing income inequality and reducing poverty, the result is the enlargement of poverty as economic stagnation remains, and the acts of corruptions, political violence and bias are practiced among the cronies, resulting in political inequality and partiality. Inequality becomes extreme as wealth is amassed by the political leader and the cronies, while mass poverty persists as the economy becomes uncompetitive and investment is not forthcoming. In socialist countries, political inequality could even be more detrimental as the party members are the most powerful groups of politicians, rent seeking the public in the allocation of resources and consumables.

An economy's fiscal policy is the direct reflection of the elected political leader's desire to promote and help the economy or preference to exercise tight control and enlarge government administration. Experience shows that leaders who desire to pursue genuine and effective economic growth and development would use the fiscal policy to enhance competitiveness and allow the economic multiplier to function and expand positively. As the economy improves, there shall be policies to avoid economic overheating or crises to minimize potential economic recessions and that growth, however moderate, shall proceed steadily with stability. Income inequality could be addressed using economic instruments, such as human capital enhancement through provision of training and apprenticeship for the low-skilled workers and young school leavers, and formal education for the younger generation so that they can be equipped with skills and qualifications and become marketable when they enter employment.

V A Fiscal Model

In small economies, there is only one national government and a single fiscal budget is involved. However, in large countries where the nation comprises provinces, states, districts or regions, there can be multiple fiscal levels where provinces or states will have their own annual budget, while the nation will have a separate budget. Residents and citizens may have to pay the same tax twice at the province level and at the national level. Similarly, there can be a duplication of government administration at the provincial level and at the national level. Complications arise between the national and provincial/state government, especially when some provinces/states are richer than the others, and the national government would have to manage the sources of revenues from richer regions but aid the poorer regions. One can imagine the magnitude of politics involved in the negotiation and allocation of government resources, especially when the regional leader and national leader hold a different ideological view from one another.

A typical fiscal argument is that the local regions would like to keep their own resources and may even obtain more from the central government. The central government, on the contrary, would like to levy more revenues from local regions but would equally be ready to keep more resources for the central government. The "national–local" issue is certainly political and consumes much resources as administrative duplication appears at the local and national levels, and the outcome may not be favorable to the tax payers and residents. There should be clear cuts in the sources of tax revenues, for example, taxes can be levied at the national level, while other taxes are levied at the local level. Usually, there is a lack of clear cuts, but rather a duplication. In income tax or sales tax, for example, the tax payers would have to pay a certain percentage of their income or consumption spending to the local government and another percentage to the national government. Duplication in tax revenue and fiscal spending at various government levels is costly because the funding will have to provide for two or more levels of government bureaucracies.

A fiscal model that incorporates many of the elaborated features can be simplified and is summarized in Table 5.1, where the fiscal policy is divided between the revenue side and the expenditure side of the equation. The sources of tax revenues come mainly from direct tax and indirect tax, and there are other sources of revenues. Reserve funds are the "balancing item" as funds are accumulated and can be set aside when there is a

Table 5.1 A Fiscal Model

Fiscal revenue		Fiscal expenditure
Sources	Features of tax	Classifications
Direct Tax: salary & profit tax. Indirect Tax: sales tax. Others: fines, interest. Reserve funds: past savings. Foreign borrowing: foreign countries, IMF.	Rates: % charge. Items: spread of taxable. Efficiency: avoidance, underreporting, etc. Population: pool of tax-paying people and business.	Demand-side items: welfare, housing, social and cultural, etc. Supply-side items: infrastructure, transport, education, health, science and technology, environment, etc. Administrative: bureaucracy, economy, national security, debt repayment, law enforcement (custom, border control, prison, police), international commitments (peacekeeping, diplomatic services), etc. Crises: natural disasters and rescues, economic depression, civic unrest, pandemic, etc.

surplus but may have to be reduced in times of difficulties. Lastly, the foreign sector can be used as a source usually when the country is faced with extreme hardship and channels of assistances within the country are exhausted and foreign governments and institutions would be called upon to assist.

The capability of the tax system depends on the effective performance of the four features, bearing in mind that while the government can control tax rates, tax items and tax efficiency, the behavior of the tax population would not necessarily come under the control of the government and could behave inversely with tax rates. As an excessive tax rate would generate disincentives, the government can at best work on the "optimal" tax rate as that should maximize the tax revenue. Indeed, when corporations and individuals are setting up offshore accounts in various "tax haven" economies, it is a sign of excessive tax rates and the government is losing in revenue collection as capital and financial funds are being driven away.

On the expenditure side of the fiscal budget, the appropriate economic concept is the division between "demand-side" and "supply-side" policies.

While "demand-side" policies tend to focus on immediate targets and are aimed to promote short-term spending needs and may not have much impact on physical production and output, they should be more useful in times of economic difficulties as that should serve as a rescue to avoid extreme hardships. Under normal economic circumstances, however, the government should concentrate on "supply-side" policies that would improve the overall capacity, capability and competitiveness of the economy that promotes growth in production, output and exports. Infrastructure development shall promote business effectiveness and health spending reduces the survival cost of individuals, while education promotes human capital and reduces cross-generation poverty, environment protection shall prolong the sustainability of growth and at the same time open new opportunities, and advancement in science and technology enriches the future production capability.

It is worthwhile to bear in mind that even though "supply-side" items are government expenditures, it does not necessarily mean that the government is the only supplier. Experiences have shown that many of the "supply-side" factors can be supplied in the private market. Typical examples include health and education. Like a person's hairstyle, health is very much a personal matter, and individuals should be given a choice to take care of their own health, and that the coexistence of public and private medical entities can serve the functions of safeguarding the need and at the same time allow individuals to make their choice in attending to their medical needs. Indeed, the dual supply strategy can also allow some degree of positive competition in the service supplied between public and private entities, and that shall benefit the end users. Individuals receiving private medical attention shall ease the demand pressure in public medical units, thereby allowing more resources for those attending public medical needs.

The same principle of duality in supply can also be applied to education. While there is a need to ensure a certain standard in all levels of education, it is preferable to allow the dual existence of public and private educational entities. The advantages are that parents are given a choice in educating their children, and as some children are channeled to receive education in private entities, the government would have more resources given to education entities in the public sector. The dual supply can also increase the competition between educational entities in the two sectors. Of course, the government will have to set the education standard and regulations in line with private educational entities.

In the provision of infrastructure, it may be more appropriate for the government sector to take the lead as infrastructure investment usually is highly costly and the investment return may take decades to materialize. Furthermore, as infrastructures often do not have alternatives or substitutes, private supply may involve high charges that would defeat the purpose of such infrastructural construction. Hence, there is a need to set up appropriate criteria in deciding on the source of supply. One economic concept is the difference between "common goods" and "public goods". Such infrastructure as road networks, sewage and street lighting, environmental protection, parks, bridges and historical sites are common goods which do not have much alternative but are consumed by all citizens. Hence, government provision would avoid monopolistic price exploitation if these common goods are supplied by private entities. On the contrary, public goods are goods that can have alternatives and the end users can have a choice in their selection. There can be more than one type of supplier in public goods. Health, education, electricity and energy provisions, transport and postage, and communication and media are examples of public goods where their supplies from private entities can compete with other private suppliers as well as government provisions.

Again, the provision of many common and public goods should best be considered within the economic context, rather than inserting political considerations in their supplies. Experiences show that public provision of many public goods would easily end up in losses. Nationalization of such public goods as railway transportation and airlines often results in heavy losses in terms of the increased cost because low demand and pressure from labor unions coexist with reduction in revenue often due to a decline in the quality of service, and users turn to other alternatives and substitutes. Unlike private businesses where loss cannot be sustained, nationalized entities usually have government backup and losses would be absorbed by the government.

The economic concept is that the effectiveness of "supply-side" policies shall enhance the economic welfare of workers and their families. In turn, the improvement in their economic welfare through higher earnings and good employment potentials shall help to take care of their survival cost and their ability to accumulate wealth and assets. Such an economic and welfare improvement should in turn allow the government to collect more tax revenue and eventually spend less on welfare as the number of needy households declines. Supply-side policies are needed for the long-term sustainability and competitiveness in lifting the economy to a higher stage of development.

Other than demand-side and supply-side spending items, the government bureaucracy itself absorbs much fiscal resource because running the administrative machinery can be costly in employing civil servants, officials and administrators, and the need to budget for all the spending in maintaining the physical structure of the government and official activities. Equally, funds must be set aside for national security and law enforcement, as well as the country's role in the global economy. These spending items are inevitable as the government needs to protect its citizens and connect with the global community. A civic society blessed with harmony and free of violence would have less crimes and requires less spending on law enforcement. On the contrary, if opportunistic politicians aim to stir up controversies and extremes, divisions and dichotomies could result in civic displeasure and disgruntled individuals could engage in non-peaceful activities.

Government spending can be divided between recurrent spending where such expenditure would be maintained year after year and capital spending which is geared more to establish the physical structure. The building of a hospital would be regarded as capital spending, while the recurrent expenditure would be the amount spent on the purchase of medical supplies and payment of medical personnel annually. Hence, while attending to immediate needs, the government should therefore attend more to the future needs and the long-term improvement in service provisions. Simply put, immediate needs often occur on an *ad hoc* basis, but the long-term improvement would stay and form part of the overall structure. The judgment of a durable, sustainable and successful government policy is its focus on the long-term improvement as this is what citizens and voters would like to see.

The fiscal model discussed in Table 5.1 should provide a guideline or framework of a functional and sustainable fiscal policy, and such an approach when adopted and followed should at least minimize the negative impact of a politicized fiscal policy and at best maximize the revenue potential for the government and growth potential for the economy. An effective fiscal policy would be the "stone that kills two birds".

VI Conclusion

While politics is ideological in nature, government policies are the more "down to earth" issues as every government policy, though politically oriented, would have economic implications. However, the market is the conventional vehicle through which resources are being deployed. No market, however, can function without the government. There are mainly two government policy paths: supply-side and demand-side policies. Differences in the conceptual analyses between the two paths can be immense. The original intentions (*ex-ante*) can differ tremendously in the outcomes (*ex-post*) in policy performances. Government policies should aim at providing advantages to all sections of the economy, though priorities would be set in such a way that some sections would gain more or faster than others. It is obvious that there is a difference in the pace and magnitude of fiscal spending. While transparency and close monitoring of government policies are necessary, the outcome of any policy requires a clear conceptual understanding as deviation or ill-intended policies would lead to distortion that would cumulate to become crises, disruption and civic discontent.

This chapter gives an extensive and comprehensive coverage on the way fiscal policies could perform or fail to perform when politicized, thereby providing a clearer distinction in the discussion between economics and politics, supported by examples, scenarios and conjectures. The questions asked, the problems so raised and the concerns discussed are fully dissected to provide pragmatic recommendations and solutions. There is such a wisdom that "criticizing is easy, constructing is difficult", or "talking is surmount, doing is the reverse". It indeed is irresponsible for analysts to just bring out the problems or make complaints without providing suggestions and solutions. The conceptual analysis conducted on different government policies shall shed light on both the *ex-ante* and *ex-post* aspects of a policy. Other than the policy on redistribution and on the distinction between "supply-side" and "demand-side" policies, conceptual implications in other government policies such as infrastructure development, energy conservation, population policy and so on could be examined with the intention to provide a comprehensive coverage in conducting and implementing the fiscal policy.

Chapter Six

The Inter-Disciplinary Relationship

I Introduction

Politics and government are the two popular areas of social science studies where economics has been used extensively for their policy goals and outcomes. The previous two chapters on analyzing political economy have illustrated how economics can be and has been used in both political goals and government policies, yet often the use of economic instruments and variables may not generate favorable economic results, favorable in the sense that it helps the overall economy to grow, thereby expanding the overall economic capability and capacity. On the contrary, policies using economics are geared for political goals and when economic distortions or unfavorable outcomes appear, the result is often blamed on the poor economic performance, and the politicians could eventually get away with their policy decisions and would not be responsible for any loss. Should there be any criteria in a political election such that the politicians cannot "free ride" their position if their policies result in unfavorable economic consequences? This question poses a challenge to the traditional wisdom of political democracy and open election, as to how the elected political leader should be responsible for the deeds, and misdeeds, the leader had executed.

Civilization has advanced far to provide human beings with a high degree of survivability through practices, institutional settings, methods of communication and governance rules and laws. However, although many aspects of human civilization have been accepted and have formed part of the daily life activities, there are emerging problems in the progress

165

of civilization, as there are still misunderstandings, vested interests and conflicts among human beings resulting in war, unrest, violence, instability and sufferings. Other than natural disasters that call for rescue and cause human losses, many conflicts are artificial and manmade. Even though there is only one human race, people all over the world have somewhat been constrained by various "manmade" practices, beliefs, institutions and rules. The difference in calculation of a new year around the world, for example, has been affected by culture, religion and practices. In turn, people's behavior is influenced by psychological feelings and behavior.

Other than political issues, there are two other branches of study in the economics discipline that are extended to incorporate social and psychological issues in human behavior and how such behavior can impact economic decisions. Behavioral economics is the branch of study that merges psychology and economics and considers the economic impacts given certain psychological behavior (Bourdieu, 1974; Hursh, 1984; Camerer, 1999; Mullainathan and Thaler, 2000; Camerer *et al.*, 2004; Sent, 2004; Thaler, 2005, 2015; Wilkinson and Klaes, 2018). There are also specialized areas of behavioral economics that investigate different microeconomic and business areas, such as finance, health, consumer choice, entrepreneurship, poverty and culture (Throsby, 1994, 2010; Granato *et al.*, 1996; Posner, 1998; Brickel and Vuchinich, 2000; Bisin and Verdier, 2001; Bertrand *et al.*, 2004; Thaler, 2005; Guiso *et al.*, 2006; Tabellini, 2010; Towse, 2010; Klamer, 2011).

Although simulation studies have been applied to project macroeconomic performances, it is still not feasible to conduct economic experiments at the macroeconomic level. Experimental economics is another branch of microeconomic analysis that is related to scenario building and specifies the economic value within an assumed or a controlled situation, such as the use of an "economic laboratory". Observations are then made from controlled experiments and economic behavior and findings can then be deduced. Economic experiments are often conducted among unrelated behavior of individuals and firms given certain conditions or information. Similarly, psychological behavior and cultural influence have been investigated in experimental economics. It would be useful to examine the economic impact of certain human behavior observable only in a controlled experiment, hoping that such behavior can be generalized to form some measurable and quantifiable patterns for policy analysis and formulation (Smith, 1976, 1982, 1989, 1991, 1994; Davis and Holt, 1993;

Loewenstein, 1999; Friedman and Casser, 2004; Hoffman *et al.*, 2007). In many ways, behavioral economics and experimental economics can be regarded as an extension to examine economic issues when social theories are incorporated into the analysis (Parson and Smelser, 1956; Granovetter, 1985; Coleman, 1986; Elster, 1989; Platteau, 2000).

In classical economics, such terms as cultural, biological, historical, psychological and human relationships are usually assumed as they are qualitative and are not quantifiable or measurable. For example, a general equilibrium analysis has been commonly assumed in microeconomic analysis, but it cannot be proved if a general equilibrium does exist. Other assumptions include perfect information and knowledge and the same utility function applies to all individuals. Again, information changes over time and there may not be perfection of knowledge when individuals are equipped with different endowments. Hence, the reality is that variations exist between different economic activities due to the presence of other aspects of human behavior. Thus, conceptual economics can be powerful in that while economic theories can serve as the skeleton, economic analyses can incorporate ideas and behavior from related disciplines to present a fuller, stronger and comprehensive understanding of human problems and the possible solutions that follow. There is thus the need to extend economics analysis to include non-economic intangible factors. This chapter extends the conceptual discussion on the relationship between economics and other social science disciplines.

II Culture: Difference versus Divisiveness

There is only one human race with two biological genders, but over the centuries of civilization, many natural and manmade or artificial differences have developed that divided humans into categories and identifications. As the livelihood of human beings has occupied all corners of the globe and exists in different climate zones, differences that are impacted by natural and manmade conditions are visible. In the "law of first opportunity" (Li, 2002, 2017a), for example, human beings would use the first available natural materials for their basic livelihood and survival. Culture can be used as a collective term that incorporates numerous features in human behavior and relationships, including historical development, faith factors, language differences, customary practices, influence by climatic conditions and geographical limitations.

It is arguable whether culture aligns or divides humans. Children are taught differently in different cultures, ranging from how to respect the elders, the young, the sick and the other gender, the way to stay healthy, the kind of food to eat and clothing to wear, attitude toward nature and other forms of life, believing in the unknown, faith in and after life, extent of frugality and filial piety duties, preparations in such key events as birth, marriage and death, differences in the calculation of annual calendar cycles, arrangements for ceremonies and festivals, institutional practices and protocols, reaction to historical events and personal morality and ethical standards and manners.

Culture has often been used as reference points in various human practices. Similarly, in such activities as ceremonies, arrangements are conducted according to prior practices and norms which are symbolic and culturally oriented. Children learn many cultural aspects in the growing up process. Culture and religious faith provide orientations as to how one should treat the other gender in a family and in the society. One interesting question is whether culture has contributed to human progress and civilization, or culture has been a constraint in limiting human progress and civilization. In some cultures, one gender is preferred to another, and one gender receives more education than the other. The advancement in certain human races led many to take it for granted that one kind of human race is better than the other. The historic method in calculating the calendar cycles differs among cultures. Numerous cultural examples can be found to have influenced human beings' economic activities.

Other than natural factors, such as weather and seasons and the features affected by the universe, there are a host of manmade factors and cultural practices that humans have developed and adopted. While some of these practices have been taken for granted, such as the calendar year, days in a week and hours in a day, many other practices and attitudes have often caused conflicts and misunderstanding among people in the same ethnic group or people between different ethnic groups. For example, nature does not say that one gender should receive more education than another, nature does not say one race is better than another, nature does not say one has to pray in order to improve one's blessing and what would happen after death, nature does not say water from one river is holy while water in another river can be used for irrigation, nature does not say how different ethnic groups and genders should dress, nature does not say which plant and flower and color should be used for national symbols, nature does not say which hour of the day and which day in the calendar month is luckier than the other.

Cultural practices are mostly manmade, and people often unquestionably follow and uphold these practices as if they were part of nature. One can conveniently dissect such a large spectrum of culture into two broad categories: the "different and non-divisive" category and the "different but divisive" category. The "different and non-divisive" category simply shows the differences among humans, but such differences will not divide or do harm to other people. People live in different tropical zones and the kind of food they consume can be different. The way parents educate their offspring can be different among ethnic groups, and the way parents dress their daughters is different from the way they dress their sons. The way humans celebrate their festivals and ceremonies can be very different as material items and choice of color would have different symbolic meanings. The duty of filial piety can differ among ethnic groups, so too the behavior on frugality. The dialects and languages ethnic groups develop over time are different. The standard on beauty, ethics, virtues and vice can differ among ethnic groups. These cultural differences are often impartially accepted and respected as they would not instigate conflicts among the different practices.

Many "different and non-divisive" features can scientifically be explained by numerous reasons. The lack of modern forms of communication and geographical limitation in the olden times had thwarted connections and restricted cordial movements between ethnic groups. Lack of support from scientific and technological innovation in the past imposed high degree of vulnerability and insecurity to human settlements. In the pre-modern era, without advancement in medical science, the life span of humans was much shorter, and it would be costly and risky to venture out to the unknown world then. A self-contained lifestyle seemed most reasonable as survival was the order of the day then. Advances in technology and scientific discovery have provided many answers to questions previously considered as unknowns, such as the formation of the moon and other planets in the universe. More and more human mysteries have been scientifically removed, and new knowledge has been formed.

On the contrary, activities in the "different but divisive" category could produce numerous undesirable and unintended outcomes because many manmade cultural aspects are not only different but they also can be divisive among humans, thereby restricting potential human progresses. History has produced numerous lessons for different human groups and countries, but both human virtues and vices have been recorded in modern history. Wars and territorial conflicts have been recorded in the history books, showing the dark side of human civilization. However, instead of looking at the bright side of history and learning from human mistakes and how to avoid future conflicts, some people, who could have been supported indirectly by authorities with specific political intentions, tried to live with history by exercising the wicked side of human behavior and thinking of revenge as the feasible outcome. Thus, instead of promoting peace, war-like conflicts continued and fostered, and the cost to humanity was not only the loss of innocent lives, but economic development was delayed, and the economy remained unstable and uncompetitive. It would require an expression of selflessness and broadmindedness for an aggressive country to apologize for the mistakes made in the past. Equally, people in a war-inflicted country would have to accept and swallow the bitter past and embrace the new generation for a better and peaceful future. Indeed, the grave mistakes committed by one generation should not be passed to the next generation, and revenge would not be the solution. History is there for people to learn about the mistakes of the past and treasure the bright side of human civilization, and not to repeat the sad chapter of history and produce more human conflicts.

Despite the lengthy path of civilization, the color of one's skin, unfortunately, serves as a divisive instrument among humans. The skin color of a person shows a visible difference. However, such a difference has led to some unfortunate chapters in human history, where people with one skin color discriminated against the other. In the history of imperialism, for example, some European countries conquered land and people in other continents, turning them mainly as supplier of raw materials and labor. Many colored people from Africa and Asia were sold in the slavery trade across the oceans to serve as hard labor in North America. The slaves had to go through tremendous hardship and suffering, and numerous deaths and casualties were not even accounted for. Racial difference became a divisive device, and history should hold those wrong decision makers accountable.

However, one should also look at the bright side of history. The city of Rome built by the Roman Empire provides many historical sites for tourists. The history of Greece has developed many ruins as tourist attractions today. The Great Wall of China was built with immense amount of human hardship. Indeed, historical sites in some countries have been considered not only as tourist sites but also as the "wonders of the world". However, with the progress of civilization and equitable development in human values, especially in the rule of law and market competition, many jobs have been professionalized into formal employment and working conditions have continuously been improving, such as jobs in construction and manufacturing industries, and mechanization in farming activities. With economic freedom and the growth of small-scale businesses and industries, many individuals have started their own businesses and compete openly in the market.

In the Emancipation Proclamation executed by President Lincoln of the United States of America in 1863, all slaves were freed. Since then African Americans have been free to learn and be educated, take up their businesses and train to become professionals. As such, people with different skin colors should lead their life more positively by taking part in the economy on a competitive basis rather than holding a remorseful attitude on the historical past. President Lincoln had formally, politically and legally discontinued the divisive aspects between humans of different skin colors, thereby ending one unfortunate chapter in human history. Similarly, most former European colonies have gained political independence and sovereignty since the end of the Second World War, but except for a few, many newly independent countries remained stagnant in their economic development and human progress has been slow. Hence, with decades of independence and the choice to decide on one's destiny, the history of colonialism should be a foregone issue and economies should establish their own development path to show to the world that they can master their economies to make new progress. Holding a remorseful attitude and continuing to use imperialism as a scapegoat for low development and lacking progress should not work anymore.

Gender shares a similar problem with people in a different manner. The biological difference between the two genders has led to some specialization of labor at home as well as in the professional space. The male gender tends to focus more on work that requires much energy and physical strength, such as firemen and construction workers, while the female gender specializes more in retail and personal service professions. Beauty contests, for example, are conventionally focused on females, while sports are conventionally taken up by males. There is thus some natural divide in job specializations between the two genders, though increasingly parallel or similar jobs are taken up by both genders. Such a natural biological difference has often led to divisive arguments as one gender has been favored over another. Nonetheless, it is still true that the biological difference between the two genders has led to sexual violence in some urban cities and discrimination in educational attainment by the female gender in some religions and customs.

On the contrary, the biological difference between the two genders should complement each other. However, humans should take another giant step in their modernization and civilization process to accept the equality between the two genders, knowing and acknowledging that there is fundamental difference in some jobs, which should be regarded more as difference than as discrimination. In employment, it often is decided and directed by the market forces, though there are increasingly calls for humanistic ideals, such as equal pay for equal work and improvement in work environment for both genders. The right and opportunity to receive education from an early age should be made equally available to both genders. Such a desire to have equality between the two genders should be confirmed with the legislation of relevant national laws and there should be a close monitoring on the implementation of equality and equity in the entire educational process.

In the choice of religious faith, people should be given their freedom to choose their religious faith. There is also a difference in religious teachings and beliefs in faith, but while most religions preach peace, tolerance and pursuit of personal path, some religions advocate for "holy war" when the religion is under "threat" which unfortunately may not have been clearly defined and stated, resulting in possible abuses that could end up with violence and distort the preaching of the religious faith. Most civilized nations allow the presence and practice of legalized religions. In some religious states, however, religious practices and beliefs are written into their constitution and law which could be used as political instruments for oppression and coercion, for example, between the two genders as one gender is considered superior to the other. The divisiveness of a religious faith began where equality among humans and between genders would not be achieved or maintained due to certain instituted religious practices and beliefs. One observation is that many religions were created by the male gender, and most key offices in contemporary religious organizations are held by the male gender as well. Gender inequality probably has been religiously incited and has remained permanent through the centuries. In any case, a divisive situation occurs when one party through political maneuver, religious practice or cultural norms "rent seeks" the other party, while the disadvantaged party suffers due to the unfair practices which were culturally instituted.

Other than the presence of a religious state which specified in the country's constitution the legality of a certain religion and restrictions on another religion, most civilized countries allow the presence of different religious practices. In a free and open world, the pursuit of faith is a personal choice as it could have an impact on the person's life permanently. In many countries, religion still occupies an important activity within the social and family circles, in moral and ethics teachings. However, with modernization and contemporary forms of life where civic institutions are increasingly gaining relevance and importance in people's daily life, pursuit of faith has very much become a private and personal affair. Indeed, many people see some similarities across religious faiths. Thus, there exists competition among different faith-oriented organizations, as each of them would like to improve their "market share" in capturing the number of supporters, pursuers, believers and donors. For example, the way to express one's religious faith also differs among religions. The dress code, the symbolic objects used in religious ceremonies, the frequency and the geographical directions of making spiritual contacts are distinctively different among religions. In short, while the pursuit of personal faith should be open and allow individuals to have their own choice, religion should not be used as a controlling device that creates division among people.

To conclude, the "different but divisive" features in cultural life could be detrimental as these features would be exploited by one group of humans to control the other. This is particularly so when the controlling group is endorsed by the authority. Indeed, the divisive aspect in different cultural aspects has unfortunately but conveniently been capitalized by politicians when they look for issues to promote their political ambition. While economic inequality has been an "evergreen" topic used by many politicians, gender, religion and race are the other more common topics politicians utilize as political instruments. Gender and racial discrimination can always be a political argument, but the unfortunate thing is that politicians often focus on the divisive aspect in the gender and racial differences.

While politics produces the divisive aspect of cultural differences, economics serves more as the commonality among all cultural activities. The way humans express their culture is conducted through economic activities. For example, different products and goods are consumed in the celebration of new years, ceremonies and festivals among different cultural groups. The retail sector is influenced by major cultural festivals, and the consumer goods and services which are produced must fall in line with the retail cycle. Culture can affect birth rates even in the choice of gender births, and competition in school entrance subsequently. There are cultural artifacts that serve more as symbols to a better future or a more prosperous new year.

There is thus the presence of a "culture industry" which has become an economic pillar in terms of employment, investment and business development. There are, however, several distinct features in the cultural businesses. One relates to the size of the business entities. Most cultural businesses, either in the form of production or in service, are small- and medium-sized enterprises (SMEs), where entrepreneurial management skill is needed most. In the production of many cultural artifacts, skill in the craftmanship is highly needed. While other artifacts would be supplied through mass production, the cultural artifacts and goods would be produced largely by SMEs. Secondly, given that cultural activities are repetitive annually, the cultural industry should remain as a steady sector in the economy, though its growth would be slow when compared to the rapid expansion in other economic sectors and productions. Due to its traditional nature and a lagging career aspect in the business, many businesses related to the production of cultural artifacts and goods are facing a decline, as young people are not attracted to join these businesses. It therefore remains as a small sector with little growth potential. Furthermore, because of its repetitiveness and seasonality, the demand for cultural goods tends to be small but limited. The value added in the production of artifacts remains low and price cannot be too high.

The "rule of law" versus the "rule of man" is another key cultural principle in civic societies. Human divisiveness can best be avoided through the rule of law, where all individuals are equal before the law, and no privileged person can be above the law. However, the institution of the rule of law must come from the state, where leaders would accept and respect the rule of law as a civic principle in the first instance. And prosecutions would be conducted fairly on every citizen, including the political leaders. There are at least two problems with the rule of law. One is the implementation problem, as different political regimes and characteristics of leaders would introduce variations to the rule of law. A political regime that does not respect freedom, democracy and accept diversity may prefer the rule of man. A religious state would allow the monopoly of one faith and religious laws could have some discriminatory elements.

III Economics of Culture

While the "culture industry" may not be a dominant sector in many contemporary economies, cultural behavior in its entirety and collectively does influence the path of economic development and growth in many economies. While there are numerous studies that explain why some countries perform stronger than others economically, the study of culture has not been applied to explain the differences in growth and development among countries. Culture is broadly considered to include customs, religious belief and pursuit of faith, ethics and moral standard, philosophy, work attitude, approach to education and science and family responsibilities.

One can begin with the discussion on the "economics law of first opportunity" where economies are faced and endowed with different intensities in resources, typically in land and labor. While farming and agriculture have been the traditional activities in land usage, the availability of labor could be crucial for the development of science and technology. In the early stage of economic development, countries with abundance of labor were inclined to concentrate more on labor-intensive economic activities. Small family businesses and various personal services were common. On the contrary, in countries where labor was in shortage, the need of mechanization led to technology advancement, and large-scale industries were developed.

Culture can influence how people work. For example, some traditional communities are still not receptive to modern technology and insist on human labor as the more reliable form of production and communication. Their distrust and suspicion toward modern technology have naturally delayed their development as other economies have caught up with the technology ladder in the process of modernization. The same attitude arises in education, and many traditional communities and families for religious and cultural reasons do not accept the modern form of schooling but have faith only in domestic education where children would be educated at home. Religious purity could be the reason but that has robbed a child from receiving other aspects of life through education in schools. It is true that modern education may not be perfect, but it is still the route through which human capital can be created, increased and nurtured.

The attitude toward individuality in some cultures and customs can have an impact on the economy's growth path. People with a strong sense of individuality tend to be more independent, enterprising and not too reliant on others. Turning to government assistance would only be the last resort when all possibilities have failed. A strong attitude on individualism would usually generate an enterprising character, which would then be translated into the desire to take up business ventures, tolerate risk and business fluctuations. Self-reliance would be the principle held by people with a strong sense of individuality. The economic consequence would be the increase in the number of entrepreneurs who are prepared to start businesses or take up a skill to stay independent economically.

Conventionally, legal immigrants usually hold an enterprising attitude in their desire to start a new life in the host country by either starting up a business, learning a skill or involving in trading activities, hoping the new opportunities would give them new prosperity, economic independence and peace. Their hard-working attitude and enterprising behavior would transcend all difficulties in the process. Legal immigrants thus provide not only a stable source of labor, an additional source of capital brought into the host country but also a readiness or preparedness to start businesses or take up a profession as their source of living support. In turn, individuals with an enterprising behavior tend to earn sufficiently to support their families and prefer to remain self-reliant.

Even though many enterprising individuals are likely to begin with the establishment of small businesses, the impact could cumulate to form a market-friendly business environment to attract foreign investment and pressurize the government to adopt competitive economic policies. The result is the growth and expansion of the private sector, and improvement in economic competitiveness. In turn, the growth in private business would lead to new job opportunities and further employment potentials, thereby creating a pro-growth economic environment. Thus, a culture that promotes an enterprising attitude would result in economic prosperity. Furthermore, because of the confidence held by people with an enterprising spirit, they would value their effort and outcomes more in absolute terms, meaning that even though the resulting gains and benefits they receive could be stronger or weaker than others, few would complain about the inequality or difference in outcome, knowing that the result in the future would be better than what is currently achieved.

It is further argued that in an enterprising economy, the comparison of income or economic inequality is seen as an "absolute" basis where the individual will do better over time, rather than on a "relative" basis of comparing one individual with all others in a snapshot manner. In other words, even though the economic outcomes differ among individuals, enterprising people would not consider that as a hindrance to their growth knowing that things could be better in the next round of economic activities. Hence, economic differences or "inequality" will not need to be politicized to become a divisive instrument in polarizing individuals into rich and poor or bourgeois and proletariat because all enterprising individuals would control their own path of life and accept the outcome of their own efforts.

Another cultural aspect is people's attitude to frugality. While the way individuals earn depends on their enterprising behavior, individuals' frugal attitude and behavior can have a huge impact on the aggregate level of consumption and savings in the economy. The economic interpretation of frugality would be a situation where the individual spends only on what is earned. Although borrowing from banks is common in property investment, for example, economic frugality would imply that the individual would ensure the ability to repay before borrowing or spending. Thus, it is unlikely for a frugal person, and the economy to that effect, to accumulate debts and not the ability to repay.

In many cultures, frugality is considered as a human virtue, and its behavior can be passed down from one generation to the next through cultural education. Another possibility for the development of a frugal attitude would be in times of difficulty, when there is insufficient food or materials for basic needs, and people would learn to save and accumulate to cover the period of material shortage. Enterprising and self-reliant individuals tend to take up a frugal attitude readily as they do not want to be dependent on someone else, either on another family members or the government. In contemporary times, personal finance is the subject often taught at universities to remind the younger generation to manage their spending behavior and to avoid severe personal debt.

The human attitude to frugality can generate an economic impact on the overall growth trend. At the individual level, a person's spending behavior can be seen from their use of credit cards as overspending is easy without checking one's ability to honor the credit card payment. Individuals without a strong sense of frugality would overspend by using their credit cards and the resulting high interest payment could easily lead to personal loss and debt. Different age groups would face their spending needs differently and the extent of frugality would differ. For young families who are working hard to make ends meet, frugality is needed especially when they start to invest by taking up mortgages for their home purchase. The ability to repay a mortgage depends largely on their employment that provides them with a steady income. However, when the critical period of their home purchase has passed, additional spending could be made to improve their quality of life.

A more interesting phenomenon in the discussion on frugality is the spending behavior of the retirees, who would have accumulated quite a sum of money after decades of employment and work, and they are no longer the breadwinner in the house. These people would have behaved frugally all their working life, but the question facing them is whether they should continue to be frugal and keep the wealth for their children and grandchildren, or they should spend their retirement asset, enjoy life and leave nothing for their children.

The determining factor in a person's utility of money function would depend on the extent of economic and social security available. In an economy where social security provisions are high, any individual could turn to the government for assistance when faced with the difficulty of economic survival. In such a society, the need to save is reduced or people's marginal savings rate would be lower as the government becomes the last economic resort. One major implication can conceptually be found in family relationships. In economies that lack welfare, for example, couples tend to have more children as a sign of security when they age, hoping that they could seek support from their offspring. Hence, in an economy where social security provisions are absent, and individuals would have to fend for themselves, especially in their old age, individuals would have a stronger desire to save and ensure that they would be looked after in their old age either from their accumulated wealth or by their children who would inherit their wealth and assets anyway. In such a scenario, the family bondage tends to be strong, and parents would be more prepared to invest in their children's education so that they can achieve a better economic future.

On the contrary, when people know that they can always rely on the government in a strong welfare economy, young couples may not have a strong desire to have children and raise a family. Similarly, when young people are equally aware that they can turn to the government for assistance, their need to depend on their parents would be reduced. Such a behavior as the lack of a frugal attitude could have undesirable social consequences, because relationships within a family could become less cohesive. Broken families and divorce rates might rise as the economic bondage within a family becomes less vital. In such a scenario, it is expected that retired people would be more willing to spend with a lower desire to save, knowing that there is no need to pass their wealth and assets to their children. This trend should be more common if people do not have offspring of their own.

Because most people shall officially retire around the age of 60, many retired people are physically healthy and can still be active and energetic. One popular trend for the newly retired people with some savings is to travel for holidays and join tours before they become too elderly. This of course concludes that the person has saved sufficiently to spend on holidays. There are two theories that can be used to explain such a trend. One is the aging theory, and that since nobody knows when a person's life ends, one needs to save to ensure adequate asset is available to cover one's post-retirement life. Frugality therefore constitutes a part of a person's life insurance policy. In economics jargon, a person's frugal behavior can be related to the "marginal utility" of money and asset one holds, and the marginal utility of money to the same person obviously changes as the person ages. When a person is faced with a low level of wealth and asset, one extra dollar will produce a high marginal utility. A wealthy person, on the contrary, will have a much lower marginal utility of money as one extra dollar will not increase the person's satisfaction much.

The discussion on frugality at the individual level can be extended to the discussion on the macroeconomy. In a growing economy where individuals are given the opportunity to progress through business development, work as a professional or seek employment in a firm, it should be normal for any frugal individual to save and invest through acquiring assets. This is how wealth is generated and accumulated through frugality. Once accumulated, assets would be reinvested to produce a bigger economic safety net as the person ages. This shall be the scenario on how a frugal individual behaves, and the accumulation of assets would mean greater financial independence. With frugality and personal savings, there will be less need to seek social support. And the government shall then have more resources for other purposes rather than the need to spend on the elderly.

On the contrary, a strong welfare-prone government may not encourage frugality as welfare assistance would always be the last resort. Personal savings may not be valued that much as the state would bail out individual difficulties. This results in a low aggregate savings rate, and in times of a crisis individuals would not have their own savings to fend for their difficulties. The rise in state financial rescue could easily lead to government debt as welfare spending mounts, especially in a time of crisis. A lack of frugal attitude on the part of both the individuals and the government would easily result in the overspending and accumulation of personal and national debt, which could easily magnify into other economic and social difficulties.

The culture and attitude regarding people's frugality, their desire to save and willingness to spend do have a subtle role in determining the direction of the macroeconomy. Indeed, cultural and custom practices could equally generate waves in economic activities. Production and consumption are often culturally based or biased. This section has conceptually raised the concern in the relationship between economics and other social issues such as culture and religion, suggesting that economic activities have been the vehicle in these social dimensions.

IV Psychology in Economics

One major contribution in a formal education system is the training and development of a scientific mind. Scientific discovery and advancement in technology are meant to promote objectivity and impartiality in human life. Instead, many people are still innocently confined to their own beliefs which often are psychologically oriented and would carry a certain degree of superstition. For example, there are superstitions about certain numbers and a certain Friday in the week, though there is no scientific proof of the viciousness or the demonic nature of the number or the day of the week. There are numerous cultural, religious, customary and ethical examples where people's behavior is influenced by their psychology without scientific support. The "locust theory" can be applied to understand the psychological force in people's behavior, where the act of one person would lead to many followers acting in the same manner. The action of one person or behavior of one group or an opinion of a leader can disseminate and produce a psychological force on many others, leading people to behave and act in a similar manner or have a similar belief. The "locust theory" can best be seen in such situations as a capital flight where individuals and investors take most of their currency out of the country in fear of devaluation or the case of food hoarding in a war-torn country.

Because the future always remains unknown, one simple psychology held by many individuals is to secure a better future. The desire to have a better future could imply improvements in various senses and dimensions, including one's career, study, health, wealth, security, family, marriage, giving birth, living standard and quality of life, as well as burial arrangement and recognition after death. A "better future" can also imply a lower risk one faces. In other words, the intention of every individual would be to "maximize" outcomes but "minimize" risk. Outcomes could either be visible and tangible as shown by physical materials or invisible and intangible but can have psychological implications. On the contrary, risk would usually be invisible, intangible and could even be immeasurable, but would be felt in real psychological terms.

The visible and tangible aspects of outcomes are usually shown in material terms, which in turn are often expressed in economic languages, jargons and calculations. There can be numerous outcomes that individuals would like to maximize. The outcome of personal achievement can usually be seen from the formal qualification obtained, such as university degrees, professional qualifications or skills acquired through vocational training. Such kind of qualification maximization ensures the individual's future career path. For workers, maximization of wage earnings should be the norm. Wage payment in economics should correlate positively with productivity. Others prefer to maximize job satisfaction, or the working schedule of the job. Wealth maximization through investment forms the basis of a society composed of free individuals. Accumulation of assets would be turned into wealth, which is usually regarded as a form of economic protection or security. While wage earnings differ between individuals and professions, wealth accumulation would also differ among individuals due to differences in the amount invested, the mode of investment and the investment return.

While individual celebrities aim at maximizing their personal fame, firms maximize their outcomes in the form of business revenue and market share. Different professions will maximize their various activities, such as the number of clients, number of voters and supporters, extent of exposure within the profession, and in the rescue profession, the number of lives saved. Consumers will shop wisely to maximize their utilities or satisfaction. Economies maximize their competitiveness, level of employment, exports, growth and productivity. The pursuit of maximum outcomes has become a psychological instinct among all human beings. For the unwanted goods, such as violence, natural disasters and crises and environmental decay, the human instinct is to minimize them. In competition, the idea of maximizing one's outcome would mean the minimization of another person's outcome. The rise in the market share of one firm would mean the decline in another firm, unless there is corresponding increase in the market size. Hence, the firm's strategy that maximizes its outcome would also contain elements that would destroy or lower the outcome of its competitors. Similarly, in political elections, one party would advocate its best but at the same time criticize other political opponents, hoping that would create a negative image of the opponents.

The discussion on the invisible and intangible outcomes is more challenging, because these outcomes are often influenced by people's psychological and spiritual behavior and belief. In pursuing the outcome of a better and secured future, for example, the invisible instruments could include the advice from fortune tellers and spiritual leaders and the use and display of certain symbolic materials, such as an animal, a natural product or an artifact. It is not possible to verify scientifically if advice from fortune tellers and symbolic materials did produce positive outcomes, or just served as psychological healings and provided spiritual comforts. Indeed, while it is difficult to know if the future life could be improved, the bottom line would be a situation with no deterioration in one's current way of life. On the contrary, if a person faces hardship and feels helpless at a difficult time, the various forms of psychological healings and comfort could help to ease the pain, difficulty and frustration suffered physically and mentally. In other words, when an individual is at the weakest and most vulnerable point in life, psychological healing and support would be a strong instrument in rescuing and boosting one's moral, strength, determination and recovery. The psychology is basically a personal wish, because if all the calls and wishes of a better future were satisfied, the world would certainly become a much better place, but there were still crimes, violence and disasters occurring in different societies at different times affecting different people.

Sailing along with the intention and desire to have a "better life" in the future is the reduction of risk in one's life. In material terms, risk has been counterbalanced by the amount of insurance a person acquired. There is also the psychological dimension in handling personal risk, especially in the developing countries. Having as many children as possible is thought to be an insurance policy as the offspring will take care of the elders. In a monetary economy, the wealth and assets one has are an insurance policy. In primitive societies, the number of poultry a household had formed an insurance policy. In times of war, the amount of food amassed would provide assurance from risk of starvation. In situations of atrocity with civic unrest, a foreign passport or the amount of gold bars one possessed could be a survival assurance.

Psychological healings through cultural, spiritually oriented and customary activities were meant to alleviate one's risk in life. In many instances, the psychological demands and feelings would go beyond one's life after death. There are cultural, spiritual and customary talks on one's life after death, or related to one's current life to his or her previous life, as if humans were immortal and would experience one life after another. Searching for a better life and the intention to reduce risk have sometimes been commanded by individuals' superstition on what to do or what not to do, as the fear of an omen could be strong enough to deter people from some activities. People's psychological behavior resulting from cultural, spiritual, customary and superstitious beliefs can have an impact on their economic activities. Resources such as land usage could be geared to religious purposes. Products could be consumed for cultural activities, such as new year celebrations, funeral arrangements, religious festive occasions and so on. Holidays would be assigned for religious and customary purposes. Even some political leaders and parties have made use of certain religions as part of their political orientation and platform.

One economic argument is that resources catered for cultural, spiritual, customary and superstitious activities relate more to the demand side in the economic equation. Such resources as land used for these purposes would no longer be used for other purposes, though they may generate some historical value and serve as a tourist attraction. Manufactured goods so produced are consumed for special purposes. In the case of religious institutions, for example, their source of income would often be considered as charity and may be exempted from tax payments, thereby raising a possible accountability problem. The economic question is whether the revenue and income of charitable organizations should also be subject to tax and reporting the accounts, as that would serve as a form of monitoring for the financial activities of these institutions and organizations. Indeed, like all other institutions, there could be the "agency" and "asymmetric information" problem as the managers and administrators in charitable organizations could also "rent seek" their organizations. Working environment could also be affected by cultural and religious behavior. For example, some religions specify the number of times a follower will need to pray daily, or the working possibility and conditions between the two genders.

The fact is that economic performances at both the resource end and the product end are often affected by the psychology of people, which are shown in different kinds of behavior related to culture, religion, custom, history and superstition. Although it is not possible to quantify the impact of these economic activities, it is fair to argue that these behaviors and norms are practices handed down from one generation to another, and because they provided invisible and intangible "advantages", few would have queried about their desirability or relevance to modern life, bearing in mind that some norms and practices project inequality and discrimination between genders, races and classes of people. They thus serve more as a divider than a harmonizer among different groups of people. The worst is that their differences have been dichotomized by politicians and issues are then created because of differences, rather than harmonizing to reach consensus to achieve a higher stage in the development of humanity.

V Conclusion

Other than government policies, there are numerous aspects in social science that require a clear conceptual understanding in relation to economics. The term culture is used to incorporate differences in race, faith, history, geography, social norms and so on. Each of these cultural aspects does have a conceptual relationship with economics. A certain religious faith would result in various kinds of travels, production and pattern of consumption. Different social norms may look at some natural resources differently. For example, while water is used to generate energy in one country, it is regarded as holy in another country. There is only one human race in the world, but such factors as skin color, language and culture exist to divide humans. In short, while culture symbolizes advancement in humanity, culture also serves as a restricting instrument in many scenarios in human advancement and understanding.

By examining on a pairwise basis the conceptual alliance between economics and three other social science disciplines of culture, psychology and politics, a cross-disciplinary approach has been used in understanding how economics can be affected by activities in other social science disciplines. Serving as a vehicle to other social science disciplines, economic outcomes are often determined by non-economic causes and intentions. Furthermore, the economic activities dictated by other social science disciplines are seen mainly on the demand side of the economic equation, involving spending, consumption and production that have been geared to specific markets. It has been argued that activities in other social science disciplines are often artificial or unnatural and various cultural practices are simply passed down from one generation to another; there is a lack of scientific proof on the truthfulness of many cultural behaviors and customary beliefs. Sheer differences in people's cultural behavior can be tolerated as they may not impose harm on others, but cultural differences can be divisive, segregating and dichotomizing different groups of people to be exploited for political purposes.

Armed with the powerful conceptual analyses, the greater understanding among social science disciplines can be enhanced. Subsequently, such international issues and conflicts as terrorism, financial crisis and national debts could equally be analyzed using economics combined with cultural factors. Indeed, many contemporary issues and problems have been prolonged as there are too many factors and involve many stakeholders. Using economics as a pivot in the cross-disciplinary approach to examine these issues would first disaggregate problems into various controllable and comprehensible dimensions, and solutions would then be catered to each dimension, with the aim to arrive at a global, effective and functional solution.

Section III

The Intensity Dimension

While most economics analyses look at the *"ex-post"* end of economic outcomes and their differences, the discussions in the following three chapters take a "vertical" approach to explain the *"ex-ante"* nature of differences in economics. The differences in all economic outcomes have been politicized or criticized as the differences may benefit some and not all, but one would have a new perspective on economic outcomes when one examines the differences in the input end of the economic equation. Hence, understanding the *"ex-ante"* aspect of any economic activity shall help to explain the fact that *ex-ante* differences shall also produce *ex-post* differences. Thus, while one is lamenting *ex-post* differences, there is a need to know that the origin of the *ex-post* differences can be due to *ex-ante* differences. It should therefore be more appropriate to address *ex-ante* differences in the first instance.

Each of the three chapters in this section has its own theme in the discussion on *ex-ante* differences. Chapter Seven begins by looking at the concept of value in economics as well as in human sciences. The argument focuses on quantifiable, behavioral and normative values in human sciences. A "value scale" has been proposed as a ladder through which human values can be promoted and improved, though there are "clogs" or forces that delay its progression. The discussion on endowment and opportunity in Chapter Eight is core to the discussion on *ex-ante* differences. Endowment is a comprehensive concept that incorporates individuals' attributes, which are different from one individual, one firm and one economy to another. Differences in endowment are the foundation of *ex-ante* differences. However, whether such differences can be improved will depend on the creation and availability of opportunity, which would be another scarcity.

Chapter Nine wraps the discussion on Conceptual Economics by arguing that economics should be given its proper role and pace, as economic activities are apolitical. Yet political ideologies have exploited economics for their own goals, favorably or unfavorably. The chapter ends by elaborating civic capitalism as the more acceptable ideology. It is most important to allow economics to do its job, rather than be exploited for non-economic purposes. "Give Economic Performance a Chance" shall be the message in Conceptual Economics.

Chapter Seven

Measurement of Values
in Humanity Sciences

I Introduction

The conceptual analysis can start by elaborating the "value" term considered in various social science disciplines. By its very nature, "value" can be expressed both quantitatively and qualitatively, and there is a conceptual need to consolidate the arguments into a standardized format for the purpose of analyzing human behavior divided into different social science disciplines. The understanding of "value" across social science disciplines helps to set the intellectual scene in studying and analyzing the conceptual intricacies between the economics discipline and other social science disciplines.

In the first instance, the term "value" has often been expressed in dollar signs. Others would argue that values could have diverse meanings and implications in different scenarios and contexts. Some values may not be entirely quantifiable, and values can be intangible and intrinsic. One may value a bottle of drink, a vehicle, a diamond or an antique, but one can also value friendship, relationship, connection, brotherhood, parenthood, kindness or gratitude and so on. Very often, it is the presence of intangible values that leads us to have diversity in economic transactions. A close family relationship, for example, would lead the household to buy a minivan to ferry the family members to various places rather than a small coupe car. The birthday of a loved one would urge other intimate ones to share a birthday cake. Although minivans and birthday cakes are differently priced in monetary terms, there are intangible values inherited in the relationships. It is the presence of such intangible values that leads to numerous economic transactions expressed in dollar terms.

As the study of economics involves the allocation, deployment and distribution of resources, each economic transaction has a monetary value attached. At the input end of the economic equation that involves the use of raw materials, other intermediate inputs such as machinery and labor are individually priced so that producers and investors could calculate their cost of production, which is then used as a guideline to decide on the price of the final output. At the output end of the economic equation, it is the consumers who would have the choice to buy whatever produced, and consumer preference would provide an indication on the appropriateness of the price set by the producers. Between these two circuits, it is the market that serves as the "invisible hand" in linking the producers and workers in the input end and consumers in the output end of the economic equation, giving an indication as to the level of supply and demand to the producers and consumers.

The producers would face the business risk and invest in the hope of making profit gains in the production process but could face loss should their investment fail. Investment serves as the first step in the economic chain of production, where various resource inputs and labor would be needed. Workers offer their services and respond to the availability of jobs once investment has taken place. The investor or producer employs but must take the business risk arising from the ups and downs of business cycles and the market sentiments. With the presence of economic freedom and freedom to enter into markets, individuals can invest and start a business or work for another investor as employees. Thus, to invest to become a business person or to gain expertise and work as an employee has become a personal choice, as both have their role in the economic chain.

This chapters examines the conceptual power of value in understanding human economic relationships, activities and transactions. According to Dictionary.com and Merriam Webster dictionary, the noun value is defined as follows: (1) the monetary or material worth in trade and commerce; (2) something that gives a relative worth, a merit or an importance; (3) a fair return in exchange; (4) something that people desire intrinsically and unavoidably; and (5) a measurable numerical quantity. Value can be seen from a physical possession, an intrinsic behavior or an intangible activity that people have a great desire to have, to own and to choose given the alternatives, and such a human desire can be measured either in monetary terms or in behavior explicated through human activities.

The value concept has been discussed extensively within the economic context, but this chapter shall elaborate on the "scale of value" that goes beyond economics and incorporates other behavioral ideas and acts, which can be normative, intangible but intrinsic. A "value scale" can be formed by identifying five levels of quantifiable and non-quantifiable measures. The first level in the discussion begins with the Marxian discussion of labor value as an input in the economic equation. The next level in the "value scale" would be expanded to other monetary measures in market capitalism that incorporate both inputs and outputs in the economic equation. The "value scale" shall then be extended to three levels of non-quantifiable measures that include normative factors, behavioral measures and humanistic qualities.

Figure 7.1 shows the graphical presentation of the five levels of value measures beginning with labor input as the simplest, proceeding to values in the market economy, extended to normative factors, behavioral qualities and finally to humanistic values. Each level shall expand the measure of value, increasing its size from one level to another, giving a comprehensive and complete valuation eventually. Each of these five levels will be discussed in the following sections. However, so long as there are humans, there are problems. Thus, while values are defined, they may not be kept or followed, and there can be clogs and restrictions in the progress from one level of measurement to another, or even within the same level of measurement, thereby limiting the materialization of human values. The chapter ends by suggesting that the economics discipline should be

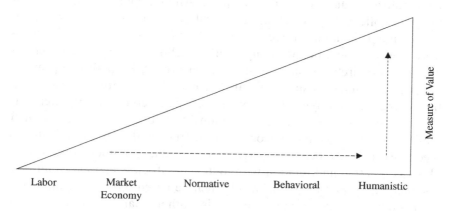

Figure 7.1   The Scale of Value Measures

the most appropriate carrier of value, as freedom in conducting economic activities allows individuals to participate, contribute, choose, accept and respect human values.

II Economic Value Measures

The ideology of Marxism advocates for political absolutism with the state being the owner of all resources and all production activities would be conducted by the state and controlled by the party members and government officials. As there is no private ownership, human workers and laborers are all "state owned" and form part of the state resources, and jobs and employment are designed and assigned or designated by the state. The entire process of production comes under state directives. Workers' jobs are allocated, consumers' household materials are allotted according to what is produced and what not, consumer preference as a choice would not be available, and the situation could get worse at times due to material shortages. Under communism and the absence of private ownership, the state would have absolute control over individuals' economic activities. Choices, preferences and alternatives would not be provided freely to individuals.

The political orientation of Marxism is that under communism, economic gains are thought to have been equalized, as the absence of resource ownership would mean that no one individual can have economic power over another in the form of job hiring, payment of wage, market fluctuations, control by private producers and the absence of wholesale and retail in deciding the price. All individuals would work for the state collectively. As such, individual creativity would not be entertained, and personal incentives have no place as there is no effective business. Hence, economic inequality would be eliminated as the economy is dominated entirely by state production. However, inequality appears in the political arena, as state officials become all powerful and manipulation, corruption, cronyism and vested interests emerge. As party membership is selective, having a good relationship with high officials or their family members would become an instrumental privilege. Political inequality appears between party members and non-members, and in close association and relation with high state officials and their families. Personal and social judgment would then be based on one's relationship with high-level government officials rather than one's ability or intellectuality.

The communist ideology is political in its essence and argues that in the class struggle between the bourgeois and the proletariat, human exploitation appears in market capitalism as employers would not reward the laborers fully. Economic production should only be seen in the form of labor input included in the production process. Labor value becomes the sole relevance in value measurement and scholars have used mathematical presentation to elaborate on the theory of labor value, though there are also criticisms on the lack of clarity in Marx's labor value theory (Okisio, 1963; Morishima, 1973, 1974; Rubin, 1973; Bowles and Gintis, 1977; Cohen, 1979; Wolff, 1981; Keen, 1993). The essence in the theory of labor value is that the economic value of a good or service is determined by the total amount of "socially necessary labor" required to produce it. In his discussion on *Value, Price and Profit* in 1865, Marx distinguished the number of hours needed in the production of certain products from the total number of hours the laborers worked for the capitalist. A certain number of hours would be needed to produce a certain product, but Marx argued that the capitalist would have acquired the rights of use value of labor power and would make the laborer work for longer hours which would exceed the amount of wage paid. Marx claimed that the difference was considered a "surplus labor" exploited by the capitalist.[1]

Marx's ideology of communism was based on the early years of industrialization in the 19th century in Europe when laborers spent much time working on the factory floor and had little time to attend to their own affairs. Training was minimal and career development was absent. Laborers were said to have been alienated from their social life circles. Furthermore, the goods the laborers produced were also priced by the capitalist producers, and the wage the laborers received practically had to be paid back to the producers through the consumption of household products; thus, the workers spent their labor for the producers and returned their wage back to the producers in the form of spending on the material products. In short, the capitalists exploited the workers through the control of their labor and working hours and of the materials spent through the goods produced and sold to the workers as consumers.

In the early age of industrialization, education was not common, industrial training was based mainly on apprenticeship, and social welfare was minimal even if it existed. Social class was seen dichotomously and

---

[1]"Labor theory of value", *Wikipedia.*

was divided mainly between the capital owners and the proletariats. However, Marx erroneously injected a political idea into an economic relationship. The simple economic relationship is one of complementarity as capitalists deployed their financial resources, while workers offered their labor service in the production process. Capitalists could not produce without the workers, and workers would not get employed if there was no investment. In the production process, then, both parties gained as workers needed to be paid for their labor contribution and capitalists needed to be rewarded for their investment.

The capitalist mode of production has been modernized considerably since the 20th century. With education and the growth of professionals as jobs became more specialized, the growth of the middle class meant that individuals could work as independent professionals, and the growth of services provided new jobs away from hard labor in industrial manufacturing. The advancement of technology and automation replaced many low-skilled jobs in the production chain. New businesses appeared and competition among investors and producers mounted. Social welfare has been developed to assist the needy households. Thus, Marx's description of exploitation and alienation has been reduced drastically, or even eradicated. With the election of some pro-labor governments over the years in some European countries, labor power has risen to check the producers' economic strength; it was the turn of the producers to complain about the "reverse exploitation" where high labor wages eroded their business competitiveness, and businesses closed or were faced with bankruptcy in economic recessions. The rise of newly developed nations effectively meant that business had become more competitive, and "latecomers" in the global economy could enter the market and compete successfully with the matured nations (see discussion in Li, 2017a).

Marx's theory on the value of labor as the sole input in the production process has been criticized. Industrial production requires labor input and other "means of production", known as intermediate goods. Tools and capital are needed, and there should also be a value arising from the production of tools and capital accumulated previously. Production requires a combination of materials inputs, and it would be simplistic to claim that labor is the only input that creates value. In contemporary business, the "surplus labor" that Marx advocates would simply be considered as part of the "value-added" content along with capital and other inputs in the production process. Employers and employees should be seen more as complements than as dichotomous to each other. One can argue that Marx had wrongly imposed a political interpretation into otherwise a pure economic relationship. In politics, relationships are opposite and dichotomous to each other as politics often produces absolute outcomes, while in economics, relationships are more relative and complementing to different actors.

Other scholars also noted the inadequacies in the theory of labor value. Morishima (1973, pp. 11–12) noted the mathematical duality in the two definitions of value in Volume 1 of Marx's *Capital* (Pilling, 1980; Marx, 1993), and concluded that duality existed between "the value determination system and the input–output system". In the production process, the economic relationship involves a system of "inputs" that includes labor, raw materials and other intermediate goods. Similarly, the "output" system requires other related components of wholesale, retail and transport services in the distribution of the final product before it reaches the consumers. The market price may reflect not only the labor cost but also the "value-added" content of each component in the entire production process.

Within the economic sphere, two types of value measurement are discussed. The Marxian measure using merely labor value in the production is a much narrower measurement and ignores other inputs in the economic equation. Marx advocated that state ownership could eliminate economic inequality arising from private ownership of resources, but not knowing that political inequality could be deadlier in socialism and communism because individuals would not be given their freedom to choose their own welfare. Market economies allowed private ownership of resources and property rights so that individuals are free to make their own individual progress through investment, education and improvement in individual endowment. Market signal can be freely available as an indicator in resource deployment. The state serves only as a mediator and ensures the effective functioning of the rule of law.

In capitalist market economies, value measures are dispersed, though they are all expressed in monetary terms as the price serves as the median between actors in all transactions. The term "value added" will be the relevant concept in market economies. In production, the use of certain raw materials such as wood and other intermediate inputs such as paint, nails and labor as a skilled craftsman would produce a piece of furniture that should carry a price higher than the combined cost of all inputs. The difference should be the "value-added" content that the use of material input has generated. In a restaurant, a certain food input will be used by the chef to produce a dish for the customers who come to patronize the restaurant. Hence, the food input may cost $5, while the wage payment to the cook could be $14 and the dish sells at $25, for example, so the additional $6 should be seen more as the increase in the "value added". It is true that the difference is regarded as the "profit" for the restaurant owner, who would be the investor in the restaurant business and is responsible for the business risk involved.

Similarly, a school-leaver with no skill or work experience will receive a much lower pay but should the young school-leaver learn a certain skill or trade, the person shall receive a higher hourly pay. With skill acquisition, the young person will receive more than an unskilled worker. Such a difference in pay reflects the "value-added" content as the person gains a higher marketable skill. Education and training primarily serve to improve the "value-added" content of the workers. The use of technology can similarly be considered as a means to improve the product's "value added" and to sell at a higher price. Mobile phones, electric vehicles and computers are technological products that are aimed to increase the "value-added" content in the production process. Mere production is not final in contemporary businesses, because there can be a host of supplementary work that needs to be conducted. Production gives rise to a host of related services. The writing of a book is production, for example, but the author does not do the publication, and the publisher requires the use of material inputs, and by the time the book is printed, sales promotion is required to get the book out to the interested consumers. At each stage, the "value-added" content of the book increases. Hence, by the time the book eventually is sold at the bookshop, the author only gets a certain percentage of the sale price, the rest goes into the other cost of production.

A contemporary business person engaging in production must get involved with multiple tasks in improving the "value-added" content, which includes not only the labor cost and material cost, but the market trend, the risk in the product's "life cycle", changes in demand pattern, competition from other producers, source of finance and exchange rate stability in case of exports. In business, whether it is in manufacturing or services, there is the need to put together required inputs, including labor, and no single input is indispensable, but rather inputs are complementary to each other. Indeed, all forms of economic activities are meant to improve the value-added content of materials, goods and services. The society spends huge amounts of funds on education aiming to increase the value-added content of human capital, research and development activities aim to improve the value-added content of manufacturing production, businesses engage in advertisement and aim to enlarge their market share enhancing the value-added content of the business, and national economies pursue market-friendly policies with the intention to allow the economy to stay competitive so that the economy's entire value-added content can be improved. The provision of effective infrastructure, for example, will promote business activities more efficiently, and that already can raise the value-added content of many business transactions. A reliable banking infrastructure shall promote efficiency in cross-border payment. An efficient road transport system shall improve the catchment areas of various businesses.

In short, it is the improvement in value added that drives individuals, businesses and corporations, institutions and governments to perform and achieve a better result over time. Economic outcomes are relative to each other, and so long as the market is open, market entry will not be restricted. Indeed, in the process of getting educated, young students are effectively looking for their best interest in choosing their subject studies so that they can end up in certain businesses or professions that will provide them with the highest possible value added in their future career. Workers are permitted to change jobs and employment should they think another job provides them with a higher value-added outcome, namely, a higher wage payment. Entrepreneurs shall identify market possibilities as it would allow them to gain a high value-added content in their business as they enter the market. Hence, even though large corporations exist in different trades, individual entrepreneurs can make use of the freedom in market entry to start their business and can survive along with the large corporations, which in turn will have to compete with other corporations. Individual ingenuity, creativity and an innovative mind are the elements of diversity and sources of progress in economic activities.

In a capitalist economy where the rule of law and a level playing field are maintained, the market mechanism allows all individuals, be they the workers or entrepreneurs, to strive for the highest possible value added in their activities. Putting it differently, a higher value added will give a higher monetary reward that promotes individual welfare and ultimately economic security. Because individuals differ in their ingenuity and endowment, the outcome of their value added shall differ from each other. Hence, so long as individuals and businesses are given the opportunity, the difference in their value added reflects the nature of the trade, business or profession. It is unwise to politicize the difference in value added as income inequality. The society educates and trains people for different jobs, individuals have different goals and mentalities, and jobs are paid differently; the difference in the value added among individuals reflects the *ex-ante* nature in trade, businesses or professions, and should not be used as a political tool to advocate inequality in one's income. Given the differences in *ex-ante* conditions, income is bound to be unequal, but it is more important for every individual worker to receive an income.

The market is open to all and there are no market boundaries, as new products are created to replace old products and new firms are established to compete with existing firms. The market can expand in all directions to allow diversity and progress. New jobs are created as technology progresses. In microeconomics theory, one discusses the utility or satisfaction of a good or a service, and that the market value tends to be governed by the marginal utility of the good or service. This explains why water is cheaper than a diamond because the marginal utility of water is lower than the marginal utility of a diamond, even though water is more vital as a good than a diamond. The utility analysis is based on how much satisfaction the consumer gets in consuming the good. One can equally ask how value added is formed. Given two similar goods, why does one sell at a higher price than another? Two motor vehicles with similar functions produced from different brand manufacturers can have different prices.

There is thus the intermediary through which the value-added content of a resource, a good or a service is formed or conveyed. In an open and legal market, market information can be obtained by all market players. Consumer loyalty can be formed through the availability of market information, and that could explain why one brand of the good is more favorable than another. Other than advertising, media broadcasting can be an effective vehicle through which the value added of a good or a resource can increase. For example, all news broadcast includes the sports news, and the faces of sports players are shown on the television screen. Why is sports considered as part of the daily news? Why not include in the daily news the number of cars produced, the number of pizzas consumed or the number of patients admitted to hospitals? If sports activities were not included in the daily news and promoted by the media, would the sports players be paid so highly? Are the sports players taking a free ride on daily news reports? Should sports players be valued more than technicians, academic professors or government officials? Which profession would be worth more to the society? News is supposed to report things that affect the public, and weather is a good example, but the behavior or personality of a certain celebrity, for example, reported in the news may not be of public interest. Other than creativity, talent can also be valued highly. Hence, the conclusion is that the vehicle, instrument or means through which the value-added content can be increased has become an important source, reflecting the diversity that the market permits.

While the market serves as a platform for every economic player to use, the price mechanism serves as an indicator of value, which can change due to time, space, opportunity, available information, shocks, endowment and product life cycles. Individuals engage in activities that enhance the value-added content of all economic resources that would finally be transformed into goods and services. The market allows value to be created, and the achievement of a higher value added will mean not only a higher monetary reward to the individual, but a higher level of economic security in terms of personal welfare, and a higher level of competitiveness and sustainability for the entire economy. Economic activities are meant to promote the value of resources so that a higher welfare can be achieved for all market players. Economic outcomes tend to be relative, as differences in *ex-ante* material inputs will naturally produce *ex-post* differences in material outputs. It is important to ensure that opportunity is made equally open and available to all players, and not based on the differences in the gains among individuals with a different endowment.

III Qualitative Value Measures

Most economic resources can be quantified in monetary terms, mainly because resources are tangible, visible and realizable. However, the mobility of economic resources requires individuals, businesses and policy decisions that are conducted ultimately by human beings, though the intention of resource usage differs among individuals, businesses and officials. However, although economic resources are mostly quantifiable, there are numerous non-quantifiable qualitative factors that are included in the decision-making process. For example, why are sports included in the daily news and not any other non-sports activities? How much free daily air time across the world has been devoted to sports news? The understanding of quantifiable value measures thus may not be adequate as other non-quantifiable values are embodied in the deployment of economic resources. In other words, there are numerous factors that influence the deployment of economic resources, leading their usage to certain outcomes.

There are broadly three categories of human factors that can affect the value outcome in the process of resource deployment, either by additionally inserting an invisible value or directing the resources to certain higher value-added usage. One set of human value arises from the "gift of nature" where lives are governed by biological or environmental factors. Many of these "normative" value factors are visible, such as race and gender. There is only one human race on earth, and as such, all humans are born equal. Unfortunately, due to historical factors, administrative convenience, physical appearance or political decisions, humans have been grouped according to ethnical differences. Due to the human events in different historical and political epochs, such as imperialism, slavery trade, ethnical or territorial wars and disputes, various obstacles and rivalries have emerged to divide humans, and unnecessary and unintended conflicts still exist. The case of gender difference among humans is similar, and the differences in the two sexes has led to differences in human norms. There are other visible factors, typically the geographical environment where people live in different climate zones, and that are seen in the way people dress and the kind of clothing products produced. Ethnical and environmental factors can affect agricultural produce in different geographical zones.

Other than monetary measures, the value arising from visible factors in goods and services is often dictated or directed by human norms, which have been taken for granted. Many of the practiced norms are human creations which can be traced back to long historical times when civilization began, and our forefathers had practiced and passed these norms from one generation to another. While the changes of seasons are the forces of nature, the decisions on calendar months, weekdays and years are human creations and the norms were accepted since the dawn of modern civilization through generational practices. There are festivals in different ethnic groups, and the norms arising from the festivals have direct and indirect economic impacts. For example, different ethnic groups may have different days as their new year. And for Christmas, a tree would be chopped and used for indoor decoration, to be surrounded by gifts and other folklores. Certain dresses or costumes and the consumption of certain types of food would be a part of the norms in different human festivals and occasions. Numerous examples in human norms would generate economic impacts. Hence, a certain product would have been made for occasions and would convey different value implications. Many artifacts and traditional foods are produced for the new year or on marriage occasions for different ethnic groups with the intention to convey blessings of one sort or another.

Although human norms are practiced, normative values cannot be easily measured and quantified. However, human norms do have an impact on different economic resources, goods and services produced and consumed. Furthermore, the norms and value they bring could change as the society develops. For example, Sunday was conventionally regarded as a day off for holy activities and gatherings. In contemporary societies, shops, restaurants and other service businesses are open on Sundays, thereby providing more choices and alternatives to consumers and households, especially in metropolitan areas. Firstly, some people may prefer to work on Sundays so that they can have a day off on another weekday. Others may work to get extra earnings instead of staying idle on the weekends. Secondly, when shops and other service businesses are open on Sundays, life and personal welfare can improve should one find the need to do shopping on weekends. In short, changes in practiced norms could further enhance individuals' welfare, so too the value attached to the norms.

The next level of non-quantifiable values aims at extending the practiced norms to other behavioral ingredients, such as cultural, moral, ethical and religious practices. Different ethnic groups have developed diverse cultural beliefs over the centuries and generations. However, many behavioral and cultural practices are "manmade" and beliefs are at times the result of superstition or inability to explain some natural phenomena. The treatment of some natural resources can be different among cultures. In one part of the world, river water is regarded as "holy", but in other parts of the world, river water is used for irrigation, or dams are constructed as an infrastructure to generate energy. The use of color can be considered as a cultural aspect in major events across cultures. In one culture, the color red is used extensively in traditional weddings to symbolize prosperity and festivity, while in another culture, white is used as a symbol of purity and transparency. Like practiced norms, cultural behavior does exercise a value impact on human activities, which in turn is translated into economic transactions in resource usage, production and consumption.

Closely associated with behavior and culture is one's chosen religion, if any. Religion provides psychological answers to individuals' faith, which can be demonstrated with different expressions and requirements. One religion encourages followers to do their prayers in a church, while another religion chooses to face a certain direction during their prayers. The number of prayer times differs among different faiths. Most religions promote peace, harmony, acceptance and coexistence, but there is one religion which advocates holy war if the followers think that the religion is threatened or criticized. The kind of faith promoted could vary among religions. While one religion considers one's afterlife as the faith element, another encourages followers to have good behavior in their current lifetime to prepare for their next life, or the followers' unpleasant experiences in this life is regarded as suffering resulting from the mean behavior in their previous life. Another religion asks followers to adopt the religious principles regardless of the outcome. In some religious states where one religion has officially been adopted, the holy book has become the prime source of education. Instead of leaving one's religious faith to personal choice, religion has been used also as a political instrument to control the nation. Indeed, not all religions preach equality in gender. Nonetheless, in religion-free societies, religious faith could be regarded as a form of psychological healing, as individuals look to religious preaching for mental solutions.

Religious activities do carry economic, psychological and social values in contemporary societies (Iannaccone, 1992; Fase, 2005; Tan, 2006, 2013). Many religion-related festive activities have resulted in variations in economic values. Airline tickets are typically more expensive before than after Christmas. Similarly, retail businesses are busier before and after Christmas day. Land has been used for religion-related constructions. Religious teaching in schools could influence the children's subsequent moral judgment, thinking and behavior. Most religions adhere to moral teachings and principles which have been transformed into accepted civilized human behavior. Indeed, the rule of law in contemporary civic societies has been established based on such moral issues as trust, non-violence, individuality, property right, privacy and externalities to guard against harm and wrongdoings. Other than religion, another source of moral principles is derived from famous philosophers, as their teachings often form the basis of human wisdom and reasoning (Dover, 1974; Donagan, 1977; Raz, 1986; Gert, 1998; Haidt, 2008). Close to morality is the ethics practiced in civilized societies (Kohlberg and Hersh, 1977; Etzioni, 1988, 1996; Raz, 1986, 1994; Friedman, 2006; Schwartz, 2007).

Presumably, most theologies preach followers to behave in a civilized human manner so that they would acquire a lasting faith that would extend to their next lives; others argue that religions serve as a psychological and sociological healing in human behavior, especially during one's tough times. Studies show that in Western religions a person's religiosity can provide spiritual and social solutions, as the person could feel protected and gain psychological strength in overcoming atrocities and unfortunate events. Thus, religiosity does present positive, but invisible, values to the person as that could direct the person to behave in a socially acceptable manner (Schwartz and Huismans, 1995; Hill and Hood, 1999; King and Crowther, 2004; Ysseldyk *et al.*, 2010).

Studies often combine morality and ethics as philosophical issues (Hart, 1963; Fuller, 1069; Frings and Funk, 1973; Gewirth, 1978; Kagan, 1989, 1998; Boone, 2017; Harvey, 2000; Bank, 2012; Thiroux and Krasemann, 2012). Both morality and ethics are often taught in schools at an early age, while parents and elders of a family often pass on ethical judgment and code of conduct in activities when their children are growing up (see, for example, Kirschenbaum, 1995). Both morality and ethics are teachings that direct individuals to have correct reasoning in their thoughts, behavior and acts and that harm should not be done to others.

There is a conceptual difference between morality and ethics. Morality tends to relate more to individuals' own thinking, and how an individual should think and act righteously. It follows that with a correct mentality in thoughts, ideas and reasoning, the individual shall behave in a non-harmful manner in the society. A non-harmful individual does promote social value, as a non-harmful individual can lead to a reduction in social violence. Ethics is the behavior of an individual that gets reflected when it is shown on others. The presence of good ethics shall then be materialized when one individual shows good treatment toward another individual. What constitutes politeness, for example, or the way children greet their parents and elders would have formulated the children's ethics standards. The thinking of being polite is moral, but the actual expression of politeness is an ethical issue. To have filial piety is a moral thought, but the act of expressing one's filial piety is ethical. Morality remains in the mind of the individual, but ethical standards are to be practiced by individuals.

Other than personal ethics, there are also other kinds of civic morals and ethics applicable to different professions (Abbott, 1983; Brien, 1998; Campbell, 2000). The basic idea of professional integrity is that the person should not abuse the power, position or knowledge one has over another person who does not have the same. In most civic professions, such as medical doctors, lawyers, accountants and educators, there are written rules, codes of conduct and standards that govern the various practices in their own professions. In the legal profession, for example, the same lawyer cannot represent both the plaintiff and the defendant. Similarly, business ethics has become important in the contemporary business world in that moral consideration and code of conduct must be incorporated in business transactions to avoid abuse and manipulation (Solomon, 1992; Stark, 1993; Sternberg, 2000; Crane and Matten, 2016).

The presence of ethics imposes an invisible but accountable value in many humanistic transactions and relationships, as it ensures certain qualitative achievements and standards, and preserves the ingredient of a civic society so that individuals are protected by the "good practice" in professions and businesses. Such ethical values add to transparency, security and trust in professional activities. Returning to economic analysis, the presence of morality and the exercise of ethics in fact serve to reduce the agency cost and uncertainty resulting from the acts of the intermediaries in transactions. Once every party is playing with similar rules, a level playing field can be instituted and equality in treatment can be assured, and special privileges will be eliminated. In other words, when all agents are acting and behaving in a *bona fide* manner, a high degree of trust and confidence will be built into the transacting parties. Trustworthiness becomes a value in human transactions.

However, the practice of ethics can be unpredictable. Political ethics can be difficult to enforce, as it is quite impossible to know if the elected politicians and leaders are acting on a *bona fide* basis, or if there were vested interests for the politicians to engage in elections. Were the politicians looking for an opportunity to serve the people, or an opportunity to become famous and get rich from the authoritative position? Would the elected leader show good ethics in managing the economy or use the elected position to victimize the opponents? In many ways, ethics is a "common good", meaning that if everyone keeps to the high ethical standards, the society would generate and spread many good practices. But, when only some individuals follow the ethical practices while others do not, the overall ethical standard could suffer and even deteriorate. For example, one household took care of its garbage disposal carefully, but if the neighboring household did not, the quality of life would depend on how each of the two households reacted ethically. Poor ethics and bad practices shall add to the "social cost" in the daily life of a community, thereby reducing the quality of life and raising life hazards. In short, the extent to which ethics is practiced is debatable, as there may not be clear guidelines as to the limit of ethical practices. Thus, even though it is highly desirable, inclusion of ethical values in human activities can become a judgment that differs among individuals, businesses, political leaders and ideologies.

Perhaps the highest level of qualitative measure of value should be the various judgments exercised by humankind. The rule of law and not the rule of men, for example, has been a human value upheld in all civilized societies (Scalia, 1989; O'Donnell, 2004; Tamanaha, 2004; Leoni, 2012). With the rule of law, individuals are equal before the law and a level playing field can be achieved to ensure non-discrimination and the eradication of privileges. Other humanistic values include the respect shown to other human ethnic groups, equality in job opportunity and education opportunity between the two genders, environmental protection and cutting waste. Protection of animals and elimination of animal cruelty has become an acceptable human value. At the global level, peace keeping and rescue efforts in troubled regions in the world and providing aid and assistance to regions and people suffering from natural disasters have been established as a cross-border human value. There is only one human race, and to accept and respect the rights of a human should be the ultimate value.

The three levels of qualitative values (visible and normative, behavioral and cultural, and humanistic values) discussed in this section point to the importance of humans as a survival race, and the mutual respect shown on humans by all humans is the greatest value that transcends all kinds of living materials. On the contrary, the various kinds of disrespect shown and exercised on some humans by others due to artificial barriers and practices in the form of discrimination, politicization, mistrust, vested interest and uncivilized behavior have not only lowered the human value but have resulted in violence, suffering and other manmade disasters.

IV A Value Scale in Human Science

A total of five aspects of values have been discussed. While labor value as a unit of measure has been proved to be simplistic as there are equally other valuable inputs in economic activities, the economic method is calculating value using the market that touched on both the input end and output end of an economic equation. The primary purpose in all economic activities concerns the "value-added" content in the production process. Value is added from one stage of production to another stage, and the progress in the value-added chain is expressed through the price mechanism that serves as an economic information to both suppliers and consumers.

While value can be quantified using economic instruments, there are more important qualitative values in human activities. Such qualitative values can be classified into three related aspects. The visible factors are related to the "gift of nature" and include ethnical groups, gender, dress, food and environment and probably innate ability and intellectuality. The behavioral values include culture, religion, morality and ethical standards and practices. The highest level of value relates to how humans are treated and respected, and the qualities include the rule of law that provides a level playing field that all humans are equal before the law, while discrimination and victimization will be cursed and despised as they bring human suffering and disrespect to humanity.

A value scale that is composed of all the quantifiable and non-quantifiable qualities is elaborated in Figure 7.2, which is an extension of Figure 7.1. Figure 7.2 assumes that there is an equal weight to the five categories of value measures, though the weight given to each category can differ among nations. As discussed, labor value serves as the first level of the value measure, the scale rises to include market economy measures and the three qualitative measures from normative to behavioral and humanistic measures. The measure of value progresses from one level

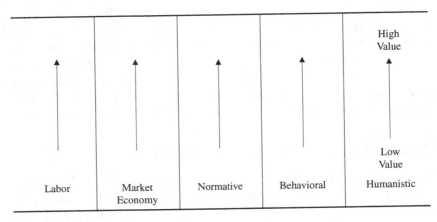

Figure 7.2   High Value and Low Value Economies

to the next and the humanistic measure forms the ultimate and comprehensive measure of value.

With these five progressive levels of value measures, a scale or an index can be constructed based on the value performance of each world economy. In Figure 7.2, two extremes are given. The economy with the High Value index should first show a decent performance in labor value, for example, in the provision of job safety against industrial hazards and non-discrimination in job provisions. Secondly, the market economy shall reflect fully the value-added content in the entire production chain, and that market players are well informed and would not be exploited or misled. The normative values are well respected in a High-Value economy, with no visible and administrative and political discrimination in gender and ethnic groups. Openness and freedom provide an alternative source of security from political elections. The high values related to the performance in the behavior category include religious pluralism, and religion becomes more a choice of individuals than the presence of a religious state. While good moral values govern the thoughts of individuals, the strong ethical standards ensure the drive to respect other individuals as well as other living life and materials. All these qualities should eventually be brought to a high standard in humanistic values of non-discrimination, absence of victimization, while the rule of law ensures equity and a level playing field.

On the contrary, a Low-Value index would show that the economy does not provide a safety net to workers, including the presence of child labor and occurrence of industrial hazards. At the same time, economic policies do not ensure a market-friendly economy, which could be dominated by the presence of corruption, cronyism and political vested interest. The lack of civic institutions allowed political leaders and officials to "rent seek" the public. The normative values are poor, including the practice of gender and class inequality, as one fraction of the population receives privileges, while another fraction of the population suffers in silence. Some of these visible and normative inequalities are backed up by the religious laws in a religious state, where some leaders use religion as a source of control. Other behavioral values would perform poorly as the practice of bias would burden both moral and ethical standards. Public or social security cannot be guaranteed as one fraction of the population is constantly in conflict with the other, and prolonged periods of violence and civil unrest had nurtured a "hate" attitude between the fractions. Political leaders lack impartial judgments and a weak governance results in economic collapse. People only looked for survival means, including the possibility and risk of fleeing the country to become refugees or illegal migrants. The humanistic values would surely not be able to perform decently. The absence of the rule of law, social distrust, unreliable institutions and disrespect of other citizens in the nation and violation of human rights occur daily in multiple dimensions. Human value is still a remote object for countries with a low-value index.

With the discussions on the two extremes of High-Value and Low-Value countries, one can piece together the performance of different global economies using these five categories of value measures. It is probable that one country performs strongly in one measure but is weak in another. The idea and intention are not only to see how strong or weak different countries perform but also how the weak areas could be improved in the "value ladder". Various indicators can empirically be used to show the performance in the five categories. The labor value category can be seen from, for example, the presence and practice of work safety codes on industrial hazards, whether child labor is disallowed and the possibility of flexible working hours. The provision of maternity days for couples with newborns is given in some countries. Babysitting facilities are provided in some modern mega corporations.

Indicators for a market economy can easily be located. The presence and proper implementation of anti-competition laws, for example, ensure market openness, freedom of business entry and against market and price manipulation. Trade and professional associations provide the code of conduct and promote good ethics and practices in trading activities. Economic forecasting reports by key financial corporations and other non-profit civic institutions produce warning of economic crises and suggest solutions should an economic recession occurs. The easiness of establishing a new business could reflect the extent of market maturity and reliability. Measures on the provision of physical and financial infrastructures that facilitate market activities can be another indicator.

Normative values can be seen from whether there is discrimination between gender, class and ethnical groups in employment, education and ownership rights. Are there civic organizations which are established to eliminate discrimination and promote openness to ensure equality in opportunity? Together with behavioral measures, one can see if there are establishments, laws and practices that favor one fraction of the population against another, such as treatment between the two genders in different religions and cults. Would some traditional cultures, religious faiths and other folklore beliefs have already formed the basis of differences, even though the differences have been taken for granted over the centuries? To search for indicators, one can see the ratio between the two genders in education attendance, especially in the developing countries. The presence of cultural diversity and religious freedom can be another indicator in measuring behavioral values. The presence and institution of civic organizations which are non-political, non-religious and non-governmental that existed to promote humanistic values can be another indicator.

Numerous indicators can be used to examine humanistic values. The independence of the rule of law, political openness and participation, freedom of speech and the impartiality of the media, together with reports on the number of social unrests and demonstrations, are good examples. However, there is still a lack of indicators to examine the few truly qualitative measures, such as respect shown on others and individual ethics practices. How and who do we judge for good ethics and moral? Such proxy indicators as provision of moral and ethical education in schools can be used but the outcomes may not easily be quantified. Some examples can be observed, such as the presence of ethical value on the priority in road usage between vehicles and pedestrians. The number of pedestrians killed in road accidents could be used as an indicator of driving ethics in road usage. In some urban cities, the signals of the traffic lights may not be respected. In others, pedestrians have the priority in crossing roads and streets. While punishment could be the short-term barrier, moral and ethical education on social disciplines would be the long-term instrument in fostering humanistic values.

Nonetheless, the conceptual discussion on the measurement of values does clarify how economic relationships are extended or implanted in other social and psychological issues. It would be proper to argue that it is not the economics that determine the social, psychological and political outcomes, but rather these outcomes are often expressed in economic terms. Economic activities serve as the vehicle or conduit through which social, psychological and political activities are to be realized and materialized, though often the economic outcomes have been used as a scapegoat when problems originated in the social, psychological and political circles.

V Clogs in Human Values Progression

Like the discussion in economic development, why are economies endowed with rich resources generally poorer, and why do economies short of natural resources tend to be industrially and technologically stronger? It all depends on how the resources are deployed and it is often the productivity of the resources that counts. It follows that the deployment of resources depends on the intention and direction of policies (whether they are "demand-side" welfare oriented or "supply-side" growth oriented) and the kind of institutions that decide and implement the policies. And policy decisions often rest with the ingenuity, broadmindedness, selflessness, knowledge and wisdom of the leaders and their associates.

Having a high human value is a "common good", in that people would treasure the highest possible value the society can achieve, but its success equally depends on the participation of all citizens in the society. As such, there is the possibility of externality, free riding, rent seeking and abuse. Human values do ultimately benefit the humans, but progress in arriving at a higher value could also be contained and thwarted by humans. There are thus "clogs" that would prevent or delay the society from securing and reaching a higher position in the "value ladder". Clogs could appear in various forms and can be found within the sphere of human behavior. Natural disasters often result in human loss and destruction, while there are also geographical limitations. But there are manmade situations that are the result of wrong decisions, ineffective policies and poor leadership. The knowledge in advancing the achievement of value could equally be lacking. Human ignorance and the slow pace of scientific advancement would thwart progress in creating, applying and treasuring values.

Consider the following two examples in understanding human values. When a natural disaster, such as a devastating earthquake, strikes a certain country, through the efficient global media reports, international institutions and countries particularly those experienced with earthquakes would come to rescue and support the earthquake-affected country with the intention to avoid human loss and sufferings, especially in the first 48 hours. International agencies and governments would airlift necessary medical and mechanical supplies, followed by individuals and organizations mobilized with the intention to raise charity funds to aid the earthquake victims. All the existing technology in earthquake rescues and all the medical equipment and materials needed to save lives are immediately sent to the earthquake-affected zone. Together with an effective local government, the rescue process would be conducted in high spirit, showing the relevance and importance of human values.

On the contrary, a country would have been ripped by such "manmade" factors as civil war and unrest, territorial disputes and battles between different ethnical fractions. The corrupt political leaders engaged in rent-seeking activities, resulting in weak governance and an ineffective government, but the leaders remained in power and refused to hold elections or step down. The local citizens suffered as the economy plummeted. Riots broke out and citizens clashed with the "law enforcement" bodies, followed by outbreak of violence, deaths and injuries, and a prolonged period of instability. Nationals attempted to flee to nearby countries as illegal immigrants, thereby creating social cost to the host country.

The situation could be reversed if leaders chose to lead and adopt effective policies to reduce hardship and improve overall economic performance. Instead of allowing corruption to root in the government, the alternative would be to institute an anti-corruption agency, and at the same time choose a body of able and delegated people to join the government to draft effective policies and produce fruitful results. Unlike a business leader whose goal would be the size of the earnings and profits, the goal of a political leader should be the well-being of the citizens, not the amount of monetary gains so obtained. A high attainment of human value can be achieved if a political leader becomes selfless and introduces policies that promote the overall well-being of the citizens.

The difference in these two examples shows that human value could be kept high in times of natural disasters but could also be reduced by artificial manmade barriers. It would be fair to argue that the attainment of an elevated level of human value is mostly restricted by humans. Other than the "gift of nature" and geographical features, clogs in the advancement of human values can easily be grouped into historical, cultural and institutional factors. Historical factors would include the result or the aftermath of unfortunate historical events, such as clashes between different ethnical groups, territorial disputes and ethnic annihilation, civil unrest and military wars. The unfortunate event occurs when one group of people takes advantage and imposes hardship on another group, and the suffering becomes a source of unhappiness, disharmony and revenge. Where there were lessons to learn in all unfortunate events, it would take generations before historical wounds could be healed and a new beginning could start and that the conflicting groups could move forward and make a positive move in their lives.

Human conflicts are often "zero-sum" games, as one group of humans take advantage of another group, and the gain of one group is achieved totally at the expense of another group. As history cannot be unfolded and the historical process cannot be reversed, the one possibility to reduce or remove the suffering of the losing group would be to institute and deploy equal economic opportunities for all to gain. Economic openness and the provision of opportunities can serve as a better alternative to provision of compensations. Thus, removing human conflicts through peaceful means can turn a "zero-sum" game into a "positive-sum" game as harmony could exist as different human groups would be working on their economic fronts.

Cultural activities do help to preserve various human norms and morals, but some cultural activities could also impose rigidity and restriction in promoting human values. As cultural activities are often "manmade" or practices descend from previous generations, few would question the validity of many cultural activities, which could be discriminatory and discourage people from thinking "outside of the box". In extreme cases, human values were demoted due to discrimination between genders, education and material deprivation due to class origin and physical punishment from the requirement of different cults. Indeed, the performance of many cultural activities was intended for the purpose of certain consumptions. Some cultural norms do at times serve as a "save face" mechanism in unpleasant moments in human behavior. Cultural activities, norms and practices could serve as a "double-edged" sword, depending on which culture one is referring to and how the culture is received. Some cultures do convey and practice acceptable moral and ethics standards, sounding out disciplines for citizens to follow and preserving such social units as families and business entities. However, activities in other worldly cultures tend to be restrictive and divisive, while privileges and discrimination are practiced.

If culture is not meant to be an instrument in restricting human progress, culture should not be conducted as a static activity in societies, but a dynamic process of modernization is needed to align culture in the contemporary society with the aim to improve human values so that individuals' welfare could be enhanced. Cultural leaders should turn culture into "manmade" virtues, where moral and ethics are mixed with respect, dignity, trust and honesty. The strategy is to remove culture as an instrument of political control but instead deploy culture as an instrument for societal harmony, progress and mutual coexistence on equal grounds.

Other than the police, the military and other uniform personnel, civic institutions in general are established with the aim to improve the civic aspects of human life. Such non-political institutions as the consumer council, the law society and accountancy associations are meant to provide civic guidelines and protections to professionals as well as those in need of professional services. However, politically oriented institutions, including the government, may have their own agenda if they were intended to serve different interest groups. Politics is a game with absolute, "zero-sum" outcome and usually is divisive in nature. Usually, what one political institution advocates would be for the benefit of its supporters and may not benefit other interest groups. The situation could be worse if different political institutions advocate for polarized views.

It would be difficult to assess how different political leaders and political institutions could do damage or promote the process and progress in achieving higher human values. A major feature in political election is its *ex-ante* nature, meaning that the process of selection and voting takes place prior to the work of the elected leader, but *ex-post* there is no guarantee that the elected politicians would do a *bona fide* job. In some countries, the process of political election is not that open and transparent, and faults could result in abuse. It is difficult to govern the political ethics of leaders. Whether the elected politicians aim to serve the country or rent seek the office as an instrument to amass wealth is a risk that voters would have to take. But it would be too late to make changes in case the elected leaders misbehave, because the damage done would be difficult to measure and corrections or unwinding of policies could be costly.

Careless political acts and decisions could hurt the society, the economy and delay the progress in achieving a higher human value. The piling up of national debts, for example, could reduce the chances of the future generation. The policy of raising the minimum wage would hurt economic competitiveness. The larger the welfare pool, the greater the amount of tax and the greater the need for more government administrators and consequently a larger government spending would be needed, as this process could become "self-fulfilling". Morality and ethical standards differ among political leaders, among political institutions and among nations.

A business leader usually decides on the business policy and strategy, and the business leaders will have to face the business consequences as to whether the business was successful or otherwise. Loss would appear should the business perform poorly, and the business leader will suffer. The same is not true in politics. A political leader decides on a certain policy, but the ultimate performance of the policy may not affect the position of the leader, as the leader would still receive his salary. Indeed, the political leader effectively would not need to be responsible for the result of the policy decisions. It may take a long time for the policy results to be materialized, and the political leader would have left the office by then. If the policy turns out to generate positive results, the leader would take the credit. If the policy turns out to generate negative results, the leader would not need to pay for any policy compensations to the voters. The country just suffers, and every citizen would have to shoulder the burden left over from the deficient performance of the policy. This naturally would impose damages to human values. It is exactly because political leaders would have this "advantage" over business leaders that careless, unintelligent and biased political leaders could get away with their deficient performances.

Human value is a "common good", like the cleanliness of a public park. People enjoy the beauty and tranquility of the public park, but if someone dumps garbage into the public park, the overall quality of the park would be affected. A problem with "common good" is its difficulty to monitor and police, as destructive acts could not be caught. Similarly, the improvement of human value rests with all individual citizens, but it is difficult to monitor the polluters and destroyers of human value because the treatment and interpretation of human value varies among individuals. The impact of "clogs" in the improvement in human values may not be tangible, visible or quantifiable. For example, in some professions, foreign experience would not be considered for a local job. It would have to depend on the ethics of the recruiter in exercising equal employment opportunity. A graduate from an "ivy league" university could have received more attention than other graduates in job applications. As such, how could one monitor equality in job opportunity? It will only be the drive to produce more graduates that would dilute employers' view of university graduates. The same is true regarding admission to some primary schools, as parents could be influenced by their peers and social media. The institution of a broad-based system is needed to promote and adhere to equality of opportunity, as well as the appreciation and respect of human values.

In many ways, the establishment, practice, nurture and dissemination of human values boil down to ethical and moral behavior of the individuals. The execution and implementation of human values and virtues often appear as "spillover" when the virtues and values practiced by one individual have an "externality" impact on another individual. For example, when one household did a respectable job in tidying up the garbage disposal, the good practice would spillover to its neighbors. The "micro behavior" in the performance of human values would have a multiplier effect, and its spread to the rest of the neighborhood could raise the standard of human values eventually. Of course, there could be a "negative externality" as the acts of some individuals would delay or thwart human values from prospering, growing and disseminating. In aggregate and on balance, it is hoped that the impact of "positive externality" exceeds that of the "negative externality" in the society and in the global community. While "positive externality" should be encouraged, there should be means through which "negative externality" could be stopped. For example, the various formal channels of communication and contact could include a clear message of law and order, moral and ethics education in schools at an early age and the rules and standards upheld by civic institutions, while the informal channels should include personal disciplines taught within family circles and the amount of positive information and knowledge one can obtain through the unbiased nature of the media.

VI Role of Economics in Human Science

Given the discussion on the complexity in the nurture and promotion of human values, it would be appropriate to ask which individual person, institution or system could help maximize the pace in the progress of human values. The promotion of human values is a cumulative process, and the behavior of every individual adds to form a bigger picture. Historically, prominent philosophers and religious establishments have served as moral leaders in nurturing human virtues. The norms and belief so developed have often been taken for granted in our daily activities. The presence of a fair and functional system has become the more reliable vehicle through which human values and virtues can be promoted and protected. The advantage in the establishment of a system is that it constitutes a set of rules and practices that are likely to be established cumulatively through time, rather than by any single leader or political party. In a well-defined system, it allows improvements through practices and the gains will be shared and implemented. A system itself should provide a "level playing field" so that privileges are eliminated while opportunities are kept open. Thus, respectable human values can be instituted in a system.

An effective and functional system must fulfil several criteria. A system must be fair, open and adhere to non-discrimination, and no single individual or party can manipulate to arrive at certain outcomes. A system must be consistent and can be tested against time. The system must allow access to all participants, and information and knowledge shall be made available to all participants, and no participant can be privileged as all participants have equal rights in the system. While an individual will not last forever and leaders may change within an institution, a system is "timeless" as new participants are included while the accumulated values can be expanded and shared. A respectable system should function on its own like a "self-propelled" engine.

The market economic system shall serve as a "timeless" vehicle through which human values can be accumulated in achieving a higher standard in the value ladder. The free market shall be open to all, and participants can achieve their gains and rewards according to their own endowments and risks. The market economic system preserves the rights of all individuals and respects their legal transactions. Economic freedom allows participants to have a free entry or exit from any markets, and the market information shall be freely available for participants to make their economic decisions. Through economic activities, individuals can fully interact with each other in a peaceful and fruitful manner. Furthermore, economic activities are not operating in a vacuum, but are supported and protected by a host of institutions, typically the rule of law and the ethical practices exercised in various professional institutions and organizations.

The market economic system therefore produces a "civic" system that allows all individuals to participate freely and in a manner protected by numerous professional practices and ethics that shall transcend the influence and power of any single individual or organization. It is the civic system that provides trust and protection to all individuals, and it is the civic system that stands between the people and their leaders. As such, individuals with difficulty could rest assured that they are taken care of by the professional institutions within the civic system and do not necessarily need to turn to seek aid from political leaders. The civic system provides the most reliable form of civic protection. Human values and virtues can then flourish unhindered in the civic system.

Even though there are unquantifiable values in the form of norms, culture and humanistic behavior, they are indirectly incorporated into the economic system in the form of product supplies, work habits and employment patterns and property rights practices, as well as through other economic transactions. For example, tailor-made products are produced and consumed in religious and cultural events, while days off over the weekend are originally structured for religious reasons. In other words, various kinds of human values can be expressed through economic arrangements, activities and transactions. Cultural norms and practices, human sentiments and behavior can be conducted through economic instruments. Economics becomes the common denominator in the expression of human values. That said, there is also a need at the micro level for an individual to make sound judgment, exercise self-control and discipline in conducting economic affairs. The use of credit cards is a good example. While the credit card holder can do shopping conveniently and payment will have to be made at a later day, but if the card holder formed a poor judgment and lacked self-control in spending, the convenience would easily result in overspending and the accumulation of personal debt when payment could not be made at the appropriate time. Self-control, discipline, frugality and the art of making ends meet are crucial human values in personal financial decisions.

As the vehicle in the exercise of human values, economics is fluid and dynamic in that economic activities can change according to the kind and level of human activities and behavior. The ups and downs of a business cycle reflect the different movements among economic participants. If economic activities are biased or lean toward certain directions, there would be other activities and economic decisions that counteract the existing trend, and activities and transactions could provide a new balance and create new opportunities. The free market economic system shows the succession of "activity waves" with dynamism and mobility. Individuals who can take up their distinct roles in the community can engage in the economic activities of their own choice, based on their endowment, ability, behavior and adherence to values. Economic freedom allows alternatives to be available and individuals can make their own economic choice without the fear of coercion. In making their choices and choosing their alternatives, different human values would be incorporated into their decisions. In short, the existence of a market economy enables values to become quantifiable through economic decisions, and calculations become explicit and transparent, thereby reflecting different proportionalities and allowing openness and equality in participation.

VII Conclusion

Values in the contemporary world go beyond financial terms and ideological implications. A new conceptual understanding of the "value" idea is needed. It may have to consider non-monetary aspects, such as ethics, humanity and civic development. In countries with strong ethics, for example, vehicles stop when pedestrians are crossing. In countries with weak ethics, vehicles compete with pedestrians in using the road space. The difference rests in the understanding of "values". Conceptually, values should not only be measured in pecuniary terms but also measured through the presence of humanity, including ethics, responsibility, respect and equality.

The discussion on the "scale of value" identifies five ingredients in the value ladder, ranging from the simplistic discussion on the labor value to the more complete set of economic transactions in the form of inputs and outputs. The three non-quantifiable ingredients start with the normative issues which are often visible, but the discussion is extended to the behavioral aspects where "manmade" practices are exercised on a regular basis, and finally to the humanistic values when the treatment and interaction with other individuals are considered. Examples are given in the text to illustrate how human values have been conducted. Such discussion effectively provides an integration between economic and social dimensions in human science.

The ingredients in value would ultimately include the features of measurability, ethics, morality, equality in opportunity and acceptance of humanity. Norms and behavior are often artificial which are practiced and passed on from one generation to another. The concept of openness and equality and the virtue of the rule of law in ensuring mutual respect and equality under the law are crucial behavioral contributions for human values to prosper. Economics has been placed as the "medium of exchange" in human sciences, as it serves as a vehicle through which all kinds of human values can be conducted, calculated and are reflected through economic activities, decisions and transactions. The market economy provides the channel where opportunities are created, and chances are provided to all participants. The economic system transcends other non-economic systems that could be exploited by leaders for their own interests. In other words, thinking of giving others a chance and creating opportunity through economic transaction versus the leaders' ambition to look for instruments to control others shall present vast differences in promoting and nurturing human values. Economics is not a religion, but it provides a set of instruments that allow participants to preserve, nurture, promote and achieve a higher position in the ladder of human values.

Chapter Eight

Endowment and Opportunity: The Origin of Economic Differences

I Introduction

Economic activities are directly related to other social disciplines. As it has been pointed out in previous chapters, economics is a passive discipline and economic resources cannot be mobilized without decisions made by humans. On the contrary, other social sciences do not have their physical form, and they need a vehicle through which their desires can be materialized. Economic variables have become a convenient instrument used to achieve other social goals. By contrast to the discussions shown in the previous chapters, this chapter focuses on the "intensive" nature of the conceptual discussion by examining the depth in the differences between economics and other social sciences. Instead of examining the "outcome end" of an economic activity, the focus goes deeper by looking at the "input end" of an economic activity, which shall give fresh insights into the relationship between economics and other social disciplines.

There is only one human race, but with two biological genders and several ethnicities. Historical origins and developments in the living environment in different corners of the world have led to diversity in languages, cultures, customs, spiritual pursuits and beliefs. Diversity itself suggests a sense of difference, but it is up to humans how to deal with these differences. Should human differences be dealt with harmoniously or dichotomously? Should we accept and embrace differences to reach compromise and harmony, or should we use differences as instruments to divide and generate conflicts? Historically, there were leaders who united people and countries; parallelly, there have been leaders who exercised extreme coercion to take control to the extent of annihilating other ethnic groups. The existence of differences is inevitable, but what matters is the way people deal with these differences. Should differences be incorporated into a common good or used as a channel to create divisiveness? Normally, a common good is all-embracing such that people everywhere would benefit, though the extent of the benefit could differ among the recipients. On the contrary, divisiveness is dichotomous, and as people are divided into different categories based on different criteria, division could result in conflicts, disagreements, and ultimately war and violence. While the end results may not be desirable, it is often the process that one must watch out for because one may not know the intention of the instigators. Would their intention be a pure personal ambition, a desire to make gains due to the presence of a vested interest, or a drive to protect cronies and promote patronage? On the contrary, would a broadminded and selfless leader prefers to work for the good of the people to attain a higher level of development and civilization? In short, how to deal with differences is an art, requires skill, knowledge and patience, could be highly political, manipulative and humanly damaging, or result in the emergence of charismatic heroes.

Virtually all economics analyses and studies have focused on the outcome side of economic activities. Beginning from data on income, trade, investment, consumption, production and government spending, all the analyses employing these data are *ex-post,* in the sense that they are the results of numerous economic activities conducted by individuals, firms and business entities, public institutions and government official activities. It shows a "spaghetti bowl" effect as the results of all economic activities are mixed together. In the difference between nominal and real GDP, for example, there can be a distinction between nominal performance due to inflation and price change and the real performance due to actual growth. There are studies that have attempted to isolate the effect on growth by certain activities. The impact of financial market activities, for example, on the real economy could be studied, but the resulting findings cannot be exact, as there could be a secondary effect, as other factors could have contributed to the growth. The idea behind the "spaghetti bowl" concept is that identifying which flavor comes from which food ingredient is difficult.

Likewise, in economic growth, how much output and income were contributed by a certain economic activity may not be identified easily. There could be chain effects and reactions, as demonstrated by the theory of the "income multiplier" (IM), in that, one activity could lead to another, such as increase in investment will always result in more jobs. On the contrary, one activity could have thwarted another activity. The theory of the "crowding out effect", for example, argues that government activities and investment could "crowd out" similar activities from the private sector. Government investment in an airline, for example, would mean the same investment would not occur from the private sector. Another example is that when the government dishes out welfare, retail shops may certainly not reduce their price, rather they may even increase their price, knowing that welfare recipients received financial subsidies.

There are overwhelming cases and studies that have concentrated on the outcome side of all economic activities. What is the level and growth of GDP per capita and the level and rate of unemployment? Why is wage rising in one type of employment and falling in another? Why are people faced with different earning abilities and how much welfare should be given to the low-income earners? Why do investors get profit earnings and workers receive wage earnings? Why are celebrities paid much higher than other professions? Why does one product, one shop or one restaurant perform much better than another product, shop or restaurant? Why is one country more competitive than another? Why are some "resource-rich" countries are poor but other "resource-poor" countries are rich? Why would such social problems as a single-parent family, drug abuse, drunk driving, domestic violence and run-down neighborhoods produce unfavorable economic and social consequences? Why is government intervention not an answer, but could even create more problems with a larger bureaucracy?

One can easily pose numerous questions on human economic activities, and there may not be satisfactory answers because the available answers would only focus on the outcome end of the economic and social activities and problems. The solution, on the contrary, would require analyses on the input end of an activity. An individual's ability to earn, a firm's profitability and an economy's competitiveness are due more to the input end of activities. In a person's ability to earn, the relevant input end questions are whether the individual was skillful, educated, healthy and disciplined. In the firm's ability to gain profit, the questions would be the "value-added" content generated in the production process. In an economy's competitiveness, the concern should be the economy's resource availability and productivity, relevance of the government policy and how enterprising the population is in nurturing business.

In other words, the missing link in the intellectual pursuit in the understanding of economics is the need to analyze the issues in the input end of the economic equation. But then, that is easier said than done, because there are so many types of inputs, and the inputs may neither be related nor connected with each other. How possibly could the analysis on all economic and material inputs be scientifically studied, generalized and conceptualized into something intellectually understandable and applicable? In the English dictionary, the term endowment refers to "the action of endowing something or someone" in the form of "an income or form of property given or bequeathed to someone" or "a quality or ability possessed or inherited by someone". The term endowment does convey a sense of acquisition with the desire to own, accumulate and save something, both materially and immaterially, so that such acquisition could be deployed for benefits or as a source of security in the future. In other words, a person must have a certain endowment before doing anything.

Endowment can be an intellectual term used to indicate the input end of economic activities. Indeed, endowment can have an aggregate meaning that incorporates numerous input factors, such as the entire availability of natural resources, amount of qualitative human capital, market-friendliness policies and technology advancement. It can equally refer to individual possession of endowments, such as the kind of formal qualifications achieved, wealth inherited, suitability of economic environment, job opportunities, physical and mental health, innate ability, social encounters and family conditions. The analysis then is how an individual, a corporation, an institution or a government acquires an endowment which could be deployed to produce results eventually. The content, size, richness and relevance of the endowment could indicate the quality of the endowment, upon which outcomes and results could then be generated.

Endowment has not been studied as a topic, though the earlier study on factor endowment concentrated on the price a factor can fetch in the market (Rybczynski, 1955; Solow, 1974). In more recent studies on behavioral economics, the discussion on the "endowment effect" argued that if players were given an endowment in the first instance, what happens to the economic behavior of the player would form intellectual contributions to behavioral economics because it examines the psychological effect in an economic experiment (Davidson, 1979; Levy, 1992; Knetsch, 2001; Carmichael and Macleod, 2006; Bischoff and Meckl, 2008; Morewedge and Giblin, 2015). The idea is that if players are provided with different levels of endowments, their economic behavior would be different in the experiment, so also the eventual outcome. In many ways, it is like the game of monopoly where players are given "seed money", and as the game proceeds, individual players can acquire assets and the game ends when one player has acquired all the endowments and assets of the other players.

Instead of relating to the discussion on the "endowment effect" which was assumed in behavioral and experimental economics, it would be fundamental to examine the endowments possessed or acquired by individuals singly or by societies in aggregate. This is essential as differences in economic inputs would generate differences in economic outputs. This is surely the "missing link" in understanding economic relationships and how the outcomes would or could have misled decision makers and politicians. Indeed, when a politician was complaining about income inequality and poverty, what the politician failed to understand was the fact that economic outcomes are different because economic endowments among individuals and societies are different. The root of "inequality" should actually be traced back to the original difference in individuals' endowments. Thus, it would be more fruitful to concentrate on improving the endowments of individuals and societies, rather than politicizing "inequality", knowing that inequality could not be solved without improving the input end of the economic equality, namely the level and quality of endowments.

II Economic Endowment

In microeconomic analysis on firms and production, the inputs refer to physical materials, labor and investment capital, and the output refers to products to be sold in the market. In the process, service inputs are also required, such as banking and financial arrangements, shipping and transportation, retail and marketing and numerous administrative tasks. Endowments therefore go beyond simply the measurable discrete inputs required for production.

Endowment is an all-embracing term that includes numerous physical and mental, quantifiable and non-quantifiable, visible and non-visible, tangible and intangible attributes that individuals, entities and economies have acquired, and these acquired attributes function as "resources" to enrich the economic survivability of individuals, entities and economies so that they can compete, take part, make progress and pursue development within their own sphere of activities. Endowments can be discussed at three different levels: individual, entities and economies. The intuition and the functionality of the attributes would be similar at all three levels, but the actuality of the endowment would appear differently, giving a sense of diversity and variation.

At the individual level, the first attribute is the physical person at birth. As the child grows, the person's endowments develop as attributes start to accumulate. The child's health, innate ability and intelligence, experience in the family, and ability to digest and absorb formal education would be the attributes that contribute to the child's endowments probably up to his or her maturity. The chance of receiving higher education or learning a vocational skill could be the critical step every young individual faces, and the outcome could crucially add to and determine the person's endowments, because the person's formal education and training eventually define the career path or professional life of the individual. As the person enters adult age and completes formal education and training, the next step is to enter the employment stage when the person can exercise his or her attributes to maximize potential.

To the individual, the personal endowments would include the individual's formal qualification and professional knowledge, but there are other "growing up" factors which may affect the individual's cumulative endowments either positively or negatively, including physical and mental health, personal characteristics and interests, and peer group pressures, which can exert independent impact on endowment quality. Family background in a person's "growing up" process would expose the individual to both favorable and unfavorable influences in regards to his or her endowments. Wealthy and highly educated parents, for example, would in principle provide good guidance to the learning life of their children. Cultural, religious and customary factors could impose additional conditions on the individual's endowment. For example, a girl who grows up in a religious state that suppresses the educational opportunities of the female population would end up with lower endowments as she would not have attained too many attributes. In a class society, a brilliant student from a lower-class family might be robbed of the chance to receive higher education, thereby limiting significantly the student's endowments.

A person's innate ability can certainly help in building up one's endowments. People with special skills and talents could expose their endowments in an early period if their skills and talents were discovered. Celebrities are people with either talent or special skills, though they could also be trained, polished and catered to different celebrity professions. In short, both the formal qualifications and the macro-environment in which the person was brought up would constitute the person's whole endowments acquired through hard work and influences of other people as well as the environment. Typically, the positive factors that determine a person's endowments should include the chance to be educated, favorable family conditions and such positive characteristics as hard work, enterprising spirit and creative personality. On the contrary, negative factors include poor health, bad company of peers, unfavorable habits such as drinking and gambling, laziness and being unintelligent, as well as having an unhelpful or unsupportive family.

One thing worth noting is that there is no standard formula that promotes a person's acquisition of endowments. As such, every person has different levels of endowments because attributes attained differ among individuals. In a class of students, some students attain better academic results than others, and the education system that cherishes the brighter students may not provide suitable additional help to the weaker students. In the academic ladder, some young students receive higher education, while others do not, thus their future career paths would surely differ. The training and demand for human capital differs among professions. Economic dynamism would require different professions and job skills in different periods, and skilled professionals would always be in much demand. Differences in family background produce young individuals with different exposures, resulting in a difference in the attainment of endowments and personal attributes. The health of every young individual, including their physical ability and unsound habits such as smoking, gambling and drinking, could impact the individual's endowments independently. The endowments of all individuals are different from those of others, some would have acquired stronger endowments, while others do not manage to attain enough endowments. Naturally, individuals with stronger endowments would do better, while those with weaker endowments could face survival problems. In other words, there are only differences and no equality in the attainment of endowments by individuals.

Entities also need to enrich their endowments frequently and regularly, or else they could equally be eroded by competitors. Entities can be a business enterprise, a public institution or a government bureaucracy. A business enterprise can range from an entrepreneurial firm to a large corporate listed in the stock exchange. Firstly, entities exist because they have a cause to serve and the need to survive, either in the production of goods and services in businesses or serving the public in various professions or administering official duties in government departments. With their goals and targets in mind, entities must establish and formulate an endowment that would enable them to achieve their goals and targets. In a business entity, production inputs of materials and human labor including management are essential components. There are other non-physical endowments in a business entity. The knowledge and experience of the business owner or management shall be the soul of the business entity. Productivity-enhancing policies within the business enterprise would promote employee satisfaction considerably. The extent of value added in the production is important as it would reflect on the technology deployed in the production. The marketability of the goods and services can be another endowment because goods and services face different market sizes and dynamics. Market-friendly policies could help production considerably. Similarly, the easiness in obtaining financial support should provide a sense of security and confidence in the business enterprise. Collectively, these attributes shall form the endowment the enterprise possesses.

On the contrary, there are also negative forces which diminish the endowment's effectiveness in a business entity. The various political demands imposed by political parties and pressure groups could work against business and economic calculations, especially demands that resulted in higher cost and dampened productivity. In entrepreneurial sectors, unfriendly government policies in the form of high tax and ineffective bureaucracy would restrict the business entity's endowments considerably, making them less competitive and hard-pressed to survive. In the world of technology, rapid changes in technology would shorten the "product life cycle", thereby making the business less sustainable. Other negative factors included limitation on the inputs of materials in the production process, for example, due to the need for environmental protection.

The endowment of a professional or non-profit-making entity arises from the need to contribute to the society. Non-profit-making entities include social enterprises, religious organizations, non-governmental organizations (NGOs), neighborhood organizations and many others. The services provided to the public would be the greatest contribution of a professional entity, while many non-profit-making entities serve different public interests or groups of people. Professional entities often specify their operational rules, including the ethical standards that members must follow and adopt. Many professional entities charge membership fees, while non-profit-making entities look for donations. Financial soundness is another endowment which institutions must consider. By the same token, high membership fees and restricted membership to professional institutions may not be considered favorable by the public. Some professions operated through entrance examinations which would be costly, with memberships being restricted.

In some non-profit-making institutions, various conditions could be imposed on members. Examples include either the compulsion to donate or seek assistance in market promotion by getting new members for the institution to expand and survive. Indeed, some conditions "imposed" on members by the so-called non-profit-making entities may not be that ethical, and the financial contributions collected through donations may not be totally accountable to the government, leading to potential misuse and abuse of funds within the entities themselves. There could be possibilities in the lack of non-financial accountability, and unethical cover-up could lead to mismanagement that, when disclosed, could destroy the civic trustworthiness of the non-profit-making institutions, especially when huge funds collected through donations are squandered by the managing agents. Examples of financial embezzlement, violations of ethical standards and mismanagement could indeed be found in some non-profit-making institutions and entities.

Governments exist in all modern economies, but not all governments are successful because governments are also faced with their own endowments. The richness and appropriateness of the endowments held by governments determine how a government is performing. The first and foremost in any government's endowment is its leadership. Either through a democratic political process or otherwise, the leadership reflects the performance in various policy directions, pace of development, degree of social consent and content, and the extent of public and international acceptance. A devoted and selfless leader who has worked for the common good of the economy and society would provide a sound endowment background for the country to progress. Along with the effective leadership, the efficient functioning of government bureaus and departments, which conduct policies fairly and efficiently, would serve as a showcase to other civic institutions.

Included in the economic endowments of a government is the adoption and practice of market-friendly economic policies to encourage investments, promote jobs and enhance economic growth. Wealth creation through investments and the enterprising attitude of the individuals shall be promoted as individuals shall then rely less on the government, who could then concentrate their efforts on promoting and enriching social capital, such as infrastructure development, education and technology advancement, and social harmony can be reached when individuals and households are occupied and contended with their jobs and businesses. In other words, governments exist to ensure the provision and enlargement of economic chances and job opportunities for people to grab, as that shall in turn empower the earning ability of all individuals and households.

On the contrary, the government shall experience a depletion of its endowments when many of the aforementioned factors appear at the opposite end. For example, the leader is self-centered and focused on promoting vested interests surrounded by cronies who practice patronage. As such, the adopted policies shall be biased or distorted as they are meant to serve only a specific group of people. An ineffective leader would probably be assisted by a huge but ineffective government bureaucracy, and red tape would emerge to delay policy performance. Instead of promoting societal harmony, the government may weaken its governance by pursuing fractional divisions and social fragmentation could lead to politicking among divisions, resulting in the polarization of social and economic issues. A lack of economic responsibility and financial accountability would result in mounting debts and overspending, leaving the debt burden to the future generation. Any of these negative factors would serve to deplete the endowments of a government.

At the economy-wide level, the endowments of an economy may go beyond simply material calculation, to include other invisible and intangible factors. Although the quantity and quality of the basic production factors shall form the primary endowments of an economy, other secondary endowments include the presence of reliable and appropriate infrastructure provisions, the trustworthiness of its government and adoption of competitive economic policies for businesses and professionals to progress and prosper. A low-debt economy is always seen to be more favorable, in addition to a high degree of individual freedom and openness to allow freedom of movement of capital and people. Armed with the rule of law, an economy that accepts and respects diversity shall adhere to the practice of a level-playing field such that all individuals are endowed with equality in opportunity and all forms of discrimination are eradicated. Lastly, the extent of entrepreneurial or enterprising attitude held by people can be considered as another important endowment, as the ingenuity, innovative and creative attitude shall mean that people are prepared to stand on their own feet and face difficulties rather than seeking assistance and complaining and expressing their disgruntlement without considering the wider picture and the economic cost involved.

The opposite end would be the factors that deplete an economy's endowments. These depleting factors include the presence of instability resulting from bitter fragmentations among groups of people. Inefficient and uncompetitive economic policies could lead to wastage of resources and even a rising level of national debt. A corrupt government and its administration surely would weaken the economy's endowments, as corruption would lead to unfairness, distortion and promoting the dark side of humanity. The economy may experience a lack of individual freedom and openness, and a weak infrastructure would restrict growth and development. The absence of reliable civic institutions could lead to an abuse of the rule of law and the presence of double standards would mean some groups of people will be privileged and above the law.

Table 8.1 presents a summary of factors which either enhance or deplete the endowments of individuals, businesses, institutions, governments and economies. One can note that many endowment factors are intangible but could be the result of various behavioral practices. Some worldly philosophies preach family values, individual hard work and self-reliance. Some religions promote respect and mutual acceptance among humanity. Various social science disciplines teach students to become educated and seek economic independence and there are social, political and economic ethics that promote peace and harmony. However, the world is not perfect; there are others who adopt bad behavior, the wrong set of personal attitudes and inappropriate characteristics for self-aggrandizement rather than serving others.

Nonetheless, Table 8.1 does provide a "recipe" for individuals, entities, governments and economies to improve their endowments if they would want to make progress within their own areas of operation. That said, the dynamic world shows tremendous differences among individuals, businesses, institutions, governments and economies. It is the difference in their endowments and the different performance of their endowments that result in the notable differences in outcomes. The endowments indeed serve as the *ex-ante* factors, which have often been

Table 8.1   The Factors Impacting Endowments

	Enhancing factors	Depleting factors
Individual	Formal education and training Innate abilities Talents and special skills Family heritage Enterprising personal character	Poor health Bad habits Weak personal character Restrictive culture, religious and customary practices

Business	Material inputs and human capital
	Knowledge and experience
	Productivity-enhancing policies
	Value added and technology
	Market size
	Favorable government policy
	Reliable financial support
		Imposed political demands (minimum
		    wage, unionization)
		Lack of market friendliness (high tax,
		    inefficient bureaucracy)
		Unsustainable products and markets
		Constrain on production inputs

Institution	Serving public interest Rule of law Professional ethics Financial soundness	Membership fee Restricted entry Lacking accountability Mismanagement
Government	Effective, functional bureaucracy Market-friendly, sound policies Appropriate institutional support Opportunities promotion Vibrant and enterprising population Devoted, selfless leadership Social harmony Economic wealth and social asset	Red tape, ineffective bureaucracy Self-centered leadership Promote cronyism and vested interest Social fragmentation, politicking Economic burdening Lacking accountability Financial irresponsibility

Economy	Quantity and quality of production
	    factors (land, capital and labor)
	Reliable infrastructure
	Trustworthy government
	Competitive policies
	Low national debt
	Openness and freedom of
	    movement
	Presence of a level playing field
	Accept and respect diversity
	Adhere to "rule of law"
	Enterprising and entrepreneurial
	    attitude
		Instability and bitter fragmentation
		Inefficient use of resources
		Corruption, double standards
		Uncompetitive economic policies
		Unreliable infrastructure and services
		High and rising national debt
		Dictatorship and "rule of man"
		Lacking freedom and openness
		Unreliable institutions

overlooked in analyses, while the worldly differences are the *ex-post* results that occupy and attract much of the contemporary analyses. As such, complaints on the different resulting outcomes have often been made by social activists and politicians without trying to understand the origins of the differences. Of course, it is easier to use the resulting differences in such popular arguments as income inequality or discrimination because the resulting differences are often measurable, quantifiable and visible, while the original endowments are not. It follows that arguments based on the resulting differences could dichotomously be used repeatedly but would not lead to any effective solution, because the problem is always vested on the *ex-ante* input end of the resource deployment process. As such, complaints on the *ex-post* outcome end of the process will obviously be in vain unless and until corrections are made at the input side of the equation.

III Economic Opportunity

Economic endowments cannot function on their own and need a vehicle or conduit through which results can be produced, materialized and realized. Economic endowments can only be made useful when there is the emergence of economic opportunities which are created through various economic channels, typically through investment, production and demand. The desire to demand would provide signals to producers, who would then gather enough funds for investment. Investment activities typically deploy funds and human labor is required in production. Economic opportunities are then created invisibly but materially through the process of investment, the process of production and the process of market demand.

As economic opportunities are typically invisible and intangible, they have hardly been analyzed. Nonetheless, it is the presence of economic opportunities that allows economic endowments to flourish and become useful for production purposes. Indeed, differences in economic endowments would generate different economic opportunities. Li (2014) pioneered the idea of economic opportunity and pointed out that economic opportunity indicates "the degree of effectiveness between *ex-ante* economic situation, where production factors are available, and an *ex-post* economic situation, where opportunity outcomes are generated". He defined economic opportunity as the "process or channel through which economic possibilities and chances are created from the extensive and intensive applications of production factors". The argument is that as a latent variable, economic opportunity can serve as an "internality" in promoting growth and development.

Economic opportunities exhibit several features or characteristics as they are invisible, intangible, non-quantifiable, immeasurable, but are realizable, cumulative and multiplicative. Economic opportunity cannot be seen or perceived as it does not have a physical form. Economic opportunities can be realized through time and more are always preferred to less. Economic opportunities can be multi-dimensional and cover several operational levels because one economic opportunity would give rise to another opportunity in the same or different level of economic operation.

The multiplicative and cumulative features in economic opportunity are the most powerful as economic opportunities so generated would be infinite. As the rise of one economic opportunity leads to the emergence of another, the process of generation in economic opportunities would multiply through time, performing like a healthy tree that grows and branches out to create more opportunities. The multiplication process would mean that opportunities would be kept by the first recipient, who would then generate the next opportunity for another recipient, and so on. Hence, the recipients would value the opportunities. Economic opportunities would become cumulative as recipients value and treasure their opportunities. The cumulative feature can be seen when recipients maintain their economic opportunities, while the multiplicative feature can be seen when recipients utilize their economic opportunities that eventually would generate more opportunities. There is the presence of an "economic opportunity multiplier" (EOM).

Li (2014) further distinguished between the extensity and intensity channels through which economic opportunity can be materialized. Extensity relates to the "width" of resource availability, namely the quantity and kind of resource endowments available for economic opportunity to emerge and materialize. The extensity channel consists of natural resources (land and raw materials), artificial resources (machines and technology) and human resources (creativity, intelligence, entrepreneurial spirit and risk taking). The intensity channel relates to the "depth" of available resources, indicating the environment through which the "width" factors can be deployed productively. These typically are the socio-economic and political factors that have an impact on the exercise of the "width" factors. Socio-economic factors consist of factors such as infrastructure provisions, policies that nurture individual drive and an enterprising attitude, reliability of institutions, and peaceful coexistence and social harmony among population groups, while the political environment could be seen from the degree of political openness and stability, market friendliness, policy orientations and fiscal performances.

Both the extensity and intensity channels complement each other. Indeed, economic opportunity can arise only when both channels are showing positive signs. Economic opportunities shall emerge when there is an abundance of natural, artificial and human resources complemented by market-friendly policies, a reliable political regime and a healthy fiscal performance. Indeed, political instability and cronyism in leadership would limit economic opportunity. Lack of socio-harmony and the presence of discrimination could fend off and reduce all kinds of economic opportunities. Of course, the worst scenario would be a negative sign in both extensity and intensity channels. The lack of natural and artificial resources coupled with political instability and a war-prone society would be the graveyard for an economic opportunity.

As economic resources are passive and cannot be made productive without action taken by humans, the act of investment plays the role of turning the passive resources into an active economic process through which economic opportunities emerge, and the different kinds of economic opportunities in turn require different individual endowments, and together they produce jobs and employment possibilities. This is where and how the analysis of opportunity contributes to the understanding of economics, as the emergence of opportunities supplemented by the endowment of individuals shall lead to creation of jobs and employment. The act of investment serves as the "push" that gives rise to an entire economic process through which opportunities are combined with individual endowments to produce employment possibilities, and through employment and job provisions, physical outputs are produced that eventually contribute to the dynamic process of economic growth, progress and development. Economic opportunity is a core concept and serves as a conduit in the entire provision of human welfare improvement.

There is the presence of a powerful EOM that works prior to the IM which is elaborated in all economics textbooks. The conceptual and theoretical difference between the two multipliers is that EOM is *ex-ante* and possesses the various features of economic opportunity, while IM is *ex-post* that shows the final quantifiable outcome of the entire growth process. Figure 8.1 summarizes the whole argument on economic endowment and opportunity. While the role of the extensity and intensity factors

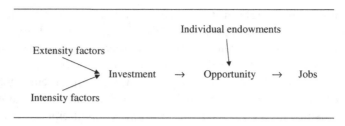

Figure 8.1   The Role of Economic Opportunity

can be made useful through investment activities, economic opportunities are generated and together with the attributes arising from individual economic endowments, jobs and employment possibilities can then be materialized.

IV   Categorizing Work and Employment

Labor is considered as an input to production just like other factors such as land, natural resources, capital and technology. Within the sphere of economics, it is obvious that the returns on production factors differed due to differences in the endowments possessed by individuals and economies. This is probably the reason why one production factor gets a higher return than another, and such a difference can even occur in the same production factor. While conventional mainstream studies on labor economics examined labor market behavior and policies, studies on the formation of human capital have increasingly become more relevant as it relates to policy on education and training in the context of economic growth (McNulty, 1984; Romer, 1989; Becker, 1994; Sweetland, 1996; Borjas, 2013; Ehrenberg and Smith, 2016).

Both labor and human capital are collective terms representing a certain group of workers and professionals. Discussion on economic endowments, however, can simplify into different types of individual labor whose work will mainly be dominated by either their sheer physical presence or acquired knowledge and willingness to take risks. This is important because while the discussion so far has been related to differences in economic endowments, there are differences in endowments which were owed to the very nature of the job each worker faces. Jobs and employment can be simplified into three categories of work, though there can be vast differences in terms of earnings and rewards between jobs in each category. The three categories of work can be classified into physical body-related, knowledge acquired and risk taking. Jobs which are physical body-related can be subdivided into three types namely talent-related, unskilled and trained skilled workers. The next category of jobs which require the acquisition of knowledge includes all kinds of professionals, scientists, technologists and innovators. The risk-taking category of workers covers entrepreneurs and businesspeople, and people who live on inheritance.

The first category includes people with talents, such as celebrities from the entertainment and sports industries, who rely exclusively on their physical body and talented abilities, and such successful celebrities can make enormous earnings and can live their life luxuriously. At the other extreme, the unskilled workers also rely exclusively on their physical strength, but they are paid on an hourly basis as their earnings will be based on the number of hours worked. Wages for unskilled workers are usually low as unskilled workers lack a highly marketable endowment. However, economic assistance in the form of social welfare would be provided in case unskilled workers and their families face economic survival problems. Economic security to unskilled workers tends to be low, unless these workers attempt to improve their endowments through training and acquiring a skill. Skilled workers are better off as they could have acquired some skills and training for a trade or job. Traditionally, apprenticeship has been the path through which unskilled workers are turned into skilled workers. As experience accumulates, their earnings should increase, and they will achieve greater economic security. In modern industries, factory workers are the more common terminology, but increasingly job rotation has become common where skilled workers would be trained for different jobs to enrich their skills and job prospects, thereby improving their marketability.

The second category of work that requires the acquisition of knowledge should include all kinds of professionals who have acquired formal qualifications and expertise and training before being able to practice their professions. With acquired knowledge, the individual endowments of these professionals should be higher as their qualifications are marketable. Indeed, modern educational policies that are aimed at increasing the quality of human capital do effectively enrich the endowments of individuals, who in turn earn different rewards and earnings as different professions are paid differently, depending on marketability, demand for the profession and age of the workers. Nonetheless, the formal education system that enriches young people's personal endowments effectively creates differences in earnings and "income inequality" among recipients. It would be ironic to argue for "income equality" when the formal education system is the vehicle through which "income inequality" is created.

Among the different professions, scientists and technologists, together with innovators, are the workers who help to expand the frontier of science and technology, providing scientific and intellectual answers to many human problems. The evolutionary approach to science and engineering would crack many human superstitions and anomalies as new answers are discovered and found backed up by scientific proof and findings. By using their brain power, innovators and creators visualize human complexities and reduce them into understandable and manageable ideas. Indeed, their creations shall open many more opportunities and job dimensions in the future, thereby infinitely expanding the economic and production frontier for the benefit of mankind.

The risk-taking category of work involves people with an entrepreneurial mind and an enterprising business attitude, and through risk taking, these workers can see and have pride in their own deeds as their business entities grow and expand to become mega enterprises. Risk-taking jobs may not be successful all the time. While there are only successful businesses that are reported and recognized, there are thousands of unsuccessful but unreported businesses that have faced loss and suffered consequences. Thus, while one can complain about how much a risk-taking business has made in terms of profits, and unlike unemployed workers who often receive welfare aid, there is normally no welfare assistance given to failed businesses. Many failed businesspersons just suffer in silence. Whether a business is successful or otherwise also depends on its own endowments, seen in terms of marketability, availability of capital, seasonal factors, input constraints, management style and product life cycles. The other type of risk takers includes people who live on inheritance, either in terms of wealth and assets, customary practices or constitutional rights. People who inherited wealth, assets and reputation face risk as they may lose their wealth and assets in case the phase of an economic cycle changes, or amendments in the instituted practices would require them to give up their inherited titles. Thus, these people also must work hard at least to retain their titles through, for example, charity work and expand their wealth and assets through investment activities.

By understanding these three types of work, one can think of a total of four layers of employment and job provisions. Workers who offer to work through their physical body and time probably form the largest group of workers. This is followed by professionals who are well educated, highly trained and have acquired knowledge which allows them to achieve a high degree of economic security as their acquired endowments become marketable. The next higher layer shall be the different forms of businesses that take risks and provide employment opportunities to other workers (skilled and unskilled) and professionals. The business risk may not necessarily be all successful, as failed businesses are often disregarded. Nonetheless, through their investment, businesspeople enlarge the job and employment frontier of the economy; the employer and employee relationships are contemporarily seen as complements and employers are increasingly taking care of their workers to boost job satisfaction and promote productivity. The highest layer of workers shall be the scientists and innovators who push the technological frontier to new heights that allow new opportunities to develop.

However, having discussed the four layers of work and employment, it does not necessarily mean that one layer would have a higher earning than another, and earnings could even differ among workers in the same layer. There is thus no uniformity in wage payment and earning by workers, as jobs require different knowledge and skills and experience. Diversity in jobs and employment opportunities shall naturally lead to diversity in job recruitments, preparations of individual endowments and choices and opportunities in taking up professional training. Furthermore, different kinds of employment and jobs would enrich and expand different economic frontiers. Typically, scientists and technologists would enrich the technical frontier. The businesses shall expand and extend the investment frontier, while professionals and skilled and unskilled labor shall enrich the human capital frontier.

Perhaps a short discussion on retirement is appropriate. The conventional wisdom is that employees must retire at a certain age, say at 55, 60 or 65 years depending on the type of employment. The traditional argument on retirement is the health factor and the need to give more jobs to the younger workers. However, most of the advanced countries are faced with the aging problem and medical advancement has promoted a much healthier population. Thus, spending on the aging population is rising rapidly. One alternative is to delay retirement and allow workers to stay in employment for a longer period provided the health condition is satisfactory. Hence, the dilemma is how to promote job opportunities for the young while retaining employment for the experienced and aged employees.

One probable economic solution is to reduce the wage payment of the aging workers when they reach the age of 60 or 65 because by then they shall not be the breadwinners in their households, and they can survive on a reduced wage to keep their jobs. Such a "breadwinner" argument can form a new theory in the economics of retirement. It takes a policy formula to be worked out. For example, after a certain age, the aging worker will have a gradual reduction in wage annually with a cap. For example, a 10% reduction for 4 years and the workers would receive only 60% of their wage after 4 years. The economic argument is that as the workers are no longer the breadwinners, their employment shall then be counted more in terms of experience and interest rather than the need to feed a family, while the saved earnings can be channeled to employ younger workers, thereby raising their job opportunities.

Of course, how far and fast wages can be reduced at the age of retirement depends on the agreement between the workers and employers, or there can be a statutory law if societal consensus can be reached. There must be a legal, systemic and administrative process and policy through which both employers and employees are given an opportunity to decide and choose between working with a reduced wage or retiring completely. It also depends on the nature of the job. Typically, it would be wise for the employees to stay in jobs that value and rely on experiences. Nonetheless, reducing wages but retaining employment after a certain age and making the released resources available to hire younger workers shall be an effective and workable economic policy to benefit both the aging workers as well as the younger workers. Keeping more aging people in the employment shall ease the pressure on government's fiscal spending on the aging population and the age of retirement shall become a voluntary and flexible choice. It is true that many healthy retired people can be recruited back to employment because their experience is valuable to the employer.

V The Root of Economic Differences

Due to the relative nature of economics, economic results and outcomes are bound to be different. Such a difference, unfortunately, has often been politicized and labeled as inequality. And much of the political fuss has been concentrated on reducing inequality without knowing that differences in economic outcomes and results are perpetual. Similarly, despite centuries and decades of politicization on inequality, differences or inequalities have not disappeared. Indeed, the behavior and advocacy down the generations of politicians, especially left-leaning politicians, have shown that their cry for reducing inequality has become an instrument used to attack employers and businesses and high-income earners in catchy political phrases such as exploitation and bourgeoise. Due to the differences in endowments, there are always inequalities or differences in economic outcomes, and the leftists' fight for "equality" would make them politically appealing. Yet lessons and experience show that poverty continues to exist in all left-leaning government regimes, while the worst would be that "economic inequality" is transformed to become the more devastating "political inequality", where the entire economy and resources are controlled and managed by political party members.

The truth is that the "unequal" economic outcomes reflect the *ex-post* situation in the chain of economic relationships, while the origin of "inequality" rests in the *ex-ante* conditions in the form of different endowments held by individuals, firms, institutions and societies. Hence, political-oriented battles and cries about inequality at the *ex-post* end would be redundant and inappropriate without knowing the differences in the endowments at the *ex-ante* end of the economic relationship. The root of inequality thus rests in improving or solving the differences in endowments. There is thus a new sphere in the economics discipline to study the definition, classification, forms, dynamics, implications and enrichment or enhancement of economic endowment, with the intention that narrowing the difference in endowments should be the probable and viable solution to empower individuals' assets, abilities and marketability.

The study of economics should be apolitical, because it is the intellectual media through which the inevitable and unavoidable truth in human economic connection can be analyzed, realized and nurtured. Economics does not exhibit inequalities but shows differences. Because of the very nature of differences, the "unequal input, unequal output" relationship forms the fundamental law in economics. The aspect of "unequal output" is the result of "unequal input". Thus, understanding, analyzing and improving the "unequal input" aspect should be the more appropriate and superior strategy than politicizing the "unequal output" aspect. Indeed, the problem among many socialist-prone politicians is the lack of economic knowledge and understanding, and the worst is the erroneous use of economics in fulfilling their ideological goals, thereby leading often to irreversible economic distortions, crises and downfall. And yet, they blame others for the poor economic performance, or exercise even tougher economic policies that further strangle the productive side of the economy.

Differences in economic endowments can be addressed, narrowed, promoted and improved, but one must admit that differences in endowments always exist and politicizing such differences would not be the solution, but could only add to the delay in finding solutions. Nonetheless, improving endowments is a complicated issue as it would not be the result of one single solution but would consist of layers or tiers of multifaceted solutions. The factors in the formation and calculation of endowments, the way endowments are measured and quantified, the required policies that enhance the endowment factors, the time delay in allowing the endowment factors to become effective, the opportunity through which endowment factors can be applied and deployed, and the eventual results that the endowment factors can produce show the linkage and complexity in reducing and narrowing differences in endowments.

The perpetual presence of differences in economic endowments suggests that "economic inequality" cannot be eradicated, but the improvement of endowments and promotion of opportunities suggest that more and better economic results can be produced. People with different endowments can improve their economic outcomes through time, but however much each person improves, there are still differences among economic outcomes. Thus, by simply and naively blaming unequal economic outcomes without making policy efforts in improving economic endowments is a fruitless exercise and could even lead to setbacks in human development.

Inequality, or differences, cannot be solved, but allowing more opportunities would mean that individuals and economies with lower endowments can be improved so that the enrichment in their economic welfare would mean a rise in the ability to survive economically. The existence of differences is not a deadly issue, but the lack of opportunities would delay improvements in economic and human welfare. The question then is how to promote opportunities and not complain about the differences. Enlarging the economic pie is still the more preferred strategy than how the pie is distributed, because pie enlargement means that everyone would enjoy some gain even though there is a difference in the gains received by different individuals and economies.

VI Conclusion

This chapter has pioneered the discussion on economic endowments, which have been argued as the root causes of the economic differences, as individuals and economies holding different endowments would exercise their economic powers differently, thereby producing differences in economic results and outcomes. The fault therefore lies not in the economic outcomes; the differences in economic outcomes are caused by differences in endowments. Such an understanding is crucial in analyzing the apolitical nature of economics, and it would be unfortunate if economic differences, whether at the *ex-ante* end or at the *ex-post* end, would be misinterpreted to suggest the presence of inequality. In addition, there are other economic understandings. Economic outcomes are always relative in nature. Economic resources are passive and can only be activated or made productive when such activities as investments by decision makers are exercised on economic resources and endowment factors.

The two main themes in this chapter are endowment and opportunity, which are considered as the discussion goes deeper in analyzing the relationship between economics and other social studies. Economic differences have often been politicized as "income inequality", but such inequality arises because of differences in the endowments possessed by individuals. Hence, politicians could complain about the *ex-post* situation endlessly, while the problem rests in the *ex-ante* situation. Although endowment is an innovative concept, it simply brings out the *ex-ante* factors in economic relationships. This is important as most, if not all, economic analyses have focused on the outcome, or *ex-post*, side of economic activities, whose differences would be obvious when endowment factors are different. Hence, lamenting the differences, or inequality, in economic outcomes cannot help solve economic problems because the root of different outcomes rests in the difference in endowments at the input end of all economic relationships. The attention should therefore be focused on enhancing economic endowments.

The economics of endowment as a subject of study is still young within the sphere of economics. Nonetheless, the discussion in this chapter examines endowment factors facing the five levels of economic entities: individual, enterprise, institution, government and economy. Each of these entities would have a variety of positive and negative endowment factors. The positive factors should enhance the endowments, while the negative factors would deplete the contribution made by the positive factors.

The relative nature in economics analysis shows that in understanding endowments, one must be aware that all individuals are different in their background, innate ability, environment in which they grow up, educational qualification attained, peer group influence and personality features and interests. As such, it is likely that individuals will pursue different paths in their lifetime, as some are more educated, have higher abilities and received varying returns. Enterprises are also different from each other, depending on the industry or service they engage in, amount of capital invested and sources of finance, management style and size of the enterprise, size of the market and seasonal factors and probability of the product life cycle. Institutions are different because they are geared to serve various civic objectives, such as anti-corruption, consumer protection, animal and environment protection, child abuse and adherence to the rule of law. The kinds of instituted professions differ depending on the market needs, ethical standards and available expertise, and as such, the rewards given to the professionals differ. Economies differ in their available endowments, depending on the amount of production factors available, marketability of the production factors, conducive government policies, business cycle and degree of competitiveness when compared to other economies, value-added content of products and services and so on. As such, one should not expect different economies to perform similarly, and variation in performance would be obvious, so also the economic returns and outcomes.

Understanding differences in endowments is just the beginning. The economic opportunities so generated from the available endowments are the other critical factor in producing different economic results. Economic opportunities can only be realized but do not have a physical form, thereby making analysis difficult. As a latent factor, economic opportunities are generated through the active participation of economic activities conducted by various economic agents that would then deploy the economic endowments for production and in turn reward the endowment factors accordingly. And since different endowments would have different roles in the production process, rewards and returns given to individual endowment factors would differ as a result.

Nonetheless, economic opportunity should not be another economic scarcity, and more is always preferred to less. Along with the understanding of differences and opportunities, the more relevant issue is whether economic opportunities are equally open to all and there is non-discrimination in the distribution and deployment of opportunities. The fact that economic opportunity does not have its physical form could generate two invisible relationships in terms of creation and delivery. Economic opportunities must be created, and this is done via numerous decision makers, such as investors, policy makers, financiers and other risk takers. These decision makers create economic opportunities through endowment deployment. Delivery of economic opportunity can be another problem as there may not be enough objective criteria even though the process is open and equal. A job advertisement, for example, usually states that applicants of all ages, genders and races would equally be considered. However, there is still the need to choose one applicant among many applicants. The human factor is involved in how open, equal and scientific the process to chose the final applicant remains. Indeed, that may reflect the point of difference rather than openness and equality in deciding on an applicant. Rather, no two applicants would be the same, and their differences, however small, could be the deciding factor. Similarly, in a class of students, some perform better than others, and the teacher would assign a different grade to different students, with some gaining better than others. This should reflect differences in performance, rather than unequal results in performance.

To conclude, the understanding of endowment and opportunity is crucial in economic analyses as they provided the "missing link" in understanding the *ex-ante* factors, whose performance would affect the *ex-post* outcomes, which have been the focus of numerous economic studies. The conceptual distinction between *ex-ante* and *ex-post* situations in all economic relationships is powerful, as it provides an in-depth analysis on the root of economic differences, which have often been mistakenly labeled as "inequality". Armed with such a distinction, economic analyses can then focus on the difference at the *ex-ante* end rather than the *ex-post* end, as solutions at the *ex-ante* end would improve situations at the *ex-post* end of economic relationships and outcomes. With such an understanding, the relationship between economics and other social disciplines can be more clear-cut.

Chapter Nine

Crash of Ideologies: Give Economic Performance a Chance

I Introduction

The discussion on the conceptual analysis in economics intends to provide a deeper understanding within the discipline of economics itself and its relationship with other social science disciplines. The intellectual vigor in the previous chapter takes a "vertical" approach by looking at the depth beyond superficial analyses. Typically, the analyses in the input end of an economic equation differ a lot from the output end of an economic relationship. By distinguishing between *ex-ante* and *ex-post* factors, the elaboration in endowment and opportunity shows that one can easily misunderstand the *ex-post* output aspect if one does not try to understand the difference at the *ex-ante* input aspect of an economic and social activity. Analyzing the "depth" of an economic issue shall help one to understand how economics has been used or misused when incorporated into studies and analyses in other social science disciplines.

Among the various social disciplines, political acts have extensively used economic variables as their instruments. This chapter argues that while economic instruments have been used for political goals, elected politicians should let economics serve its own cause and allow economics to perform its best. By giving economics a "chance" to perform, this chapter proposes that rightful economic outcomes are the best form of political results that voters in a democratic election would like to see as that shall enhance the economic welfare of all voters, though one has to bear in mind that welfare improvement may differ among voters as there are differences in voters' endowment.

Differences in economic outcomes are inevitable, and the discussion on economic endowment suggests that differences at the *ex-ante* end of the economic relationship are the more fundamental cause of difference when compared to the *ex-post* end of economic outcomes. Thus, effort to narrow the differences shall start at the endowment end, rather than politicizing the differences by dressing them up as "inequality" that creates dichotomies at the outcome end. On the contrary, taking a positive approach to address differences can lead to greater economic harmony. One must understand that equality in opportunity is another important attribute that helps to provide channels through which individuals with different endowment can improve their economic welfare, thereby gaining a greater economic ability to survive.

Non-discrimination and equality of opportunity have become part of the civilized ethics, like freedom, ethics, discipline and the rule of law. However, there is a "populist" debate on freedom and liberalism as to the extent of freedom and how liberal individuals can become. The wider perspective in which individual freedom and liberalism can be exercised is the limit constrained by civilized ethics, societal and personal discipline, security at all levels and the scope operated within the rule of law as that shall provide a level playing field and a shield against social inequity to all individuals regardless of their background and origin. The rule of law must be impartial, unbiased and shall not favor one group of people against another. The rule of law applies to all individuals indiscriminately, and no one is above the law, including political, business and religious leaders.

Thus, individual freedom and liberalism do not mean one can violate the unbiased nature of the law, defy civilized ethics and ignore social discipline and etiquette and security issues. An individual's freedom can be maximized if no damage or harm is done on another individual. An individual can behave freely and liberally so long as the act is legal and harmless. Ethics, disciplines and. standards are needed in ensuring that individuals' behavior is commonly acceptable and shall not act as a poor precedence to others, especially to children. This is the implication in the argument on "social cost" (Li, 2017a), where individuals should manage and be responsible for their own "private cost" so that their behavior and acts do not spillover to increase the "social cost" which would then be paid for by the public through government fiscal spending.

History is a subject where we learn of the past. Numerous tragic incidents of the past are documented in the history books. However, the behavior of many individuals has been influenced by historical incidents. It is unfortunate that some people politicize historical events and incidents, and they are often used by political leaders as scapegoats to gain power, stir up people's sentiment, create social disharmony and conduct non-peaceful acts with the aim of correcting or rewriting history. Historical incidents should be considered objectively, and individuals should have a forward-looking attitude to life. People should not live their life based on past incidents, but rather should learn from the history and avoid making similar mistakes. Otherwise, social dichotomization and non-peaceful acts would result, thereby limiting economic and social progress. Freedom and liberalism mean that one is free to conduct legal acts in one's life. Life is invaluable, and individuals should do their best and maximize their endowment through marketable activities rather than expressing remorse and let their invaluable life be dictated by wrongful and unfortunate historical events. No one should be a slave to historical events.

Building up from understanding the differences in endowment among individuals, this chapter extends the discussion to examine and clarify the misunderstanding between the two ideologies of capitalism and socialism. The following sections shall elaborate on the contemporary form of civic capitalism that has incorporated the civic aspect into the capitalist mode of production. However, civic capitalism has been attacked as there are still differences which have been politicized as inequalities and power struggles continue. The conclusion makes a pledge that despite ideological battles between political parties, it would be proper for all political parties to focus more on economics performances, thereby giving economics a chance to function and serve.

II Ideological Differences

Indeed, people hold different views and interpretations. For example, in looking at "different economic outcomes", one would consider the benefit from the "outcomes", but others would focus on the "difference" in the gains (Li, 2002). Such a difference in viewpoint is exactly the core argument between the two political ideologies of capitalism and socialism. Capitalism advocates for economic progress through investment and growth so that all individuals with different endowment are free to conduct their economic activities. People with diverse endowments will engage in different activities, as a business person or as a worker being employed. Capitalism effectively empowers the "economicability" of all individuals but accepts the different economic outcomes provided progress is sustainable and that all individuals shall benefit from the growth and progress. The uneven gains are due to the uneven endowment possessed by the individuals. In capitalist market economy, "absolute difference" in gains is acceptable so long as all parties are gaining.

The ideology of socialism or communism focuses on the "difference" part of economic outcomes, and argues that the difference creates inequalities, and those who get more would get more at the expense of those who get less, without regard for the difference in individuals' economic endowment. Instead of trying to understand the difference in endowment, socialist advocates blame the problem on the distribution of the economic pie as it gets larger. In other words, socialists focus only on the "relative difference" in gains, and such difference is considered as "inequality", and gaining less would be the direct consequence or at the expense of those who gained more.

The leftists have been using many political jargons to crystalize the differences. Though leftist leaders at times gained popularity by politicizing and sharpening the difference in economic outcomes, such differences continue to exist in economies with different political ideologies. The truth is that political popularity and ideologies are not the answers to correct the difference in economic outcomes, because the cause of difference in economic outcome rests in the difference in the economic endowment at the input end. It is dangerous when the sharpening of economic differences ended up in dichotomizing disharmony, and that inappropriate economic policies were applied for political reasons, leading to more economic distortions that ended up entangling one economic problem with another (see, for example, Halac and Yared, 2018).

The debate between the two ideological extremes of capitalism and communism has existed for a long time. In the contemporary global economy, most of the freer market economies have adopted capitalism as the social fabric of property rights to ensure private ownership, freedom of movement in both people and capital to maximize individuals' welfare, and political democracy to ensure political freedom and participation have long been instituted, though socialist policies are also applied when pro-socialist leaders are elected.

In the communist countries, economic decisions can be controlled by party leaders, and political inequality coexists with economic inequality.

A top-down approach is instituted when the communist party, being the supreme political institution, followed by the government, and individuals could at best exercise the "use rights" of all economic resources, while the "ownership rights" remain always in the hands of the state. Communist party members become the most powerful body of individuals.

Over the centuries when pressure groups and pro-socialist leaders have inserted changes to the primitive form of capitalist system, it leads one to argue for the case of "civic capitalism" where numerous civic aspects have been instituted into capitalism. On the contrary, given that there is freedom and the permission of liberal behavior, capitalism has been under attack by the leftists through politicizing and extending "inequality" to such non-economic aspects as race, gender, history, religion and immigration, thereby creating social division and fragmentation rather than working for a common good.

In comparing the two ideologies, capitalism advocates for economic performance as that shall empower the "economicability" of all individuals. And as individuals are occupied with their economic activities, growth and progress shall permit both "opportunity multiplier" and "income multiplier" to function to their maximum extent, thereby generating gains for all to share and spread to people in all walks of life. Furthermore, as people's economic welfare improves, there will be lower reliance on government or public assistance, and in turn, the government would have more to spend on building the economic capability for the future generation. In short, the pursuit of a common economic good would ensure a prosperous future for both the current and future generations.

The left would maximize the "difference" aspect by politicizing it as "inequality" and arguing that those who gain less would suffer or be disadvantaged as a result. To the leftists, and since there are differences in many things, there are inequalities in many things. Instead of looking at the common good, the leftists look for divisions and fragmentations. Social dichotomization has become the political instrument the left deploys, as that is how they can gain popularity in the name of "helping" the various fragmented groups of people. Political outcomes would naturally take priority over economic outcomes. Political power could then be gained through the votes. The leftists' way to finance their political ambition is to raise tax and rely on debts, resulting in a much weaker and uncompetitive economy. As investment becomes unattractive, job opportunities and employment potentials are low, and high unemployment would mean that more and more people would have to depend on government assistance and subsidy, giving rise to expansion in government bureaucracy and increased control and intervention in people's private life and activities.

To the capitalist leaders, the work to improve the common good will naturally incorporate and take care of those fragmented groups of people advocated by the leftist politicians, and there is no need to dramatize the so-called inequality if there are policies instituted to permit all groups of individuals to participate equally. To the leftist leaders, social and economic divisions have become their source of strength and base of power.

III Civic Capitalism

Individual freedom and liberty, property rights and private ownership, the rule of law and a market economy have been the conventional ingredients of modern capitalism. Democracy is political freedom which should be cherished together with other aspects of freedom, such as freedom of association and freedom of employment, though there are legal, moral and ethical boundaries in freedom of speech and freedom of the media. Provided the activity is legal and not socially harmful, demonizing and insulting, individuals are free to conduct their activities according to their wishes on how to improve their endowments and utilize the market opportunity through their own ingenuity.

There is, however, a subtle difference between freedom and liberty. While freedom deals with individuals' activities, liberty deals with individuals' behavior. People can behave liberally provided the behavior is legal, neutral and unbiased, and ethically and morally acceptable and is socially respected, and no harm will be imposed on another individual, including no harm on children. With freedom and liberty, the market functions to provide an "invisible hand" in allocating and matching different endowment of individuals with different job opportunities and employment potentials. As such, individuals with different backgrounds can have their choices made and rewards earned through the dynamic forces of the market, bearing in mind that the different choices and rewards earned also differ among individuals. Difference in market sentiments produces dynamism in economic activities.

Despite the differences in endowments and outcomes, the individuals have the advantage of controlling their own "economic fate", making their decisions in the endowment they would like to acquire, choosing what to do with their own endowments and enjoying the consequent benefits.

A capitalist market economy allows all individuals to show their best in their accomplishments. And since individuals have differences in "their best", there are thus differences in their accomplishments, depending on such features as age, personal background and experience, skill and knowledge, marketability and opportunity, and stage of the business or economic cycle.

As Li (2017a) advocated, the contemporary or post-modern form of capitalism has been nourished and improved to take care of the various drawbacks that existed in the early stage of pre-modern form of capitalism. Various contemporary institutions have aided capitalist development, making it more open and accessible to all. Banks and financial institutions allow individuals and businesses to conduct their investment activities through savings and the provision of loans and mortgages. The education system has enabled more young people to acquire knowledge and skills to improve their endowment, thereby allowing them to become more marketable. In the delivery of education, although the teaching aspect shall be conducted by the educationist and the provision of the educational infrastructure and system, the willingness and drive to learn and be educated, however, must come from the young students themselves, who would have to make great efforts in order to be successful in the entire learning process.

Through the work of pressure groups, democratically elected governments have become more humanistic by providing fiscal assistance to aid needy individuals. Provision of social and economic infrastructure has become the contemporary function of businesses and governments, as investment in infrastructure has become a must in promoting economic sustainability, growth and competitiveness. The establishment of various civic institutions has enhanced the quality of human life tremendously, thereby allowing social equity and openness to replace bias, cronyism, coercion and vested interest. For example, neighborhood organizations have emerged to take care of local issues, while volunteer jobs are becoming more common for people to contribute flexibly to the livelihood of their communities. Donations by philanthropists and from successful business persons are becoming a social norm, making a practical virtue.

Human life has been highly valued, and legislations have been instituted to give a more humanistic touch on employment and working conditions. Employers, especially large corporations, have improved the working environment tremendously. Typical examples include equal pay for equal work between genders, flexible working hours and "work-from-home" arrangement, increased maternity leave days, stronger hygienic and security arrangements in factories, provisions of stress-release facilities in the office area, and in hi-technology companies, days are provided for "creative activities" to promote employees' long-term productivity. Over the decades, pro-welfare governments have instituted labor protection legislations, and labor unions often negotiate on behalf of workers and members, though at times labor unions can be militant and restrict new employment. Adherence to strong ethics and moral standards has ensured the elimination of child labor. Many employers have paid more attention to their employees and working conditions, as they see the "employer–employee" relationship as complementary to each other rather than dichotomous. Indeed, no employers can survive without employees, and equally no workers can survive without employers. A harmonious working environment can only help productivity that brings absolute benefit to both sides.

It is true that unfavorable labor conditions have often been reported and advocated, as if workers are always disadvantaged and being exploited. There can be some truth in many of the reported cases and actions are needed to improve working conditions and labor regulations. Yet, the difficulties facing the employers' side are hardly noticed, reported or compensated. For example, the number of business failures, closures and bankruptcies and the resulting financial loss suffered by the employers are often ignored. Businesses and employers must take risk which cannot be measured, and their failures are usually not compensated. There is thus "inequality" in the way "economic sympathy" has been expressed and treated between workers' difficulty and employers' difficulty. Typically, there is unemployment assistance provided by many governments, but there is no assistance provided to small business and entrepreneurs who failed in their business, though there are rare occasions of bailouts by governments if the affected corporation is crucial to the industry or economy. For small- and medium-sized enterprises (SMEs), their business failures and closures often lead to loss and the business owners suffer in silence. There is uneven and unequal statistical, media and social exposure between workers' conditions and employers' conditions.

Choice is an important element in contemporary capitalism. Due to differences in people's personal, family and business background, it is a must that people are given a choice to choose between alternatives to maximize their welfare and utility. Other than the quantifiable aspects of welfare and utility, there are psychological aspects, such as which medical doctor provides more suitable treatment or which school provides a sound curriculum to their children. Welfare and utility can also be shown preferentially, such as properties in certain neighborhoods or the brand-name effect of an educational institution. The availability of choice would necessarily mean that there are also alternatives on the supply side. Housing supply can be conducted through public housing scheme as well as real-estate development in the private market. Medical and hospital facilities can be done via government spending in the form of public infrastructure and privately run clinics and hospitals. Educational institutions, airlines and banks can exercise the idea of "dual provision" or "dual supply" whereby the service is supplied through both public and private channels. People can have a choice in patronizing different sources of supply, and a sense of competition can also be generated among those "dual-supply" businesses.

Civic institutions exist and emerge to provide an additional layer of protection within the capitalist market system. Law societies are established to uphold the rule of law and to ensure a level playing field, while the legal profession conducts appropriate training. The same is true in other professions, such as accountancy, banking, health and medical, engineering and construction, as organizations are established to ensure standards and eradicate abuse. Humanitarian institutions and non-governmental organizations (NGOs) exist to rescue unnecessary human suffering due to war, atrocities, disasters and crises. Established consumer societies aim to check on product safety, quality and market fairness. Anti-competition laws have been passed to uphold open competition and freedom to market entry. In many matured capitalist market economies, there is even the appointment of an Ombudsman and establishment of institutions that serve as checks and balances to monitor the performance of the government and official departments and disclose any possible governmental misdeeds, such as misspending, cronyism and poor ethics. This is important as the public needs to ensure transparency in government institutions. There are of course the law-enforcement bodies, including the police and the military that provide security to the communities and the borders. Various social and pressure groups have been established to alleviate social discontents and grievances with the aim to promote a just economy.

The advantage of the "civic" nature in capitalism is that many of these established institutions and professions are apolitical and do not need to have any political affiliation. They exist to serve the public and people, regardless of their background and orientations. As such, personal and public security can be safeguarded without any political involvement. Civic capitalism shows the combination between the presence of civic institutions and the free capitalist political system. While people are protected by civic institutions, individual freedom and provision of choices permit individuals to chart their own life and plan their career path. The society cherishes individual success and business prosperity, but people with low endowment are faced with hardships and are taken care of through the government's welfare support as well as other civic bodies, such as neighborhood associations and humanitarian organizations. People's differences are being attended to rather than politicized into a dichotomous problem. In the capitalist system and given the differences in individual endowment, there are ways and means to improve individuals' absolute differences through time but they should not be considered as opposing forces that viciously emphasize relative differences.

There is in all economies the existence of a government, but between the citizens and the government, there is the presence of different layers of institutions that protect and secure the livelihood of individuals without being politically involved with the government. An individual under civic capitalism has the freedom of conducting any kind of legal activities while at the same time being protected by different civic institutions and professional organizations. With peace and security, individuals can perform their best for their own gain as well as attribute their work to strengthening the macroeconomy. The emergence of new businesses would lead to the appearance of new jobs as the economy progresses, thereby promoting economic diversity, social acceptance and mutual respect.

What counts crucially in civic capitalism is the presence of a reliable social infrastructure that comprises a legal system and a sustainable social structure accepted, respected and utilized by all citizens. The system under civic capitalism effectively serves as a "middle man" that liaises the various relationships between people and government, between workers and employers, between designated groups of individuals, between suppliers and consumers, and indeed, between any two or more individuals and entities.

However, as individual freedom is allowed in market economies, there are possibilities that the market will fluctuate as individuals' expectations change, and the dynamic nature of economic activities would produce periods of expansion followed by periods of contraction, leading to emergence of economic overheating in the former and recession in the latter. This is due to the chain-like relationship in economics. The rise in demand, for example, would lead to inflation, which would require a different solution. When expectations plummet, an economy could end up in a crisis and economic decline would hurt businesses, employment and wages. There are other possibilities that would steer the economy into wrong directions. Bad investments could produce losses. There are villains who are prepared to harm the economy, or people who held vested interest and take advantage of the economy for improper or unproductive activities. There are politicians who abuse economics for political purposes.

In short, the economy will be affected by two related forces. First, the economy shall be moving by its own dynamic forces, generating fluctuations on its own as a result of genuine economic activities. The second force on the economy shall include possible distortions generated by different kinds of decision makers who make use of the economy for non-economic ends. In the process, economic distortions so created would be intertwined with other normal and genuine economic activities, thereby leading to possibilities such as emergence of new economic problems, greater complexity of existing problems or produce further extremes in economic activities. Economic decisions would be dangerous if left to unscrupulous decision makers who do not know the inter-connectedness in economic complexities. As such, it would be difficult to solve an economic problem or distortion if the cause of such problems is not economic oriented in the first instance, and it would be impossible to distinguish one element of the problem caused by economics and another element of the problem originated from non-economic intentions.

Fortunately, such economic theories as externality, agency, asymmetric information and rent seeking have been constructed to investigate economic distortions resulting from bad decisions and unscrupulous behavior. Despite the distortions, however, one of the strengths of a market economy in civic capitalism is its ability to rejuvenate given the opportunities and the dynamics, as the result of proper decisions could either produce stronger outcomes and revise the direction of the economic cycle or lead to adoption of policies that would correct previous distortions. While capitalism allows for the freedom of economic transactions, the civic aspect allows for the emergence of effective and productive decision makers through civilized and democratic channels. Civic capitalism thus embraces the largest possible extent of economic diversity, allowing both genuine and distortive economic activities to be conducted by different decision makers. Since economic distortions can only create or prolong problems, their negative impact would eventually have to be corrected by non-politicized economic policies made probably by pro-economics leaders.

IV Politicization and Attacks

The problem in many social science disciplines is that an outcome can be interpreted in more than one possible way. Similarly, an economic outcome can be seen by different stake holders who could have their own interpretations. However, some interpretations are normative and based on opinions without factual support. There is a clear difference between opinion and analysis. Opinions can be based on a person's biased viewpoint, but analyses are often supported by reasoning, facts and cases, statistical support and observations. As one economic outcome differs from another, some would consider the importance of "outcomes" as that would lead to growth and progress, while others would focus on the "difference" which could be politicized as inequality or exploitation by one group on another group of individuals. Differences in interpretations and the lack of distinction between opinions and analyses can be politicized by people with a different vested interest. A businessman would obviously prefer to see more economic outcomes as that shall promote market demand and sales. Another individual who gains less from one economic outcome would probably pursue and deploy non-economic means with the aim to obtain a similar gain or reduce the gain of others.

One typical dichotomy between the two political ideologies of capitalism and socialism is the way economic outcomes are being interpreted. Political leaders adhering to capitalism ideology tend to look for ways to improve the economy at the macro level, which means that policies are applied to ensure that all citizens will benefit, though gains differ among businesses and households. Policies on business investment, infrastructure, employment, finance and fiscal spending on public goods and services aim to produce growth either at the regional and sectoral or macroeconomic levels. Economic policies will also cater to the needs of different individual groups, including the provision of basic welfare to the needy individuals and households to ensure their economic survival. One general aspect in understanding political economy is that policies are meant to benefit the people, thereby allowing individual workers, businesses and households to utilize the market mechanism fully, and that individuals endowed with their talents, skills, knowledge, education and experience could maximize their gains given the opportunity and state of the economic cycle.

Policies in capitalist economies are meant to produce a viable, sustainable and suitable economic climate so that growth proceeds as different individuals and businesses across sectors and regions can utilize and enjoy the "opportunity multiplier" and "income multiplier" function to produce benefits to all. Such "supply-side" policies as investment in physical and social infrastructure, education, health and other public goods are meant to be forward looking, implying that even though the economy could be doing well contemporarily, there is a need to "prepare for the rainy days" so that policies should aim at improving the economy's overall competitiveness and sustainability. Should economic difficulties arise when dynamic forces in economic activities could produce extremes, counter-cyclical policies can be put in place appropriately to avoid extremes and provide rescue in times of crises. Without intervention, economic fluctuations could eventually correct themselves through the forces of supply and demand as business expectations change. Suitable economic policies at best are meant to smoothen the economic cycles so that extreme hardship can be lightened or avoided.

In economic analysis, one can take a generalized viewpoint, but that could have overlooked some details when it comes to individual performance. On the contrary, if policies are catered to the need of different individuals and businesses, their benefits could become specific and would result in fragmentation and unfairness as the benefit that was given to one entity may not be made available to another entity. For example, should the government spend on subsidizing one uncompetitive or declining industry or firm to maintain its survival, or invest in long-term infrastructure so that all industries and firms can benefit?

Because capitalist policies largely aim to produce an overall result that benefits all, socialist and other non-capitalist political leaders must look for ways to seek popularity and votes in order to gain political power. Politicization of different economic outcomes has been a popular instrument captured by many ambitious leftist political leaders, as division and fragmentation among individual groups can provide them with popularity, especially where freedom of expression and association is permitted. In a two-party political system, it is usual for the capitalist party to aim at policies that produce economic performances, while the pro-socialist party tends to emphasize differences and consider the differences as dichotomous to each other.

The classic example of polarization politicized by the leftist political leaders has been the employer–employee relationship. It was true that in early industrialization, work regimentation coexisted with harsh working conditions, as the civic aspect of capitalism was absent. However, the experience gained from the industrialization age was the emergence of economic growth in the form of rising output and export, and that gave rise to new professions and employment potentials. Through education, urbanization and institution of social protection policies, workers were given the opportunity to pick up new skills and receive training for different trades, leading to an increase in their economic independence.

Instead of admitting the differences among individuals due to endowment variation, income inequality has been politicized by leftists in the "rich and poor" dichotomy. The truth is that so long as there is difference in individual endowment, there will be "inequality" in incomes received by individuals. Indeed, income inequality and poverty have been an "evergreen" issue exploited by generations of leftist advocates, and yet there is still income inequality, though the gap could be narrower due to different stages of economic and business cycles. Empirical studies on inequality and development showed that the inequality gap is larger in the developing countries than in the advanced countries. The difference mainly rests in the fact that in advanced countries there are civic channels instituted which help to narrow the inequality gap, such as openness in economic opportunities (Zhou and Li, 2011; Li *et al.*, 2016).

Income inequality reflects basically the difference in economic endowment, and such differences cannot be solved through political instruments. Numerous leftist political leaders when elected have followed the same recipe of imposing a high tax on the "rich" or the "top one percent" income earners, thinking that redistribution through politics can alleviate the "poor" or penalize the "rich", or committing large welfare spending to help the endowment low-income earners, resulting in rising national debt and loss in competitiveness. The reality is that statistically there is always the "top one percent", so too the "lowest one percent". Even without hard core empirical studies, one can observe that capitalist countries with elected leftist leaders tend to show a weaker economic performance and a fall in overall competitiveness, as the rising tax on the one hand and growing debt resulting from large spending on the other hand would dampen and discourage investors. What is worse is that investors would send their capital to invest in market-friendly countries, which in turn enjoyed higher growth and export and experienced improvement in competitiveness.

In short, the economy under a leftist political leader suffered internally as investment was dampened and externally as the economy was losing its competitiveness. As jobs were lost due to capital departure, the uncompetitive and weak economy would mean less jobs and employment opportunities. In the end, poverty remained or even expanded, and income inequality worsened. Economic realities show that difference in economic outcomes should not be politicized, but there should be more effective policies that improve the endowment of individuals. Ultimately, economic difference is an economic problem, and should not be used as a political instrument.

Other popular instruments leftist politicians used to attack the economy include historical insinuations. The history of imperialism and numerous wars and human conflicts have been used by political leaders as scapegoats in situations when their economies underperformed, especially among developing countries. As Li (2017a) argued, imperialism should no longer have much effect on poor economic performance as most former colonies have gained political independence since the end of the Second World War. The reality could be that the imperialism sentiment was exploited by incompetent political leaders as a scapegoat to cover up their weakness and non-performance in their economy. The incompetent political leaders could turn out to be corrupt and the practice of cronyism and patronage benefitted the leaders and officials. There are numerous cases where for decades foreign funds, economic aids and investments either through international agents or government and private channels that poured into the country did not produce growth as the overall economic structure and development remained poor. There are studies that pointed to the performance of international aid agents, as international aid from advanced countries could have ended up in the pockets of the corrupt officials.

Historical wars and invasions have also been exploited by leftist political leaders as an instrument to gather people to attack their "enemies" at selected times and occasions, especially when there were unfavorable political pressures at home and scapegoats were needed and applied to sidetrack people's attention. Blaming a historical enemy could help to ease political tensions or serve as a propaganda instrument. In civilized countries, a day could be set aside for the remembrance of certain wars. Indeed, it was true that countries were being invaded historically, and unnecessary death and bloodshed occurred. But if the invaded country was strong, powerful and accepted by the global world, the country might not have suffered the invasion in the first instance. Thus, while one could express remorse on being invaded, the other side of the coin was to ask why the country was weak or why other countries were strong. One could make use of the historical events and reflect on the country's weakness. This shall lead to more thought on how to strengthen the country, making it more respectable in the global economy. Thus, history should be considered positively as a reflection on how to improve and strengthen the country, rather than accusing foreign invasion and demonizing other countries. Historical events should not be politicized.

Race relationship is another divisive issue used by leftist political leaders. Again, it is true that there is the dark side of history that humans were traded as slaves and the history has documented generations of hardships resulting from slavery. Civilization has moved forward, and emancipation of slavery had taken place more than a century ago. As a divisive issue, leftist leaders would polarize the activities and history of different races for political purposes. In civic capitalism, humans of different races are free and can conduct their businesses as opportunities arise. Indeed, there are successful people from different races in different parts of the world, either in business, professions, celebrities or sports. Having a certain skin color does not necessarily mean success or failure. Indeed, one should not be a slave to his or her own skin. Like any other normal person, people with different skin colors should excel in their work performance before returns could be gained. Due to differences in endowment, people of different races can perform according to their own talent, ability, knowledge and so on. In a multi-racial society, what counts is one's ability and work performance, not the color of one's skin. It would indeed be unwise if people, especially political opportunists, use race as the reason or scapegoat to make certain gains or cover certain human weakness.

The politics of gender has been used as another divisive issue. It is true that the biological differences between the two genders have generated different outcomes. Other than the biological system of human reproduction, their physical bodies and the way the two genders are dressed show a huge difference in their appearance. There are some jobs which are mostly done or occupied by the male gender, while many jobs are better done by the female gender. The issue of sexual orientation is not limited to any one gender either. Some gender advocates point out the suffering that the male gender had caused on the female gender. But there are reverse cases and many other incidents where suffering was imposed by people of the same gender. Illegal activities must be brought under the law, and the acceptance of gender and gender equality must be promoted through education, application of ethical standards, civilized behavior and establishment of lawful civic institutions.

Indeed, gender discrimination has been considered as unethical and uncivilized, and social efforts should be made to improve the relationship between the two genders. For example, "equal work, equal pay" between the two genders has been acted upon by many employers, though there is still room for improvement. While there are challenges to traditional views and cultural behavior on the treatment between the two genders, it is still true that there is some specialization of labor between the two genders. Equal opportunity in employment should mean that the personal background of the two genders in terms of qualification and experience would be treated equally. Indeed, equality of employment opportunity has been stated in many job announcements and advertisement, though implementation can be another issue.

Gender equality must also be seen in less developed countries where the female gender tends to receive less education and is equipped with a lower level of personal endowment. Gender discrimination still appears in some cultures and religions. It would be up to the state at the national level to pass policies to promote gender equality and non-discrimination. Politicization of gender difference could be improper, unwise and biased in merely exposing the weak side of the female gender. On the contrary, there are numerous cases where females are successful in businesses as professionals and serve their country as elected political leaders. There is surely the strong and positive side of the female gender where females are contributing importantly and significantly to the society and economy. Ultimately, it is the level of endowment acquired by both genders that counts in their role in every society. More females with high individual endowment shall do good individually and for the female gender. Nonetheless, all individuals will have to face competition in the market economy, and the presence of the rule of law, civic institutions and proper policy on gender equality should provide a level playing field for all individuals from the two genders. And how successful one is shall depend on several endowment factors, and not the gender the individual belongs.

Religious pursuits have also been politicized. In economies where individual freedom is cherished, individuals are free to choose their religious faith. On the contrary, in countries where a certain religion is adopted at the state level, the dominance of a certain religion may impose discrimination on other religions, as well as the various discriminatory practices and behaviors which the religion pronounces. Individuals should be given freedom to choose their faith, and whether one should pray in a certain building or face a certain direction relates only to the different religious practices. Religion should be treated as another form of civic institution that preaches and conveys certain beliefs and behaviors to their followers. In a religious state, unfortunately, religious freedom would normally be limited. The adoption of an official religion would mean other religions would not be entertained, or even be despised.

There can be other examples of politicization other than the employer–employee relationship, race, gender and religion; language and culture can also be used as political instruments to attack certain groups of individuals who speak a certain language or dialect or share a common culture. The intention to politicize is to engage in the fragmentation game of "divide and rule". But making a political commitment to help could only be superficial and nominal; the goal could be to gain votes and support in the election. In other words, the *ex-ante* political promise would have to be tested to see how the elected leader would eventually formulate post-election policies, as that shall reflect the *ex-post* situation an elected leader conducted. That shall involve not only the nature of the policy itself but also its wider economic implications when implemented.

Armed with a high degree of individual freedom, the capitalist market system does allow individuals and institutions to express their opinions and grievances on all pertinent issues. As such, there can be individuals and institutions which have different social, economic and political goals and interests in mind, and there exist various channels through which individuals and institutions can make their voice heard. Individual freedom would not only positively allow people to do their best but also could be abused by people with negative behavior and socially disruptive intentions, thereby imposing additional social cost on other positive economic aspects.

In short, allowing people and institutions to express their different opinions is a virtue in a civilized economy, but it could lead to politicization, politicking and attacks on the normal functioning of the market economy. It is thus difficult to identify or isolate the different aspects of the economy which are the result of the normal functioning or distortion resulting from politicization and attacks. The economic situation would deteriorate should the influence of the latter exceeded that of the former. Extreme politicization and ideological-oriented attacks would eventually produce undue economic disruption and distortion, and it would require pro-economics political leaders to formulate policies that put economic results as the top political priority.

V Give Economic Performance a Chance

There are differences in economic results, but politicians should not ideologize and dichotomize the results as inequality without trying to understand and improve the *ex-ante* situation. "Inequality" will not go away as the society trains and educates people with different endowments in the form of skills and qualifications. It will be deceitful on the one hand to reinforce the education and vocational training systems which produce differences in human capital and on the other hand complain about the difference in income as a result of the difference in education received by individuals. Economic differences cannot be solved using political instruments, and the better alternative is to improve the *ex-ante* end in the economic production chain. Nonetheless, however much improvement is done in the formal education system and in vocational training, there will still be differences in economic outcomes. In a class of students, for example, some are stronger than others academically, and the difference in their future career path would already produce income differences. When politicized, differences become inequality, but the substance remains the same. Politicization could even delay the process of endowment improvement. For example, large spending on welfare may result in national debt, but the same spending could be used to improve human capital and long-term infrastructure that would facilitate businesses and work conditions.

One must truly understand that politics is a game of power only and political power reinforces the authority of the political leaders. The general public will gain only if the elected leaders execute and deliver policies that promote the economy so that jobs are forthcoming, and the rise in employment could improve the economic welfare of the workers. Closely allied with economic policies shall be the promotion of opportunity through market-friendly policies as increase in investment should aid economic competitiveness. The economic linkages that produce economic gains and benefits for all shall be the desire of all voters, because this is how they can see their benefit by exercising their freedom in political elections. In any political election, the winning candidate takes all and strictly speaking voters do not gain anything except the wish to have a better economy for them to operate either as businesses benefiting from investment or workers benefiting from employment.

It really is up to the elected political leaders to engage in policies that promote the overall economy, rather than dichotomizing the different groups of voters thinking of helping certain groups at the expense of other groups. Economics is passive and cannot perform without decision makers deploying the economic resources for production purposes. In a capitalist market economy, the economic drivers should be the investors who see production opportunities, and workers are being hired for production. With investment activities, the "opportunity multiplier" begins to function, producing many more job opportunities, requiring different endowments for different jobs, and rewarding workers differently. Expansion in one business leads to another, and the appearance of one job gives rise to another. Eventually, all investments, industries and job opportunities mingle with each other as the economy grows. And there are different growth rates as returns differ among investments, earnings differ among endowments and subsequently the gained economic welfare shall differ among workers.

All the differences in outcomes arise from differences in endowments and requirements in different businesses and investments. As the economy grows, there will be new phenomena needing to be tackled, but focusing on the endowment end in the production relationship shall be the best economic strategy. The natural economic path should be apolitical, and political leaders shall see and trust that economic forces shall produce welfare for all economic participants. Economic development for all can be confined within the economic sphere and problems can be dealt with using pure economic and non-political tools.

Although elected politicians can amass much political power, it would be best if they do not politicize economic issues or use economic tools for political ends. In other words, elected politicians should let the economy run its own course rather than imposing disruptive and distortive policies which would at best give some temporary political results but require economic corrections in the future. Economic results and outcomes are the best reward elected politicians shall give back to their voters. Economic outcomes do not penalize one individual against another; it is due to the difference in demand and supply or the different endowment that is required by different jobs that outcome differences are produced, which are natural in economics.

Such a discussion serves as the fundamental in the natural operation of a market economy, as one economic activity gives rise to another, and one economic problem gives rise to another. There could also be the "problem multiplier" in a market economy. When confined only and purely to economics, solutions to problems could come forward as the forces of "supply and demand", and together with expectations, shall lead to a revision in an economic cycle. Elected political leaders shall see to the fact that economic problems can only be solved using economic instruments, and policy decisions should lead to the effective application and usage of economic instruments.

In the contemporary world where diversity has been considered as a norm, there will be people, professionals, leaders and politicians who look for areas to extend their interest, influence and power. It is probable that people would hold different and opposing views, but support must be sought. When politicians, officials and other decision makers attempt to elaborate on their diverse opinions, economic instruments would usually be used as the means to seek support. The essence of diversity in a full democratic society is that when one leader or politician argues for one viewpoint, there is always another leader or politician offering or advocating the alternative viewpoint. In advocating for different viewpoints, economics could easily be deployed in decisions which are intended for non-economic purposes. In political elections, for example, pecuniary donations would be needed to support certain political parties and candidates, and donations would then be spent on the purpose of election canvassing. Politicians in their election campaign could make promises that require the deployment of economic resources and outcomes. However, how economic resources would be attained for political ends or what economic impact political promises had could turn out to be unimportant. Yet political and non-economic decisions in deploying economic resources do have severe economic implications, which could be unfavorable or negative and require further correction at a later stage.

The idea to "give economics a chance" is to leave economics alone as much as possible so that economic normalcy can function to its utmost, including development in the various stages of the economic cycle. Let economic development take its own course, and different types of decision makers, including politicians, government officials, businesses and professionals, should allow the market to perform. Unnecessary interference and politicization of economic results should be removed. Government intervention should at best be pro-market and pro-growth, so that policies shall be addressed to improve the overall economic capacity, capability and competitiveness. It is only through improvement in long-term economic welfare that people could enjoy their benefits. And of course, given the differences in individual endowments, the extent of benefits individuals could gain would also differ. In other words, letting the effective functioning of the economy be the political and social priority shall be the best strategy, and policies shall aim at maximizing economic results. Non-economic policies shall keep to their own areas of concern, while the implementation of such policies shall not generate unfavorable economic impacts as that could produce undue distortions on the economy.

Like any other living being, the economy has a life of its own, except that the life would end in the case of a living being, but the life of the economy is immortal and everlasting. The market mechanism shall function as the ways and means to keep the economy healthy. Proper and productive businesses and individual activities serve as the components of the "economic body", and economic health could be promoted and checked by a pro-economy government who should choose, decide and apply policies to ensure and improve the health of the economy as a living entity. There is always the existence of destructive elements in the health of all living entities, and the economy entity is no exception. For an economy, the destructive elements shall include those individuals and decision makers using the economy for non-economic ends. The destructive acts would either delay economic performance, lead to loss in opportunities, require other resources to rescue the economy's ill health, impose economic burden that impinges future development potentials or simply results in un-replenishable losses that created sufferings to all.

One must accept differences in economic results, and improvements shall preferably be conducted at the *ex-ante* end of the economic relationship. Labelling and demonizing differences as inequality is purely an act of politicization and politics can never be used to solve economic issues. Many politicians are exploiting and misinterpreting economic issues for their own political goals, which could do harm to the economy in the political process. Figure 9.1 shows a simple relationship between economics and politics. In political elections, voters can make an ideological choice between capitalism with free market and socialism or communism with economic coercion, or a mixture of some elements from each of the two ideologies. Elected political leaders would then form a government for a period specified by the nation's constitution. The debate on political

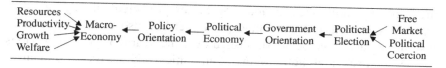

Figure 9.1   The Relationship between Economics and Politics

economy shall be crystallized when the government exercises its political power and judgment on the economy, as to whether policies would lean more toward socialism or would adhere more to capitalism. The government's policy orientation shall be crucial in reflecting their ideological goal. Consequently, policies will have the ultimate impact on the economy, which can be summarized in the promotion, functioning and use of resources, and productivity will then be generated through investment. The rise in productivity shall lead to aggregate economic growth, and it is economic growth that enhances individuals' welfare. If undesirable policies are adopted, the performance of these four economic elements would be affected negatively, thereby leading to either a low performance or a rise in economic burden for the future generation. The misuse of resources could result in wastage, while low productivity should mean the presence of unemployment or unused resources. A low productivity produces a low rate of economic growth, which in turn may not generate enough welfare for people to enjoy.

VI Conclusion

The strong conceptual message and discussion in this chapter is simply that the normal functioning of economics can be separated from political desires and goals if leaders and decision makers put economic development and people's welfare as their top priority. While economic forces shall function at their own pace and chart their own path to generate economic outcomes, there can be fluctuations as economic dynamics would generate cycles; politicians deploying economic instruments for political and non-economic ends would unnecessarily disrupt the normalcy of the economy. It is impossible to separate the economic impact from the market economy's normal functioning and the disruptive acts resulting from policies oriented for political purposes.

The bottom line in much of the contemporary world is civic capitalism. While economic activities can function based on market mechanisms, public security and progress are protected not only by political representation and uniformed personnel but also by a host of civic institutions that have been established over the years to serve the various public interests and help to maintain ethics and civilized standards, including channels through which the general public can challenge the political leaders should misdeeds be found. The more fundamental function in civic capitalism is the intention to ensure a "level playing field" for all citizens in the eyes of the rule of law, as well as economic openness, political transparency, equality in opportunity and non-discrimination. Indeed, the civic aspect of capitalism implies that many societal issues and problems are apolitical and can be dealt with professionally with strong ethical standards through non-political channels. The beauty in civic capitalism is that political pressure and bias can be removed in handling societal issues and problems, leaving reasoning, transparency and professionalism as the criteria in identifying solutions. Individuals under civic capitalism are free to perform creatively in their own profession without the need to "kowtow" to political leaders and do not need to side with certain political, religious and other pressure groups. As such, individuals can perform their best as there are no disruptive barriers.

Nonetheless, civic capitalism also allows for diversity in the expression of ideas and opinions, confined to the limit within the rule of law. This effectively means that there are people, including political and social leaders, with disruptive intentions who politicize issues as the instrument to attack others with opposing ideologies. While peace and security are an advantage for all, the emergence of chaos would also benefit those insinuators, as they might be "power hungry" and have in mind other intentions to extend their vested interests.

Similarly, experience shows that political leaders having a leftist ideology tend to deploy economic policies and instruments for political purposes, typically penalizing the able sector of the tax players as a political gesture in dealing with income inequality, rather than promoting the "economicability" for all. Leftist policies often result in piling up economic distortion with unintended and unwanted consequences, without much ability to make economic corrections, thereby leaving a larger economic mess for the future generation. Corrections on economic distortions can only be made and conducted by pro-economic political leaders who shall then implement policies that could gradually minimize the impact of distortion on the one hand and let the normalcy of the economy to take its path on the other hand. Politicization of economic issues can only be an instrument of attack on people with different ideologies but cannot serve as a means to promote economic welfare and would probably result in more economic problems or each problem becomes more severe. Indeed, many economic problems are not the fault of economic activities which could find their way out in a business cycle but are the fault of short-term political ambition with the desire to produce quick political results.

While there is always the presence of government and the possibility of leftist political leaders being elected, it is always the election of pro-economic political leaders who would "give economic performance a chance" by steering market-friendly policies to correct distortion on the one hand and indulge in growth promotion on the other hand so as to allow an increase in economic welfare that benefits all. In civic capitalism, it is the increase in economic welfare that voters should get in return for voting a certain political leader in power. The discussion on "give economic performance a chance" is an appeal to all political leaders that it is the overall economic results that count because it reflects the outcome of economic policies and the benefit that all citizens can enjoy regardless of their race, gender, age, regional disparity and religious orientation. Economic results carry a sense of impartiality to all recipients and do not discriminate one recipient against another; it is only the politicians who instrumentalize economics for their political ends by dichotomizing economic and social issues.

With this conceptual analysis in mind, people should understand that economics is here to serve all decision makers and users of economic instruments. The passive nature of economic resources is that it is only the active decision makers and users of economic instruments who would create either favorable or unwanted results. There is therefore the need to distinguish between the favorable results arising from the genuine working of economic activities and the way economic instruments are abused by decision makers, because the overall economic outcomes do not show the separate impact between the two. Hence, wrongful economic outcomes could be misunderstood as the poor performance of the economy, but the undesirable outcomes could instead be the result of the misconduct in policy decisions. It would be appropriate to understand that political freedom could end up with the election of leaders who would consider the entire economy as a political instrument. For the sake of good economic performance, it would be best to elect pro-growth political leaders who would steer economic policies to benefit all citizens, creating opportunities and enhancing competitiveness.

References

Abbott, A., 1983, "Professional ethics", *American Journal of Sociology*, 88 (5) March: 855–885.

Akerlof, G. A., 1978, "The market for "Lemons": Quality uncertainty and the market mechanism", in Diamond, P. and M. Rothschild (eds.), *Uncertainty in Economics*, Oxford: Academic Press, Chapter 15, pp. 235–251.

Akerlof, G. A. and R. Shiller, 2009, *Animal Spirits: How Human Psychology Drives the Economy and Why It Matters for Global Capitalism*, Princeton: Princeton University Press.

Amendáriz, B. and M. Labie, 2011, *The Handbook of Microfinance*, Singapore: World Scientific.

Arnott, R. and J. E. Stiglitz, 1991, "Moral hazard and nonmarket institutions: Dysfunctional crowding out of peer monitoring?", *American Economic Review*, 81 (1) March: 179–190.

Bank, S., 2012, *Ethics and Values in Social Work*, 4th edition, Basingstoke: Palgrave Macmillan.

Baumeister, R. F. and E. J. Finkel (eds.), 2010, *Advanced Social Psychology: The State of the Science*, New York: Oxford University Press.

Baumol, W., 1986, *Microtheory: Applications and Origins*, Cambridge, Mass.: The MIT Press.

Becker, G., 1994, *Human Capital: A Theoretical and Empirical Analysis with Special Reference to Education*, Chicago: The University of Chicago Press.

Bertrand, M., S. Mullainathan, and E. Shafir, 2004, "A behavioral-economics view of poverty", *American Economic Review*, 94 (2): 419–423.

Bischoff, I. and J. Meckl, 2008, "Endowment effect theory, public goods and welfare", *Journal of Socio-Economics*, 37 (5) October: 1768–1774.

Bisin, A. and T. Verdier, 2001, "The economics of cultural transformation and the dynamics of preferences", *Journal of Economic Theory*, 97 (2) April: 298–319.

Boone, B., 2017, *Ethics 101: From Altruism and Utilitarianism to Bioethics and Political Ethics, an Exploration of the Concepts of Right and Wrong*, London: Simon & Schuster.

Borjas, G. J., 2013, *Labor Economics*, 6th edition, New York: McGraw-Hill.

Botero, J. C., S. Djankov, R. L. Porta, F. Lopez-de-Silanes, and A. Shleifer, 2004, "The regulation of labor", *Quarterly Journal of Economics*, 119 (4) November: 1339–1382.

Botta, A., 2009, "A structuralist North–South model on structural change, economic growth and catching up", *Structural Change and Economic Dynamics*, 20 (1) March: 61–73.

Bourdieu, P., 1974, "Cultural reproduction and social reproduction", in Brown, R. (ed.), *Knowledge, Education and Social Change*, London: Taylor & Frances, pp. 71–84.

Bowles, S. and H. Gintis, 1977, "The Marx theory of value and heterogeneous labor: A critique and reformulation", *Cambridge Journal of Economics*, 1 (2) June: 173–192.

Brickel, W. K. and R. E. Vuchinich (eds.), 2000, *Reframing Health Behavior Change with Behavioral Economics*, New Jersey: Lawrence Erlbaum Associates Publishers.

Brien, A., 1998, "Professional ethics and the culture of trust", *Journal of Business Ethics*, 17 (4) March: 391–409.

Calhoun, C. (ed.), 2002, *Dictionary of the Social Sciences*, New York: Oxford University Press.

Camerer, C., 1999, *Behavioral Economics: Reunifying Psychology and Economics*, Proceeding of the National Academy of Sciences of the United States of America, 96 (19) September: 10575–10577.

Camerer, C. F., G. Loewenstein, and M. Ragin (eds.), 2004, *Advances in Behavioral Economics*, New Jersey: Princeton University Press.

Campbell, E., 2000, "Professional ethics in teaching: Towards the development of a code of practice", *Cambridge Journal of Education*, 30 (2): 203–211.

Carmichael, H. L. and W. B. Macleod, 2006, "Welfare economics with intransitive revealed preferences: A theory of the endowment effect", *Journal of Public Economic Theory*, 8 (2) April: 193–218.

Chang, H.-J., 2015, *Economics: The User's Guide*, New York: Bloomsbury Group.

Chenery, H. B., 1975, "The structuralist approach to development policy", *American Economic Review*, Papers and Proceedings, 65 (2) May: 310–316.

Chhotray, V. and G. Stoker, 2009, *Governance Theory and Practice*, London: Palgrave Macmillan.

Clower, R., 1967, "A reconsideration of the microfoundations of monetary theory", *Economic Inquiry*, 6 (1) December: 1–18.

Coase, R. H., 1988, *The Firm, the Market and the Law*, Chicago: The University of Chicago Press.

Cohen, B. (ed.), 2005, *International Political Economy*, London: Ashgate Publishing.

Cohen, G. A., 1979, "The labor theory of value and the concept of exploitation", *Philosophy and Public Affairs*, 8 (4) Summer: 338–360.

Coleman, J. S., 1986, "Social theory, social research, and a theory of action", *American Journal of Sociology*, 91 (6) May: 1309–1335.

Cornes, R. and T. Sandler, 1996, *The Theory of Externalities, Public Goods, and Club Goods*, 2nd edition, Cambridge: Cambridge University Press.

Coyle, D., 2007, *The Soulful Science: What Economists Really Do and What It Matters*, Princeton: Princeton University Press.

Crane, A. and D. Matten, 2016, *Business Ethics: Managing Corporate Citizenship and Sustainability in the Age of Globalization*, 4th edition, Oxford: Oxford University Press.

Cukierman, A. and A. H. Meltzer, 1986, "A theory of ambiguity, credibility, and inflation under discretion and asymmetric information", *Econometrica*, 54 (5) September: 1099–1128.

Dahl, R. A., 2006, *On Political Equality*, New Haven: Yale University Press.

Davidson, W. H., 1979, "Factor endowment, innovation and international trade theory", *Kyklos*, 32 (4) November: 764–774.

Davis, D. D. and C. A. Holt, 1993, *Experimental Economics*, New Jersey: Princeton University Press.

Deacon, R. T., 2011, "The political economy of the natural resource curse: A survey of theory and evidence", *Foundations and Trends in Microeconomics*, 7 (2): 111–208.

Devereux, M., A. C. Head, and B. J. Lapham, 1996, "Monopolistic competition, increasing returns, and the effects of government spending", *Journal of Money, Credit and Banking*, 28 (2) May: 233–254.

Dixit, A. K. and J. E. Stiglitz, 1977, "Monopolistic competition and optimum product diversity", *American Economic Review*, 67 (3) June: 297–308.

Donagan, A., 1977, *The Theory of Morality*, Chicago: The University of Chicago Press.

Dover, K. J., 1974, *Greek Popular Morality in the Time of Plato and Aristotle*, Oxford: Blackwell.

Ehrenberg, R. G. and R. S. Smith, 2016, *Modern Labor Economics: Theory and Public Policy*, 12th edition, London: Routledge.

Elster, J., 1989, "Social norms and economic theory", *Journal of Economic Perspectives*, 3 (4) Fall: 99–117.

Emmelhainz, M. A. and R. J. Adams, 1999, "The apparel industry response to "sweatshop" concerns: A review and analysis of codes of conduct", *Journal of Supply Chain Management*, 35 (2) June: 51–57.

Erzan, R., J. Goto, and P. Holmes, 1989, *Effects of the Multi-Fibre Arrangement on Developing Countries' Trade: An Empirical Investigation*, International

Trade Division, International Economics Department, The World Bank: Washington DC, November.

Etzioni, A., 1988, *The Moral Dimension: Towards a New Economics*, New York: The Free Press.

Etzioni, A., 1996, *The New Golden Rule*, New York: Basic Books.

Fama, E. F. and M. C. Jensen, 1983, "Separation of ownership and control", *Journal of Law and Economics*, 26 (2) June: 301–325.

Fase, M. M. G., 2005, "One economics and religion", *De Economist*, 153 (1) March: Article 85.

Fine, B. and D. Milonakis, 2009, *From Economic Imperialism to Freakonomics: The Shifting Boundaries between Economics and other Social Sciences*, London: Routledge.

Forni, M. and M. Lippi, 1997, *Aggregation and the Microfoundations of Dynamic Macroeconomics*, Oxford: Clarendon Press.

Frankel, J. A., 2010, *The Natural Resource Curse: A Survey*, NBER Working Paper No. 15836, Cambridge MA: National Bureau of Economic Research, March.

Friedman, B. M., 2006, "The moral consequences of economic growth", *Society*, 43 (2) January: 15–22.

Friedman, D. and A. Cassar, 2004, *Economic Lab: An Intensive Course in Experimental Economics*, London: Routledge.

Frings, M. S. and R. L. Funk, 1973, *Formalism in Ethics and Non-Formal Ethics of Values: A New Attempt toward the Foundation of an Ethical Personalism*, Evanston: Northwestern University Press.

Fuller, L. L., 1969, *The Morality of Law*, Revised edition, New Haven: Yale University Press.

Gelman, A. and K. Fung, 2012, "Freakonomics: What went wrong?". *American Scientist*, 100 (1) January/February, 6–9.

Gert, B., 1998, *Morality: Its Nature and Justification*, New York: Oxford University Press.

Gerth, H. H. and C. W. Mills, 2009, *From Max Weber: Essays in Sociology*, London: Routledge.

Gewirth A., 1978, *Reason and Morality*, Chicago: University of Chicago Press.

Gould, D. M. and W. C. Gruben, 1996, "The role of intellectual property rights in economic growth", *Journal of Development Economics*, 48 (2) March: 323–350.

Granato, J., R. Inglehart, and D. Leblang, 1996, "The effect of cultural values on economic development: Theory, hypotheses, and some empirical tests", *American Journal of Political Science*, 40 (3) August: 607–631.

Granovetter, M., 1985, "Economic action and social structure: The problem of embeddedness", *American Journal of Sociology*, 91 (3) November: 481–510.

Guiso, L., P. Sapienza, and L. Zingales, 2006, "Does culture affect economic outcomes?", *Journal of Economic Perspectives*, 20 (2): 23–48.

Haber, S. and V. Menaldo, 2011, "Do natural resources fuel authoritarianism? A reappraisal of the resource curse", *American Political Science Review*, 105 (1) February: 1–26.

Haidt, J., 2008, "Morality", *Perspectives on Psychological Science*, 3 (1) January: 65–72.

Halac, M. and P. Yared, 2018, "Fiscal rules and discretion in a world economy", *American Economic Review*, 108 (8): 2305–2334.

Harris, L., 2003, *Trading and Exchange: Market Microstructure for Practitioners*, Oxford: Oxford University Press.

Hart, H. L. A., 1963, *Law, Liberty and Morality*, Stanford: Stanford University Press.

Hart, O., 1995, "Corporate governance: Some theory and implications", *Economic Journal*, 105 (430) May: 678–689.

Harvey, D., 1996, *Justice, Nature and the Geography of Difference*, Oxford: Blackwell.

Harvey, P., 2000, *An Introduction to Buddhist Ethics: Foundations, Values and Issues*, Cambridge: Cambridge University Press.

Helpman, E., 1992, *Innovation, Imitation, and Intellectual Property Rights*, NBER Working Paper No. 4081, May, Cambridge, Mass.: National Bureau of Economic Research.

Henderson, J. V., Z. Shalizi, and A. J. Venables, 2001, "Geography and development", *Journal of Economic Geography*, 1 (1) January: 81–105.

Hicks, J. R., 1935, "Annual survey of economic theory: The theory of monopoly", *Econometrica*, 3 (1) January: 1–20.

Hill, P. C. and R. W. Hood Jr. (eds.), 1999, *Measures of Religiosity*, Birmingham, Al.: Religious Education Press.

Hirsch, B. T., 1991, *Labor Unions and the Economic Performance of Firms*, Kalamazoo, MI: W.E. Upjohn Institute for Employment Research.

Hitt, M. A., R. D. Ireland, and J. S. Harrison, 2005, *Mergers and Acquisitions*, Oxford: Blackwell Publishing Ltd.

Hoffman, E., K. A. McCabe, and V. L. Smith, 2007, "Behavioral foundations of reciprocity: Experimental economics and evolutionary psychology", *Economic Inquiry*, 36 (3) July: 335–352.

Hölmstrom, B., 1979, "Moral hazard and observability", *Bell Journal of Economics*, 10 (1) Spring: 74–91.

Holmstrom, B. and P. Milgrom, 1991. "Multitask principal–agent analyses: Incentive contracts, asset ownership, and job design", *Journal of Law, Economics and Organization*, 7 January: 24–52.

Hursh, S. R., 1984, "Behavioral Economics", *Journal of the Experimental Analysis of Behavior*, 42 (3) November: 435–452.

Iannaccone, L. R., 1992, "Religious markets and the economics of religion", *Social Compass*, 39 (1): 123–131.

Jensen, M. C., 1986, "Agency costs of free cash flow, corporate finance, and takeovers", *American Economic Review*, 76 (2) May: 323–329.

Jensen, M. C., 1994, "Self-interest, altruism, incentives, and agency theory", *Journal of Applied Corporate Finance*, 7 (2) Summer: 40–45.

Jensen, M. C. and W. H. Meckling, 1976, "Theory of the firm: Managerial behavior, agency cost and ownership structure", *Journal of Financial Economics*, 3 (4) October: 305–360.

John, J. D., 2011, "Is there really a resource curse? A critical survey of theory and evidence", *Global Governance: A Review of Multilateralism and International Organizations*, 17 (2) April–June: 167–184.

Kagan, S., 1989, *The Limits of Morality*, Oxford: Oxford University Press.

Kagan, S., 1998, *Normative Ethics*, London: Routledge.

Kaplow, L., 2013, *Competition Policy and Price Fixing*, Princeton: Princeton University Press.

Keen, S., 1993, "Use-value, exchange value, and the demise of Marx's labor theory of value", *Journal of the History of Economic Thought*, 15 (1) Spring: 107–121.

Kendrick, D. and L. Taylor, 1970, "Numerical solution of nonlinear planning models", *Econometrica*, 38 (3) May: 453–467.

Keynes, J. M., 2016, *The General Theory of Employment, Interest and Money*, New Delhi: Atlantic Publishers & Distributors.

Kierzkowski, H., 1989, *Monopolistic Competition and International Trade*, Oxford: Oxford University Press.

King, J. E. and M. R. Crowther, 2004, "The measurement of religiosity and spirituality: Examples and issues from psychology", *Journal of Organizational Change Management*, 17 (1): 83–101.

Kirschenbaum, H., 1995, *100 Ways to Enhance Values and Morality in Schools and Youth Settings*, May, Needham Heights, MA: Allyn & Bacon.

Kirshner, J., 1997, "The microfoundations of economic sanctions", *Security Studies*, 6 (3) Spring: 32–64.

Klamer, A., 2011, "Cultural entrepreneurship", *Review of Austrian Economics*, 24 (2) June: 141–156.

Klepper, S., 1996, "Entry, exit, growth, and innovation over the product life cycle", *American Economic Review*, 86 (3) June: 562–583.

Knetsch, J. L., F.-F. Tang, and R. H. Thaler, 2001, "The endowment effect and repeated market trails: Is the Vickrey auction demand revealing?", *Experimental Economics*, 4 (3) December: 257–269.

Kohlberg, L. and R. H. Hersh, 1977, "Moral development: A review of the theory", *Theory into Practice*, 16 (2): 53–59.

Laffer, A. B., 2004, "The Laffer Curve: Past, present, and future", *Backgrounder*, No. 1765 June, Washington DC: The Heritage Foundation.

Lambsdorff, J. G., 2002, "Corruption and rent-seeking", *Public Choice*, 113 (102) October: 97–125.

Lefort, C., 1986, *The Political Form of Modern Society: Bureaucracy, Democracy and Totalitarianism*, Cambridge, MA: The MIT Press.

Lehalle, C.-A. and S. Laruelle (eds.), 2013, *Market Microstructure in Practice*, Singapore: World Scientific Publishing.

Leoni, B., 2012. *Freedom and the Law*, Indianapolis: Liberty Fund.

Levitt, S. D. and S. J. Dubner, 2005, *Freakonomics*, New York: Penguin.

Levy, D. M., 2002, *How the Dismal Science Got Its Name: Classical Economics and the Ur-Text of Radical Politics*, Ann Arbor: The University of Michigan Press.

Levy, J. S., 1992, "An introduction to prospect theory", *Political Psychology*, Special Issue, 13 (2) June: 171–186.

Li, K.-W., 1991, "Positive adjustment against protectionism: The case of textile and clothing industry in Hong Kong", *The Developing Economies*, 29 (3) September: 197–209.

Li, K.-W., 2002, *Capitalist Development and Economism in East Asia: The Rise of Hong Kong, Singapore, Taiwan and South Korea*, London: Routledge.

Li, K.-W., 2006, *The Hong Kong Economy: Recovery and Restructuring*, Singapore: McGraw-Hill International.

Li, K.-W., 2012, *Economic Freedom: Lessons of Hong Kong*, Singapore: World Scientific Publishing.

Li, K.-W., 2013, "The US monetary performance prior to the 2008 crisis", *Applied Economics*, 45 (24) August: 3449–3460.

Li, K.-W., 2014, "An analysis on economic opportunity", *Applied Economics*, 46 (33) November: 4060–4074.

Li, K.-W., 2017a, *Redefining Capitalism in Global Economic Development*, Oxford: Academic Press.

Li, K.-W., 2017b, "Is there an 'interest rate — speculation' relationship? Evidence from G7 in the pre- and post-2008 crisis", *Applied Economics*, 49 (21): 2041–2059.

Li, K.-W. and X. Zhou, 2010, *A Parametric and Semiparametric Analysis on the Inequality-Development Relationship*, Geneva Trade and Development Workshop, Geneva, Switzerland, September.

Li, K.-W. and X. Zhou, 2013, "A nonparametric and semiparametric analysis on inequality and development: Evidence from OECD and non-OECD countries", *Economic and Political Studies*, 1 (2) July: 55–79.

Li, K.-W., X. Zhou, and Z. Pan, 2016, "Cross-country output emergence and growth: Evidence from varying coefficient nonparametric method", *Economic Modelling*, 55 June: 32–41.

Lockard, A. A. and G. Tullock, 2001, *Efficient Rent-Seeking*, Boston MA: Springer.

Loewenstein, G., 1999, "Experimental economics from the vantage-point of behavioral economics", *The Economic Journal*, 109 February: F25–F34.

Lowe, P. D. and W. Rüdig, 1986, "Political ecology and the social sciences — The state of the art", *British Journal of Political Science*, 16 (4) October: 513–550.

Madhavan, A., 2000, "Market microstructure: A survey", *Journal of Financial Markets*, 3 (3) August: 2005–258.

Manchin, M. and A. O. Pelkmans-Balaoing, 2007, *Rules of Origin and the Web of East Asia Free Trade Agreements*, World Bank Policy Research Working Paper No. 4273, July.

Maskus, K. E., 2000, *Intellectual Property Rights in the Global Economy*, Washington DC: Institute for International Economics.

Marx, K., 1993, *Grundrisse*, London: Penguin.

Marx, K. and B. Fowkes, 1992, Capital: A Critique of Political Economy, Vols. 1, 2 and 3, London: Penguin Classic.

McNulty, P. J., 1984, *The Origins and Development of Labor Economics*, Cambridge, Mass.: The MIT Press.

Milner, H. V., 1988, *Resisting Protectionism: Global Industries and the Politics of International Trade*, Princeton: Princeton University Press.

Mirrlees, J. A., 1999, "The theory of moral hazard and unobservable behavior: Part 1", *Review of Economic Studies*, 66 (1) January: 3–21.

Mosca, M., 2005, *The Notion of Market Power in the Italian Marginalist School: Vilfredo Pareto and Enrico Barone*, Universita di Lecce Economics Working Paper No. 70-34, Lecce, July.

Mullainathan, S. and R. H. Thaler, 2000, *Behavioral Economics*, NBER Working Paper No. 7948, Cambridge, Mass.: National Bureau of Economic Research, October.

Mullor-Sebastián, A., 1983, "The product life cycle theory: Empirical evidence", *Journal of International Business Studies*, 14 (3): 95–105.

Marx, K. and B. Fowkes, 1992, *Capital: A Critique of Political Economy*, Vols. 1, 2 and 3, London: Penguin Classic.

McNulty, P. J., 1967, "A note on the history of perfect competition", *Journal of Political Economy*, 75 (4) August: 395–399.

Morewedge, C. K. and C. E. Giblin, 2015, "Explanations of the endowment effect: An integrative review", *Trends in Cognitive Sciences*, 19 (6) June: 339–348.

Morishima, M., 1973, *Marx's Economics: A Dual Theory of Value and Growth*, Cambridge: Cambridge University Press.

Morishima, M., 1974, "Marx in the light of modern economics theory", *Econometrica*, 42 (4) July: 611–632.

Nickell, S. and R. Layard, 1999, "Labor market institutions and economic performance" in Ashenfelter, O. C. and D. Card (eds.), *Handbook of Labor Economics*, Vol. 3, Part C, Ch. 46, London: Elsevier, pp. 3029–3084.

Nishimura, K. G., 1992, *Imperfect Competition, Differential Information, and Microfoundations of Macroeconomics*, Oxford: Clarendon Press.

Odagiri, H., 1994, *Growth through Competition, Competition through Growth: Strategic Management and the Economy in Japan*, Oxford: Oxford University Press.

O'Donnell, G., 2004, "Why the rule of law matters", *Journal of Democracy*, 15 (4) October: 32–46.

Okisio, N., 1963, "A mathematical note on Marxian theorems", *Weltwirtschaftliches Archiv*, 91: 287–299.

Olken, B. A. and R. Pande, 2012, "Corruption in developing countries", *Annual Review of Economics*, 4: 479–509.

Parsons, T. and N. J. Smelser, 1956, *Economy and Society: A Study in the Integration of Economic and Social Theory*, London: Routledge.

Philip, B. and D. Young, 2002, "Preferences, reductionism and the microfoundations of analytical Marxism", *Cambridge Journal of Economics*, 26 (3) May: 313–329.

Pilling, G., 1980, *Marx's Capital: Philosophy and Political Economy*, Boston: Routledge and Kegan Paul.

Platteau, J.-P., 2000, *Institutions, Social Norms and Economic Development*, London: Routledge.

Posner, R.A., 1998, "Rational choice, behavioral economics and the law", *Stanford Law Review*, 50 (5) May: 1551–1575.

Posner, R. A., 2001, *Antitrust Law*, 2nd edition, Chicago: University of Chicago Press.

Raz, J., 1986, *The Morality of Freedom*, New York: Oxford University Press.

Raz, J., 1994, *Ethics in the Public Domain: Essays in the Morality of Law and Politics*, New York: Oxford University Press.

Robertson, G. B., 2004, "Leading labor: Unions, politics, and protest in new democracies", *Comparative Politics*, 36 (3) April: 253–272.

Robinson, J. A., R. Torvik, and T. Vendier, 2006, "Political foundations of the resource curve", *Journal of Development Economics*, 79 (2) April: 447–468.

Robinson, J., 1953, "Imperfect competition revisited", *Economic Journal*, 63 (251) September: 579–593.

Rodrik, D., 2015, *Economic Rules: The Rights and Wrongs of the Dismal Science*, New York: W.W. Norton.

Romer, P. M., 1989, *Human Capital and Growth: Theory and Evidence*, NBER Working Paper No. 3173, Cambridge Mass.: National Bureau of Economic Research, November.

Ross, M. L., 1999, "The political economy of the resource curse", *World Politics*, 51 (2) January: 297–322.

Rowley, C. K., R. D. Tollison, and G. Tullock (eds.), 1988, *The Political Economy of Rent-Seeking*, Boston, MA: Kluwer Academic Publishers.

Rubin, I. I., 1973, *Essays on Marx's Theory of Value*, New York: Black Rose Books.

Rybczynski, T. M., 1955, "Factor endowment and relative commodity price", *Economica*, 22 (88): 336–341.

Scalia, A., 1989, "The rule of law as a law of rules", *University of Chicago Law Review*, 56 (4) Autumn: 1175–1188.

Schneeweiss, C., 2003, *Distributed Decision Making*, Berlin: Springer-Verlag.

Schwartz, S. H., 2007, "Universalism values and the inclusiveness of our moral universe", *Journal of Cross-Cultural Psychology*, 38 (6) November: 711–728.

Schwartz, S. H. and S. Huismans, 1995, "Value priorities and religiosity in four Western religions", *Social Psychology Quarterly*, 58 (2) June: 88–107.

Sent, E.-M., 2004, "How psychology made its (limited) way back into economics", *History of Political Economy*, 36 (4) Winter: 735–760.

Shabbir, G. and M. Anwar, 2007, "Determinants of corruption in developing countries", *The Pakistan Development Review*, 46 (4): 751–764.

Sharkey, W. W., 2009, *The Theory of Natural Monopoly*, Cambridge: Cambridge University Press.

Smith, V. L., 1976, "Experimental economics: Induced value theory", *American Economic Review*, Papers and Proceedings, 66 (2) May: 274–279.

Smith, V. L., 1982, "Microeconomic systems as an experimental science", *American Economic Review*, 72 (5) December: 923–955.

Smith, V. L., 1989, "Theory, experiment and economics", *Journal of Economic Perspectives*, 3 (1): 151–169.

Smith, V. L., 1991, *Papers in Experimental Economics*, Cambridge: Cambridge University Press.

Smith, V. L., 1994, "Economics in the laboratory", *Journal of Economic Perspectives*, 8 (1) Winter: 112–131.

Solomon, R. C., 1992, *Ethics and Excellence: Cooperation and Integrity in Business*, Oxford: Oxford University Press.

Solow, R. M., 1974, "The economics of resources or the resources of economics", in Gopalakrishnan C. (ed.), *Classic Papers in Natural Resource Economics*. London: Palgrave Macmillan, pp. 257–276.

Spence, M., 1976, "Product selection, fixed costs, and monopolistic competition", *Review of Economic Studies*, 43 (2) June: 217–235.

Stark, A., 1993, "What's the matter with business ethics?", *Harvard Business Review*, 71 (3) May: 38–48.

Sternberg, E., 2000, *Just Business: Business Ethics in Action*, Oxford: Oxford University Press.

Stigler, G. J., 1957, "Perfect competition, historically contemplated", *Journal of Political Economy*, 65 (1) February: 1–17.

Streissler, E., 1972, "To what extent was the Austrian school marginalist?", *History of Political Economy*, 4 (2) Fall: 426–441.

Streissler, E., 1988, "The intellectual and political impact of the Austrian school of Economics", *History of European Ideas*, 9 (2): 191–204.

Sweetland, S. R., 1996, "Human capital theory: Foundation of a field of inquiry", *Review of Educational Research*, 66 (3): 341–359.

Tabellini, G., 2010, "Culture and institutions: Economic development in regions of Europe", *Journal of the European Economic Association*, 8 (4) June: 677–716.

Tamanaha, B. Z., 2004, *On the Rule of Law: History, Politics, Theory*, Cambridge: Cambridge University Press.

Tan, J. H. W., 2006, "Religion and social preferences: An experimental study", *Economics Letters*, 90 (1): 60–67.

Tan, J. H. W., 2013, "Behavioral economics of religion", in Paul Oslington (ed.), *Oxford Handbook of Christianity and Economics*, Oxford: Oxford University Press.

Taylor, L., 1979, *Macro Models for Developing Countries*, New York: McGraw Hill.

Taylor, L., 1983, *Structuralist Macroeconomics: Applicable Models for the Third World*, New York: Basic Books.

Taylor, L., 1985, "A stagnationist model of economic growth", *Cambridge Journal of Economics*, 9 (4) December: 383–403.

Thaler, R. H. (ed.), 2005, *Advances in Behavioral Finance*, Vol. II, New Jersey: Princeton University Press.

Thaler, R. H., 2015, *Misbehaving: The Making of Behavioral Economics*, London: W.W. Norton & Company.

Thiroux, J. P. and K. W. Krasemann, 2012, *Ethics: Theory and Practice*, 11th edition, New Jersey: Pearson Education.

Throsby, D., 1994, "The production and consumption of the arts: A view of cultural economics", *Journal of Economic Literature*, 32 (1) March: 1–29.

Throsby, D., 2010, *The Economics of Cultural Policy*, Cambridge: Cambridge University Press.

Towse, R., 2010, *A Textbook of Cultural Economics*, Cambridge: Cambridge University Press.

Tullock, G., 1989, *The Economics of Special Privilege and Rent-Seeking*, New York: Springer Science+Business Media.

Urry, J., 2000, *Sociology beyond Societies: Mobilities for the Twenty-First Century*, London: Routledge.

van den Bergh, J. C. J. M. and J. M. Gowdy, 2003, "The microfoundations of macroeconomics: An evolutionary perspective", *Cambridge Journal of Economics*, 27 (1) January: 65–84.

Viscusi, W. K., J. E. Harrington, Jr., and J. M. Vernon, 2005, *Economics of Regulation and Antitrust*, 4th edition, Cambridge, Mass.: The MIT Press.

Wallach, L. and P. Woodall, 2004, *Whose Trade Organization? A Comprehensive Guide to the WTO*, New York: The New Press.

Weintraub, E. R., 1979, *Microfoundations: The Compatibility of Microeconomics and Macroeconomics*, Cambridge: Cambridge University Press.

Wheelan, C., 2019, *Naked Economics: Undressing the Dismal Science*, New York: W. W. Norton & Company Ltd.

Wickens, C. D., J. G. Hollands, S. Banbury, and R. Parasuraman, 2016, *Engineering Psychology and Human Performance*, 4th edition, London: Routledge.

Wignaraja, G. (ed.), 2003, *Competitiveness Strategy in Developing Countries: A Manual for Policy Analysis*, London: Routledge.

Wilkinson, N. and M. Klaes, 2018, *An Introduction to Behavioral Economics*, 3rd edition, London: Palgrave.

Wolff, R. P., 1981, "A critique and reinterpretation of Marx's labor theory of value", *Philosophy and Public Affairs*, 10 (2) Spring: 89–120.

Ysseldyk, R., K. Matheson, and H. Anisman, 2010, "Religiosity as identity: Toward an understanding of religion from a social identity perspective", *Personality and Social Psychology Review*, 14 (1) January: 60–71.

Zhang, W. B., 2000, *On Adam Smith and Confucius: The Theory of Moral Sentiments and the Analects*, Commack, NY: Nova Science Publishers.

Zhou, X. and K.-W. Li, 2011, "Inequality and development: Evidence from semiparametric estimation with panel data", *Economic Letters*, 113 (3) December: 203–207.

Index